T0297745

Data Breach Preparation and Response

Data Breach Preparation and Response

Breaches are Certain, Impact is Not

Kevvie Fowler

Curtis Rose, Technical Editor

AMSTERDAM • BOSTON • HEIDELBERG • LONDON
NEW YORK • OXFORD • PARIS • SAN DIEGO
SAN FRANCISCO • SINGAPORE • SYDNEY • TOKYO

Syngress is an Imprint of Elsevier

Syngress is an imprint of Elsevier
50 Hampshire Street, 5th Floor, Cambridge, MA 02139, USA

Notices
Knowledge and best practice in this field are constantly changing. As new research and experience
broaden our understanding, changes in research methods, professional practices, or medical treatment
may become necessary.

Practitioners and researchers must always rely on their own experience and knowledge in evaluating
and using any information, methods, compounds, or experiments described herein. In using such
information or methods they should be mindful of their own safety and the safety of others, including
parties for whom they have a professional responsibility.

To the fullest extent of the law, neither the Publisher nor the authors, contributors, or editors, assume
any liability for any injury and/or damage to persons or property as a matter of products liability,
negligence or otherwise, or from any use or operation of any methods, products, instructions, or ideas
contained in the material herein.

The views, opinions and guidance within this book are those of the authors and not those of any other
organization or governing body.

ISBN: 978-0-12-803451-4

Library of Congress Cataloging-in-Publication Data
A catalog record for this book is available from the Library of Congress

British Library Cataloguing-in-Publication Data
A catalogue record for this book is available from the British Library

For information on all Syngress publications visit our
website at https://www.elsevier.com/

Working together
to grow libraries in
developing countries

www.elsevier.com • www.bookaid.org

Publisher: Todd Green
Acquiring Editor: Chris Katsaropoulos
Editorial Project Manager: Anna Valutkevich
Project Manager: Punithavathy Govindaradjane
Designer: Matthew Limbert

Typeset by SPi Global, India

Contents

About the Author

Kevvie Fowler is a partner and National Cyber Response leader for KPMG Canada and has over 20 years of IT, security and forensics experience. He assists clients in identifying and protecting critical data and proactively preparing for, responding to, and recovering from Breaches in a manner that minimizes impact and interruption to their business.

Kevvie is a cyber security and forensics expert who is author of *Data Breach Preparation and Response* and *SQL Server Forensic Analysis* and contributing author to several security and forensics books. He is an instructor who trains law enforcement agencies on cyber forensic and response practices and his cyber forensics research has been incorporated into formal course curriculum within industry and academic institutions. Kevvie is a SANS lethal forensicator and a member of the SANS Advisory Board and the Board of Referees for the Elsevier Digital Investigation Journal where he guides the direction of emerging cyber security and forensics research.

About the Contributors

Paul Hanley is a recognized expert in information security, with significant experience in the field. He has particular experience in aligning security functions to the needs of the business and in delivering global cyber security programmes. He is the national lead partner for cyber security at KPMG Canada.

Paul's specialisms include leading large-scale cyber security and transformation programs. He also has expert knowledge in information security risk management, technical security architecture design, cyber maturity assessments, cryptography, and security compliance.

In his career, Paul has been directly involved with a number of high profile, billion-dollar banking, government, and other programs and has built strong business relationships.

Paul regularly provides input into and comments on draft Security Standards and is the "go to" person for cyber advice for a number of regulators. He has been profiled by *SC Magazine*, the guest presenter at many high profile security events, and his activities have been shown in the media, on television, in the broadsheets, and in the specialist information security press.

Greg Markell is a leading insurance expert on the topic of cyber and privacy liability. In his current practice, he advises public, private, and nonprofit organizations regarding their risk transfer of organizational exposure to cyber-related losses.

Greg began his career underwriting for a large national insurer, starting in property and casualty before quickly moving into executive and professional risk, with a focus on director's and officer's (D&O) insurance. He then moved on to join a national brokerage, focusing on specialty insurance products for financial services companies, including D&O and cyber liability. He left this firm as a partner in 2014 and joined a top 10 global broker, where he is a resource for his colleagues for D&O and is the practice leader for cyber and privacy liability.

Greg received his Bachelor of Commerce degree with a minor in Economics from Queen's University. He is a fellow chartered insurance professional and an accredited Canadian risk manager.

Chris Pogue, Senior Vice President of Cyber Threat Analysis

Having been on the front lines of cybercrime investigations for the past 14 years, Chris has worked on thousands of Breaches, spanning the globe. As the SVP of Cyber Threat Analysis, he brings that knowledge and experience to Nuix, enabling them to build the most comprehensive, efficient, and effective Cybersecurity team on the planet.

Prior to joining Nuix in June 2014, he spent the past six years at SpiderLabs where he worked as an incident responder, a managing consultant, and, ultimately, a director. He also held a position as an engagement manager at the IBM/ISS X-Force Incident Response and Penetration Testing Teams. Prior to these roles, he served in the United States Army for 13 years as a signal corps warrant officer and a field artillery reconnaissance sergeant.

Among his many achievements, Chris was the original creator of the forensic methodology known as Sniper Forensics, a method that has emerged as the industry standard among users including the Federal Bureau of Investigation and the United States Secret Service. Additionally, in 2010, he was named as a SANS thought leader. He was the 41st security professional to have been awarded this distinction.

Chris holds a full range of professional certifications including Certified Information Systems Security Professional (CISSP), Certified Ethical Hacker (CEH), Certified Reverse Engineering Analyst (CREA), SANS GIAC Certified Forensic Analyst (GCFA), and Payment Card Industry Qualified Security Assessor (QSA). He also plays a leading role in a number of industry-relevant organizations which include the Consortium of Digital Forensics Specialists (CDFS), United States Secret Service Electronic Crimes Task Force (USSS ECTF), and the International Association of Chiefs of Police (IACP) Computer Crimes and Digital Evidence Committee (CCDE). He is the primary author of *"Unix and Linux Forensic Analysis"* by Syngress and the author of the award winning blog, *The Digital Standard*.

Chris has a Bachelor of Science degree in Applied Management from Grand Canyon University and a Master of Science degree in Information Security from Capella University.

George S. Takach (gtakach@mccarthy.ca) is a senior partner at McCarthy Tétrault (www.mccarthy.ca), where he practises exclusively in the technology law field. He brings significant value to clients in the following areas: privacy (including data Breaches), data security, cloud computing, big data, and social media, as well as tech M&A and commercial arrangements such as licensing, outsourcing, and e-commence. He is the author of three books in the computer law space, and for 20 years taught an evening law school course in computer law.

Brian West is a global managing director, Crisis Management at Fleishman-Hillard Inc. He has more than 35 years of experience in corporate & public affairs and issues/crisis management in Asia Pacific and globally, including working both in house and consultancy. He has managed stakeholder relationships and communications around many high profile crises, from litigation to product recalls and data Breaches. His work has ranged from the mining and resources sector, through the investment, financial and professional services, FMCG, and public sectors. He leads a global team of certified crisis professionals focusing on issues and crisis response, as well as crisis preparedness.

Acknowledgments

I thank my wife for her extreme understanding in my absence (again) while writing another book and for her ability to play sounding board without looking overly bored. To my wonderful kids for enduring a bit of a "disappearing daddy" routine over the past year, I thank you. This book without a doubt would not have been possible without your continued support.

I would also like to thank Syngress Publishing for supporting the publication of this book and to Chris Pogue and Curtis Rose for your invaluable guidance that helped shape the outcome of this project.

CHAPTER 1

An Overview of Data Breaches

Kevvie Fowler

INTRODUCTION

You are at home watching television when your phone rings. It's your boss, he advises you that your company has received complaints about fraudulent activity that has been traced back to your organization. He feels that there may have been a security Breach within your systems and needs you to come into work immediately to help manage the incident. Arriving at the office and on your way to a meeting that has been called, you begin to think to yourself although you've managed smaller incidents such as malware outbreaks, your organization has never managed anything like this. Glancing around the meeting room at the assembled members of the public relations, legal, IT, security, and executive team, there is a common look of despair and disbelief. No one appears to be in control and at that moment you begin to get a sick feeling in your stomach as management asks the dreaded questions; How *do you begin to investigate and manage the Breach? How do you recover? What will investors make of this?*

Unfortunately the above scenario is an all too familiar one and as cyber criminals gain greater sophistication, the number of Breaches are increasing and many organizations are no longer questioning whether a Breach will occur but understand that they will experience one or have already experienced one and don't yet know it. The impact of these Breaches can be catastrophic with the 2011 Breach of Sony Corporation's online videogame services serving as an example with reported losses of over $1 billion USD.[1]

Proactively preparing for a Breach has been proven to significantly reduce the associated impact to an organization by 23%.[2] This book can serve as both a guide to aid in the proactive preparation for a Breach to minimize impact

---

[1] http://www.wsj.com/articles/SB10001424052748703859304576307664174667924.

[2] http://www.symantec.com/content/en/us/about/media/pdfs/b-cost-of-a-data-breach-us-report-2013.en-us.pdf.

Data Breach Preparation and Response. http://dx.doi.org/10.1016/B978-0-12-803451-4.00001-0

and as a reference that can be used to reactively qualify, manage, and recover from Breaches.

WHAT IS A DATA BREACH?

In this day and age, it's difficult to ignore the fact that cyber security is on everyone's mind. Whether it surfaces in a discussion within the Boardroom or the lunch room, the discussion doesn't go far before cyber security and data Breaches are discussed. Often it's about the latest organization to fall victim to a Breach or what an organization is or should be doing to protect itself. A Google search of "data Breach" will result in millions of hits, many with conflicting definitions of what a data Breach is. I will not debate which definitions are correct or which ones are not; what I will do is define key Breach-related terms that are used throughout this book to ensure proper context and clarity.

- *Security Event:* An action directed to a system, network, or human intended to alter the target's state
- *Security Incident:* An event that violates organizational, regulatory, legislative or contractual security, or privacy policies
- *Data Breach ("Breach"):* A security incident that:
  - Involves the intentional or unintentional access, disclosure, manipulation or destruction of data; or
  - Meets specific definitions of a "Breach" as per state/province or federal laws or active contracts with clients, third parties or partners

Looking at our three definitions, most organizations have millions of events that occur on any given day, a subset of these events will be qualified as actual security incidents, and a subset of those incidents will be qualified as Breaches. It is good practice to treat all incidents as potential Breaches until they can be properly qualified, if not an incident not managed with the urgency and attention of a Breach, can later be qualified as one, and can expose the organization to increased lawsuits, fines, and reputational damage. We'll talk more about this later in this chapter.

Our Breach definition is holistic in nature and covers most known Breach scenarios. Popular examples that fit this definition include a cyber criminal breaking into a computer to steal data; a malicious insider who abuses personal access to systems and alters or discloses data to unauthorized users; or an employee or third party who inadvertently losses data contained on a backup tape, USB key, or other forms of storage media.

Breaches are not singular events that can be solved by bringing a few techno-logically savvy team members into a room. Breaches are one of the most com-plex challenges a business can face and require proper preparation in order to ensure they are managed throughout their entire lifecycle.

LIFECYCLE OF A BREACH

Cyber security for decades has been viewed by many primarily as a technology issue. This narrow view unfortunately has extended to Breach management resulting in Breach response plans being developed focusing squarely on tech-nological response. With this focus, they often center around how to quickly identify and remove a compromised server or laptop from a network in order to limit impact to business operations. Technological response, however, is just one phase of a series of events a Breached organization will need to go through in order to recover. This series of events is referred to as a Breach lifecycle. The lifecycle begins before the Breach is detected and ends long after the Breach has vanished from the headlines and business operations have resumed. We will refer to this entire process as the data Breach lifecycle which is illustrated in Fig. 1.1.

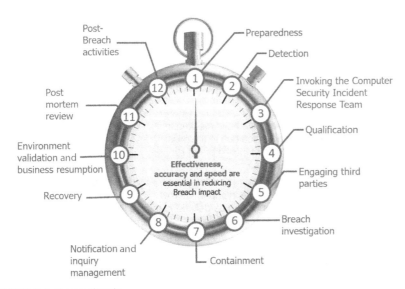

FIGURE 1.1 Breach lifecycle.

In-line with other business and technology lifecycles, there are outliers which may not traverse the Breach lifecycle in their entirety or in the same order as captured (Table 1.1). This Breach lifecycle, however, does encompass a wide range of Breaches and will be used as the basis of structured proactive Breach readiness within this book. Understanding the Breach lifecycle is a critical step in ensuring holistic Breach prevention planning for an organization.

Table 1.1 contains a description for each phase of the Breach lifecycle as well as a chapter reference that you can use to quickly obtain detailed guidance on the lifecycle phase.

Table 1.1 Data Breach Lifecycle Phases

	Phase	Description	Chapter Reference
1	Preparedness	The steps an organization takes in advance of a Breach to identify sensitive information, implement cyber defenses and detection capabilities, and to develop and test a Computer Security Incident Response (CSIR) Plan to manage an incident. Most organizations that suffer a material security incident have gone through this phase and have operated under the impression they were covered to an acceptable level. However, often errors in asset identification, security strategies, and incident response capabilities are quickly highlighted during and after management of an incident and organizations will almost always revisit this step after an incident to further improve preparedness including bolstering cyber security controls and response capabilities based on lessons learned. This phase is the beginning and the end of the management of any material incident	Chapters 2, 3, and 8
2	Detection	The moment an organization is alerted about a security incident. Whether the incident was detected by organizational security controls, staff or by a third party organization or individual. After the detection of an incident, it is critical that it is escalated appropriately to invoke the CSIR Plan. Several industry Breaches have resulted in increased impact to the victim organization due to the miss-handling of detection events which were ignored or not properly routed to the organization's CSIR Team	Chapter 4
3	Invoking the Computer Security Incident Response Team	Engaging appropriate CSIR Team members to assemble and assist in the management of the incident. Internal stakeholders should assemble and as defined in the CSIR Plan determine when to bring in third party CSIR Team members	Chapter 4
4	Qualification	Confirms the legitimacy of the incident. Detailed analysis is not performed at this stage; however, organizations should review the source, details, and determine if it is plausible that the incident did occur within their organization as well as determine the initial scope of the incident so the appropriate CSIR Team stakeholders can be engaged to manage the incident. Analysis of the information will be performed later in	Chapter 4

Table 1.1 Data Breach Lifecycle Phases—cont'd

	Phase	Description	Chapter Reference
		the lifecycle and may positively or negatively alter the scope of the incident	
5	Engaging third parties	Engaging third party team members such as legal counsel, public relations firms, and forensic response providers. Engagement of third parties should be in a controlled manner. Organizations finding themselves unprepared during an incident often bring in redundant third parties for assistance and provide them autonomy which without clear instructions and focus can actually hinder the investigation and the investigation findings and related communication can be used against the organization if not protected under attorney-client privilege	Chapter 4
6	Breach investigation	The monitoring, collection, preservation, and analysis of electronic or digital evidence in an effort to confirm the occurrence, scope, and timeframe associated with an incident. This phase of the lifecycle should follow applicable legal requirements for evidence acquisition and preservation and assist the victim organization adhere with legal response and notification obligations as appropriate	Chapters 4 and 6
7	Containment	Limiting the spread, reoccurrence, and extent of the unauthorized access within an organization. This often includes removing compromised systems from the network or shutting down compromised web applications. These steps effectively "stop the bleeding" and are driven by the analysis and qualification performed earlier in the lifecycle	Chapter 5
8	Notification and inquiry management	Identifying and notifying affected victims, regulators, and other parties about the Breach as appropriate. Identifying regulatory, legislative, contract, and industry good practices assist in determining the requirements. The analysis and the type of information contained in the incident and potential impact to the victims will further help determine notification requirements	Chapters 7 and 9
9	Recovery	Restoring trust to a presently untrusted host or environment. This may include rebuilding systems and networks containing compromised hosts or restoring destroyed data from backup	Chapter 8
10	Environment validation & business resumption	Reviewing and certifying the successful recovery of the environment is an essential step in reassuring internal staff, external stakeholders, and the industry as a whole that your organization has learned and improved from the past Breach and is ready to resume trusted business operations. This step is normally performed by a team other than those who performed incident containment and recovery	Chapter 8
11	Postmortem	Reflecting on the preparedness, detection, and management of the incident to identify what worked well and what requires focus to reduce the likelihood of a repeat incident and identifying recommendations to increase your capabilities to detect and manage future incidents	Chapter 8

Continued

Table 1.1 Data Breach Lifecycle Phases—cont'd

	Phase	Description	Chapter Reference
12	Post-Breach activities	Managing Breach related activities which manifest after the incident has been closed. These activities typically include lawsuits by impacted organizational shareholders, clients, and partners. Organizational leadership changes due to the Breach are also commonly associated with this phase in the Breach lifecycle; however, will not be explicitly covered in this book	Chapter 9

It also refers to the specific content provided in this book that will help you manage an actual Breach.

SOURCES OF DATA BREACHES

Data Breaches can occur as a result of several incidents, the most common being:

- A targeted cyber attack by a criminal specifically targeting an organization
- An opportunistic attack such as one by a criminal scanning the internet for vulnerable systems, finding, and exploiting them
- Inadvertently through errors and omissions such as an employee who loses a USB key containing sensitive data, or by an event at a third party who was entrusted to protect client data

These three incidents are the most common sources of data Breaches which we will explore in greater detail beginning with targeted cyber attacks as a result of cyber crime.

Cyber Crime

Cyber crime is a broad term which encompasses any crime committed using a computer or a network such as the internet. Cyber crime is often thought of as a criminal on a computer who gains unauthorized access to another's computer. However, cyber crime can also include the act of developing a virus for sale, storing a virus on an electronic device with the intent of using it, online fraud, and the digital exploitation of people and animals. Cyber crime costs the global economy over 445 billion dollars per year[3] with the largest impact being its damage to company performance and national economies. Behind every cyber crime is a cyber criminal which we'll explore in more detail.

The Cyber Criminals

When thinking of a cyber criminal, most people are likely to think about a recent news story about a "hacker" who digitally broke into an organization

---

[3]http://www.reuters.com/article/2014/06/09/us-cybersecurity-mcafee-csis-idUSKBN0EK0SV20140609.

and stole or manipulated sensitive information. In this chapter we will demystify the term "hacker" and refer to them as cyber criminals which better describes who they are and what they do. Any cyber crime executed in the past or that will be executed in the foreseeable future can be mapped to one of four distinct types of cyber criminals: petty criminals, hacktivists, organized criminals, and nation-state sponsored criminals. These four types of cyber criminals which we will examine in greater detail begin with petty criminals.

Petty Criminals

Petty criminals are single or small groups of criminals who carry out cyber crimes against individuals and organizations. They often use specialized software to detect and exploit vulnerabilities on publicly exposed systems and websites, they exploit these vulnerabilities and gain access to the information, and sell it for financial reward. Petty criminals are financially motivated and opportunistic, meaning they normally don't target organizations but rather opportunities. If a petty criminal is planning to steal credit card information, for example, they will take the path of least resistance and target an avenue where the risk of being caught is relatively low. If a petty criminal stumbles upon a website with strong security controls, they will often move on to another website which may host similar information but has inferior security controls.

Despite being financially motivated, most petty criminals lack significant financial or technical resources. If an organization has superior risk controls, a petty criminal will normally move on to another organization with a lower level of security. Even when petty criminals possessing specialized skills write and sell malware, they look for a quick return on their product.

The story surrounding a 2013 cyber security Breach in a leading US retailer includes an example of a petty criminal who sold malware he authored to a group of cyber criminals. The malware in question was reportedly[4] developed by a 17-year-old petty criminal from Russia, who sold it for $1800 to another group of cyber criminals who Breached the retailer's network and installed it across 1800 store locations. The malware stole a reported 40 million credit card numbers from the retailer's network.

In addition to selling custom malware, petty criminals with specialized skills serve as hackers for hire and develop computer intrusion programs such as malicious software, referred to as malware, that they sell to other cyber criminals. Fig. 1.1 illustrates a cyber criminal advertising his specialized skills for hire within an online marketplace known as the underground economy which we will discuss later in this chapter. Offense language in the advertisement has been redacted (Fig. 1.2).

---

[4]http://thehackernews.com/2014/01/BlackPOS-Malware-russian-hacker-Target.html

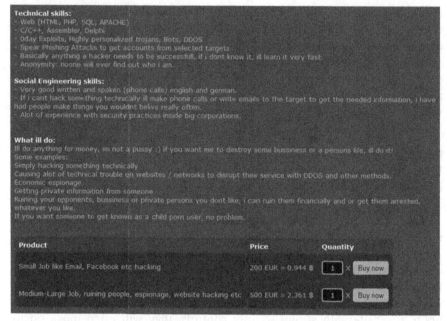

FIGURE 1.2 Cyber criminal advertising specialized skills for hire.

Petty criminals have also been known to launch targeted social engineering attacks which includes sending specially crafted emails designed to entice and trick individuals into divulging sensitive information and to circumvent procedural and technological controls to grant the criminal access to desired information or systems. An example of this is a criminal sending an email to an employee of an organization masquerading as the organization's IT support desk. The criminal may ask the user to log in to a fake site designed by the criminal to look like a website of the victim organization, but when accessed by the employee would capture their username and password. Some petty criminals may also be insiders, meaning they are legitimate employees of an organization who have access to systems and data. They abuse this access to sabotage or steal sensitive information that can be sold for financial gain.

Organized Criminals
Similar to petty criminals, organized criminals carry out cyber crime for financial gain. However, organized criminals differ as they normally are part of a large group of individuals who are well organized and very well funded. There are thousands of organized crime groups in the world. Many of these groups are very knowledgeable, are meticulous in planning and identifying organizations to target, and are highly efficient in execution. In recent history, organized crime groups have been linked to several high profile Breaches of US retailers in 2013 and 2014 and in each have compromised millions of financial and

personal data records that were later used for financial fraud and identify theft. In addition to targeting specific organizations, organized crime groups also use malware to carry out their financially motivated attacks.

It is important to note how malware has evolved. In the early 2000s malware was designed to disrupt operations and spread quickly, and this commonly resulting in saturated network connections and loss of business service availability. SQL Slammer[5] and Blaster[6] are two examples of this. Since then, malware has evolved and is now stealthy and designed to infect, monitor activity, and steal data without detection. This shift in malware has made it a popular vehicle for attacks by organized criminals. One such example is known as ransomware.

Ransomware is a strand of malware that unobtrusively infects a computer, scanning all local folders in search of data such as pictures and documents. It then turns to the network and repeats the search among network files and folders. With an inventory of documents, the malware encrypts them, rendering them useless. It then displays a message to the user informing them that they will need to pay a ransom, normally in the form of an online currency such as Bitcoin or LiteCoin, and once paid, the criminal group will send the victim the key needed to decrypt the files and return them to their prior state.

Ransomware is usually a threat that is built once and then used multiple times. The organized criminal group either purchases the malware or develops it internally before setting it loose on the internet, possibly infecting millions of systems around the world.

Despite the success of financially motivated crimes, monetary value is not a driver that is shared by all cyber criminals. The next group of criminals we will look at carry out cyber crimes in support of political causes.

Hacktivists
Hacktivists are groups of criminals who unite to carry out cyber attacks in support of political causes. Hacktivists typically target entire industries but sometimes attack specific organizations who they feel don't align with their political views or practices. In some cases hacktivists have targeted organizations not based on the victim organization's beliefs but the clients and partners they do business with. One law firm fell victim to a cyber attack from a hacktivist group due to the law firm's representation of a client linked to a high-profile legal case[7] the hacktivist group stole emails from the law firm, many of which were protected under attorney-client privilege and publicly posted them on the internet. At the time of this writing there are over 80 different hacktivist groups

---

[5]http://en.wikipedia.org/wiki/SQL_Slammer

[6]http://en.wikipedia.org/wiki/Blaster_(computer_worm)

[7]http://www.pcmag.com/article2/0,2817,2399909,00.asp

in existence. Among the best known hacktivist groups is "Anonymous," which has carried out hundreds of cyber attacks including Operation Payback,[8] which included a series of Distributed Denial of Service (DDoS) attacks that disrupted victims' websites, preventing legitimate users from accessing them. A DDoS attack is launched from multiple computers running specialized software that generates a large amount of traffic directed to a website with the intent of overwhelming the system so that it stops responding to legitimate user requests. Hacktivists typically announce upcoming attacks in advance with the goal of recruiting fellow hacktivists and raising media attention on the political cause they are supporting. Once recruiting is complete, the operation begins and hacktivists perform several types of reconnaissance to identify targets and weaknesses that can be exploited within targeted organizations. The attack is then carried out typically including the theft of sensitive information or disrupting business operations. At the end of a cyber operation, the hacktivists disband until they are recruited for a future cyber campaign. In this writer's experience of protecting organizations, hacktivists tend to attack in waves and the attacks continue for a period ranging from a few days to several weeks, sometimes long after a campaign was originally reported to end. Fig. 1.3 illustrates the stages of a hacktivist campaign.

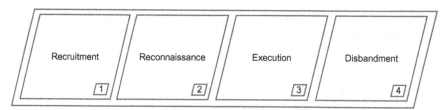

FIGURE 1.3 Stages of a hacktivists campaign.

The last group of cyber criminals we will look at are those sponsored by nation-states who carry out attack in support of a state agenda.

Nation-State Sponsored Criminals
Nation-state sponsored criminals are highly skilled individuals who are either employed by or contracted by nation states to launch targeted and coordinated attacks against their own or neighboring countries in support of a specific state agenda. When thinking about nation-state criminals, it is sometimes difficult to comprehend that some countries' governments direct criminal cyber attacks against their own citizens as well as against other countries. In the past, top

---

[8]http://www.darkreading.com/attacks-and-breaches/operation-payback-feds-charge-13-on-anonymous-attacks/d/d-id/1111819?

secret spies would infiltrate foreign governments and steal sensitive information, such as military plans. With the increased reliance on computers, espionage has moved to the cyber realm where it is commonly executed from secret computer security labs and focuses on the identification and covert extraction of sensitive digital information.

In many cases governments employ security experts who can plan and execute nation-state sponsored attacks. However, some governments also rely on external cyber mercenaries with specialized skillsets who are contracted to assist in or execute cyber attacks in their entirety. One such group of mercenaries is known as the Elderwood Group.[9] This is a group of cyber criminals who have conducted more than 300 cyber attacks over the past four years, including targeted attacks against US military defense contractors, as well as governments and large technology companies.

Considering the substantial investment in cyber security protection by governments, their military, and large technology companies, being a good cyber-criminal is not enough to ensure a successful attack. Nation-state sponsored criminals also leverage 0-day vulnerabilities. These are vulnerabilities within popular software and hardware products that the vendor and public are unaware of.

These 0-day vulnerabilities are often identified by cyber security experts within various government agencies, by independent security researchers and also by criminals. These vulnerabilities are highly sought after by elite hacking groups who need to deliver results to their high-paying clients. With this in mind it is not uncommon for 0-day vulnerabilities found within popular software packages to demand price tags upwards of $250,000.[10] In reality this high price tag can make up a small fraction of the fees elite cyber criminals charge their nation-state clients. Keeping the existence of the 0-day vulnerabilities unknown to the general public helps ensure they remain effective. To aid in maintaining this secrecy, cyber criminals often use covert channels to communicate with each other and prospective clients.

Criminal Communication Channels
The Invisible Web

The internet consists of two main areas, the first being the public internet also referred to as the "visible web." The visible web is the area of the internet that most people are familiar with. Users navigate it and use search engines to access web pages across popular domains such as .ca, .com, .org, .net, .biz, and .info.

---

[9]http://thenextweb.com/insider/2012/09/07/google-aurora-attackers-still-large-targeting-mainly-us-finance-energy-education-companies/

[10]http://www.forbes.com/sites/andygreenberg/2012/03/23/shopping-for-zero-days-an-price-list-for-hackers-secret-software-exploits/

This visible portion of the internet has been estimated to account for less than 4%[11] of the internet's total size. The other 96% of the internet can be referred to as the "invisible web" which is not indexed by search engines and requires special know-how and in some cases specialized clients to access it. Digging one level lower, the invisible can also be divided into two areas the Deep web and Dark web.

Deep web consists of millions of websites that store data within back-end databases and can only be accessed by users who enter search terms into a web form on the website. An example of a deep website would be a library which would require users to enter specific search criteria into a web form in order to see the records such as books that match the search criteria. Deep web content can be accessed by standard web browsers as long as users know where to look and what specific records they are looking for, so they can craft the query criteria accordingly.

Dark web was designed with one sole goal, to keep the identify and location of its users anonymous unlike the visible web and deep web where there are multiple sources that record users' IP addresses and other information which can be used to track their geographical locations, computer types, and, in some cases, their identity. Two of the largest and most popular networks within the dark web are the .Onion and .I2P domains. Websites within the onion domain carry an .onion extension and can be accessed using a The Onion Router (TOR) client. Websites within the Invisible Internet Project carry an .i2p extension and can be accessed using a variety of specialized clients. Using a standard computer or mobile device you can download the required dark web client and simultaneously access the visible and invisible areas of the internet including the deep web and dark web as depicted in Fig. 1.4.

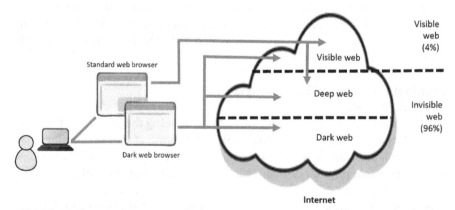

FIGURE 1.4 Illustration of the visible and invisible web.

---

[11]http://bgr.com/2014/01/20/how-to-access-tor-silk-road-deep-web/#

Because the dark web was designed to mask the identities and location of its users, it is often used by the military, investigative journalists, and the government to ensure its communication remains anonymous and difficult to track. Unfortunately it is also frequently used by cyber criminals to profit from and promote illegal activity.

Profiting From Cyber Crime

The sheer size and anonymity associated with the invisible web is a draw for cyber criminals and illegal activity. Much of this illegal activity is financially driven and comes in one of two forms, selling previously stolen data and extortion.

Selling Stolen Data

As discussed earlier in this chapter, petty criminals and organized crime groups are financially motivated. When they launch attacks and steal information, the information itself is of no direct monetary value and must be sold for financial reward. The one exception to this is ransomware that holds data at ransom until a fee is paid to release it. When stolen data needs to be converted into currency, cyber criminals often turn to the underground economy which is a marketplace consisting of large collections of websites selling illegal products and services ranging from drugs and weapons to advertisements from contract hitman and cyber mercenaries. An example of this is the screen capture depicted in Fig. 1.4 which shows an advertisement retrieved from the underground economy advertising stolen credit card numbers and online payment service accounts for sale (Fig. 1.5).

With this blatantly direct advertising and commerce one would wonder why law enforcement doesn't shut down these networks. The primary challenge is that for many of the servers involved, the advertising and commerce reside within the invisible web—which is an area of the internet specially designed to keep its users anonymous. This makes it very difficult for law enforcement to track down the physical location of systems and those who use them.

This anonymity means the underground economy serves as a thriving marketplace for criminals selling data stolen during a past cyber attack. There are several types of data commonly traded within the underground economy which are captured within the Table 1.2.

Information such as organizational trade secrets and other forms of intellectual property are also targeted by cyber criminals; however, this information is not as commonly sold within popular online forums, therefore, has been omitted from the preceding table.

Selling stolen data within the underground economy is an activity that occurs subsequent to a cyber attack. Organized criminals have also mastered another revenue channel that doesn't require them to actually launch cyber attacks against an organization, but rather to extort a fee to prevent a future cyber attack.

FIGURE 1.5 A screen capture of stolen data for sale within the underground economy.

Cyber Extortion

The most important asset to almost every organization in the world is data. Cyber criminals understand this and may threaten to launch cyber attacks that will negatively impact the availability and integrity of an organization's data, their brand, and hinder their ability to conduct business. An increasing number

Table 1.2 Popular Data Products for Sale in the Underground Economy

Data	Purpose	$\record
Usernames and passwords	Research shows that users often reuse the same username and password among multiple websites. Obtaining the credentials of a user from one website (even if the website is not associated with any sensitive data) will allow the criminal to attempt and reuse it within other websites used by that user that are associated with sensitive data	$5.60[a]
Social media accounts	Social media accounts serve multiple purposes to cyber criminals. First, they are used as a vehicle to send SPAM. Criminals are paid by advertisers to send marketing messages referred to as SPAM to as many people as possible. Traditionally SPAM is sent via email from virus compromised computers. Transmission of email-based SPAM is easily detected by basic security tools. SPAM detection mechanisms however rarely apply to the realm of social networks. One compromised social media account can be used to send SPAM to other connected social network users without detection. SPAM sent via social networks can also be associated with a better rate of success in reaching their intended audience as the SPAM is being sent from another social network user and method that the recipient trusts. Social media accounts with a higher number of followers or friends can be used by criminals to reach more unsuspecting users and command higher dollar amounts within the underground economy. Secondly, social media accounts are being used by an increasingly larger number of websites to simplify the user authentication. These websites are allowing existing social media accounts to be used as authentication as opposed to having the user create a new username and password within the website. Therefore a compromised social media account can be used by a cyber criminal to gain access to both the social network as well as other sites leveraging the social network for authentication	$.05–$8.00[b]
Loyalty rewards accounts	Loyalty rewards is a popular incentive organizations use to improve the customer experience. Points are awarded to customers who do business with an organization and can be redeemed for merchandise and in some cases monetary credits on store accounts. Due to the associated monetary value and merchandise that can be obtained by points, they have become a target of choice for cyber criminals who will transfer points from unsuspecting accounts or redeem points for merchandise that is shipped to alternative mailing addresses. Points are also being transferred using third party services that convert and transfer points between loyalty reward programs. On average loyalty reward points will allow a cyber criminal to purchase merchandise for 1% of its market value. For example a cyber criminal could spend $10 in the underground economy to buy enough loyalty reward points to buy a camera with a market value of a thousand dollars	$.50 for 50,000 points[c]
Debit and credit card numbers	Stolen debit and credit card information is sold within the underground economy to criminals seeking to use the card information for financial fraud. Stolen debit card information linked to a bank account with a high balance retains a greater value to criminals. Similar to debit card data, values vary depending on what details accompany the card number, the type of credit card, and how long ago they were stolen from an organization. A stolen credit card record containing the card number, expiry, and security code is not worth top dollar. However, combining these details with a cardholder name, address, and mother's maiden name allow cyber criminals to bypass some	$.25–$100[d]

Continued

Table 1.2 Popular Data Products for Sale in the Underground Economy—cont'd

Data	Purpose	$\record
	fraud detection systems and therefore will command higher premiums within the underground economy. In addition to the details associated, the type of credit card and age of the compromise in which it was obtained also affects the price. Credit card data belonging to a platinum credit card that was compromised recently will command higher fees in contrast to the same information and card type that was compromised weeks ago. The reason for this is that older the information gets the greater the likelihood that the organization and the card issuer will identify the data Breach and suspend or cancel the credit card as a result. With valid credit cards criminals purchase merchandise, transfer funds between accounts, and make online payments and donations	
Healthcare records	One of the most highly sought after commodities in the underground economy are stolen healthcare records. These records can contain names, birthdates, medical history/aliments, social insurance numbers and in some cases financial information such as bank account data or credit card information. This information is used by criminals for identity theft and prescription drug fraud. Cyber criminals are also using healthcare records to help create fraudulent claims which are submitted to insurers	$47.62[e]

[a]http://blogs.wsj.com/riskandcompliance/2013/06/26/passwords-more-valuable-than-credit-card-data/.
[b]http://blogs.wsj.com/corporate-intelligence/2015/03/28/whats-more-valuable-a-stolen-twitter-account-or-a-stolen-credit-card/.
[c]http://www.tripwire.com/state-of-security/vulnerability-management/how-stolen-target-credit-cards-are-used-on-the-black-market/.
[d]http://www.tripwire.com/state-of-security/vulnerability-management/how-stolen-target-credit-cards-are-used-on-the-black-market/.
[e]http://www.foxbusiness.com/technology/2015/01/15/e-bazaar-crooks-hawk-your-info-in-online-black-market/.

of organizations are being contacted by criminals who have not yet Breached their networks but are threatening to Breach them if a ransom is not paid. Cyber criminals traditionally ask for ransom to be paid in an virtual currency such as Bitcoin as it's run by a decentralized network of computers that don't collect personal information about users, and transactions are designed to be irreversible. This makes the delivery of ransom to the criminals seamless and untraceable. Fig. 1.5 illustrates the actual extortion letter sent to a US-based organization demanding a bitcoin payment to avoid a future cyber attack (Fig. 1.6).

Another form of cyber extortion occurs post-Breach when a cyber criminal holds stolen data hostage. In these cases often the victim is not aware a Breach has occurred until they are contacted by the cyber criminal and often will need to quickly investigate to discount the hacker's claims or comply with the criminal's demands. An example of this form of attack from 2007 is a large technology manufacturer[12] who was contacted by a cyber criminal who claimed to have stolen the encryption key used within several of its technology products

---

[12]http://www.techworld.com/news/security/symbian-signing-key-reportedly-stolen-from-nokia-could-have-enabled-powerful-malware-3525754/

FIGURE 1.6 Extortion letter received from a US based company. *Source: http://krebsonsecurity.com*

and would publish it to compromise the security of millions of the manufacture's devices if a ransom was not paid. The organization contacted the authorities who arranged to catch the bad guys in the act and left millions of euros in a parking lot. The criminal however was able to retrieve the ransom payment and escape without detection. The criminal has never been caught to date and the encryption key was never published.

Selling Illegal Services

Cyber criminals are collaborating to become more efficient at planning and executing attacks. Years ago a cyber criminal would develop the skills he or she needed in order to carry out a cyber attack. Today, cyber criminals will seek out other criminals with the required specialized skills and a good reputation to assist in the planning or execution of a cyber attack.

High-in-demand services offered by cyber criminals within the underground economy are captured within Table 1.3.

Table 1.3 Popular Illegal Services for Sale in the Underground Economy

Service	Cost (USD)
Hacking into a website of your choice	$100–$300
A "how to" manual on how to perform illegal criminal activity	$30 each
Access to previously compromised systems (bots) that can be leveraged to carry out your bidding	$600–$1000 for 500 bots
Launch a DDoS attack against targets of your choice for one week	$350–$600

Similar to legitimate organizations, brand reputation is extremely important and cyber criminals pride themselves on their reputation which serves as a differentiator in a competitive underground marketplace.

Cyber attacks are a large source of data Breaches; however, there are also non-malicious sources of data loss including simple errors made by employees.

Errors and Omissions

As businesses explore ways to become more agile, efficient, and flexible for employees, initiatives such as Bring Your Own Device (BYOD), globalization, and remote workforces—in concert with the inexpensive data storage costs—have resulted in corporate data being stored, transferred, and processed on noncorporate devices that can be misplaced, lost, or stolen and result in a data security Breach. To help manage the risk many organizations develop and educate employees on policies that govern what information can be copied to specific storage media, when encryption needs to be used and how information should be managed by employees. Despite these policies and awareness, humans are prone to mistakes. Sometimes they may forget proper protocol, and other times an employee may take a calculated risk to circumvent the process. Take, for example, an employee who copies a large amount of sensitive information to a USB thumb drive. The employer provides encrypted USB keys however the amount of data that needed to be copied superseded the company issued device. The employee copies the information to his personal USB key for an urgent client meeting and misplaces it. This could result in a data Breach that will be equally as damaging to the organization as a targeted cyber attack. Information stored on systems located within an organization's office or employee's possession—although in line with organizational processes—is also exposed to physical theft that can result in a security Breach. Errors and omissions security Breaches can also be as a result of system error. As many organizations modernize physical data into portals and websites, controls need to be verified to ensure data is properly segregated between users. This also ensures that one user cannot see the information of another. Whether due to a system glitch or intentional or unintentional human behavior, errors and omissions are accounting for an increased number of costly data security Breaches for organizations.[13]

Third Parties

Many organizations employ third parties to deliver services and products. In outsourced arrangements, although elements of data management or processing are outsourced, outsourcing organizations are still required to govern the third party data and systems. This governance of a third party can be more challenging than governance of information had it resided within the organization's facilities. Also regulatory, legislative, and organizational requirements the organization would face if the data was present within their facilities still apply to it when it resides with the third party.

Despite the outsourcing of service delivery, the consequences associated with a cyber event experienced at a contracted third party can still directly affect the outsourcing organization. For example let's consider an organization which maintains a customer database of one million data records that is backed up by a third party. If the database was accessed by cyber criminals due to a lack of basic security practices within the third party provider, the impact of the Breach including loss of business, recovery costs, and damage to brand would lie with the organization. If there was a contract in place between the organization and the contracted third party the costs associated with the Breach may have been covered by the third party, and better yet the Breach may have been avoided all together if there were terms within the contract that required the third party to implement and maintain good industry security practices to protect the organization's information.

Contract security terms are normally contained in a legal service agreement that defines the level of services the organization will receive and the steps taken by the third party vendor or service provider to protect the information under its management. When evaluating service providers, it is imperative to ensure that they incorporate and comply with security requirements including maintaining

---

[13]Thor Olavsrud, "Most Data Breaches Caused by Human Error, System Glitches", *CIO, June 17, 2013*

an adequate level of cyber security protection equal to or greater than that of the organization's own practices. This must include prompt notification in the event of a suspected or confirmed intrusion at the third party provider. And in the event of a security Breach, your agreement should ensure that your organization has access to your systems and data and the ability to perform digital forensic investigations if needed. Some organizations have encountered Breaches and have disagreed with the forensic findings and approach taken by their service provider. If there is an accessibility clause within a contract you would be able to bring in an independent forensic service provider to perform an investigation that better aligns to your organization's needs, goals, and objectives.

IMPACT OF A DATA BREACH

In this day and age, a security Breach is viewed by many as an inevitable event. Some argue this may be one of the most significant events that an organization can face. In support of this opinion, news headlines are dominated by massive data security Breaches that reference hundreds of millions and in some cases billions of dollars in costs to victim organizations. The impact of these mega Breaches is staggering however not typical for most organizations who suffer a data Breach. The Ponemon Institute shows that the average cost of a typical Breach in North America is 5.4 million dollars (USD)[14] or 201 dollars per Breached record.

Impact associated with Breaches can go beyond the financial implications and range from impacting your staff's morale and productivity to permanently damaging customer, partner, and brand reputation.

The impact of data Breaches span direct and indirect costs and can also result in as systemic costs to the industry—concepts we'll explore in more detail beginning with direct costs.

Direct Costs

Direct costs are the immediate costs to the organization for managing the Breach including determining the Breach scope, investigation related expenses such as engaging third party forensics and legal assistance, and the costs to identify and notify impacted customers and partners. The Ponemon Institute has reported that the direct costs on average to an organization would be $67 (USD) per compromised record.[15] Further details on direct costs are captured in greater detail within Table 1.4.

---

[14]http://www.ponemon.org/blog/ponemon-institute-releases-2014-cost-of-data-breach-global-analysis

[15]http://www.ponemon.org/blog/ponemon-institute-releases-2014-cost-of-data-breach-global-analysis

Table 1.4 Direct Costs Associated With a Breach

(#)	Phase	Description	Aprox. Cost (USD)
1	Detection and escalation	Cost associated with the activities needed for an organization to detect and reduce scope of the incident including identifying the data involved in the Breach, the cost of forensic response, crisis team management, and internal communication to corporate leadership Detection and escalation costs are typically influenced by the type of Breach. Forensic costs are typically higher if the point of compromise is not known such as with the compromise of a web application by a criminal in contrast to an incident involving a lost corporate laptop	$420,000
2	Notification	Costs needed for organizations to identify affected individuals and regulatory, legislative, and contract notification requirements as well as notifying victims of the Breach via email, phone, mail, or website advertisement Notification costs are typically influenced by the countries, states, and provinces that Breach victims reside within. Countries, states, and provinces with a higher number of notification requirements for Breach victims will positively influence the cost and timeline for notification of Breach victims	$510,000
3	Post-Breach Services	Costs associated with activities needed by the organization to address legal and consulting fees, regulatory fines, lawsuits, costs of identity theft, and fraud monitoring services for Breach victims as well as targeted product and service cost reductions to help maintain and attract new customers Internal costs such as improving cyber security in the aftermath of the Breach and organizational personnel and leadership enhancements are also included Post-Breach services similar to other Breach phases are typically influenced by the number of records involved, in addition to the amount of any public perceptions on the negligence of the organization's proactive security strategies and effective and efficient response to the Breach	$1,600,000

Additional factors that influence direct costs of a data Breach are as follows:

- *The maturity of the Breached organization's security program* will influence the cost of a Breach. An organization with a highly mature security program will typically identify the Breach sooner and have the controls and programs in place to rapidly respond and manage it which reduces the Breach scope and impact
- *Prior experience in managing a* Breach can reduce the costs of subsequent Breaches. Being familiar with the process, what worked and the pitfalls to avoid will aid in effectively and efficiently managing the Breach
- *The number and type of records lost* directly influences the cost of a Breach. With this in mind, typically, Breaches with one million records will cost more to recover from than a Breach containing one thousand records. However, looking at the type of record, a Breach of one million records of personal customer information would likely cost less than a Breach of one record, if the one record contained intellectual property that was integral in several important product lines. We will cover how to use

database forensics to better pinpoint the precise number of records involved in a Breach and minimize the associated impact within Chapter 6 of this book

Indirect Costs

Indirect costs are not cash-based and alternatively account for the time, effort, and resources employees of the Breached organization spend handling various aspects of the Breach response such as interviewing and hiring third party firms to assist in Breach management, internal investigations, and customer turnover as well as managing damage to brand reputation and investor value. On average Breached organizations have indirect costs that amount to approximately $134 (USD) per compromised record. Some aspects of indirect costs are difficult to calculate and therefore referenced with a Not Applicable (N/A) for costs within Table 1.5.

Table 1.5 Indirect Costs Associated With a Breach

(#)	Phase	Description	Aprox. Cost (USD)
1	Lost Business	An unfortunate consequence of a data Breach is the abnormal loss of existing customers as well as a reduction in target customers who will chose not to create a relationship with the victim organization as a consequence of the experienced Breach. These factors are influenced by the sheer size of the Breach, and the frustration of the victims which can be amplified by: ■ Poor Breach response such as slow and unreliable Breach communication ■ The level of inconvenience or hardship Breach victims suffer is another factor which can be tied to the type of data. For example, a Breach involving personal information can be more burdensome to victims than a Breach involving financial data ■ The age of the affected Breach victims, research shows adult Breach victims are typically less likely to do business again with an organization where their financial data has been Breached in contrast to younger consumers who appear to be more forgiving[a] ■ Lost business is typically influenced by how well an organization manages the Breach response especially the Notification and inquiry management and Post-Breach activities	$3,320,000
2	Loss of employee productivity	Breached organizations may experience a loss of employee productivity due to business systems being taken off-line during Breach-related forensic investigations as well as employees being reallocated to assist in Breach response actions such as selecting external vendors, providing counsel or assistance, and aiding in developing communication and action plans	N/A
3	Loss of brand value	Historically Breaches have a direct effect on brand value. This results in decreased share prices for a period of time following a Breach, increased customer churn rates, and a reduction in acquiring new customers as well as lost future business partnerships and business opportunities	N/A

[a]http://www.safenet-inc.com/news/2014/data-breaches-impact-on-customer-loyalty-survey/.

Systemic Costs

In addition to the direct and indirect costs Breached organizations must manage, there is also a systemic impact that needs to be considered when evaluating the impact of a Breach. An example of this is within the retail industry, if one retailer is Breached and credit card data is stolen. The Breached retailer will cover the direct and indirect costs of a Breach; however, there is a cost to cancel compromised cards, to reissue new credit cards to the affected consumers and to account for chargebacks associated with the fraudulent transactions for accounts associated with the Breach. In this example the single Breach can have a material negative impact to the Breached organization as well as a cascading impact across the banks who issued the credit cards and the merchants who unknowingly processed the fraudulent transactions.

HISTORICAL CHALLENGES WITH BREACH MANAGEMENT

Most organizations that suffered highly publicized data Breaches up until the time of this writing had one thing in common; they each had incident response plans in place that many felt were adequate. They also learned—in the heat of the Breach—that their plans were far away from what they needed. Reflecting on some of the recent Breach management challenges will allow us to improve future Breach response.

The following challenges in Breach management are compiled from lessons learned from actual Breaches that have occurred in the industry. The organizations that experienced the challenges will not be named; however, the challenges they faced will be of benefit to the industry as a whole.

1. **Waiting too long before disclosing a Breach and notifying customers**
   When a Breach is experienced timely notification is essential to ensure victims can be kept informed on the Breach and are aware and informed of the potential impact to themselves. Breached organizations need to ensure they understand legislative, regulatory, and contract notification requirements for affected customers and partners and to ensure investigation details are accurate prior to communication. A balance should be struck between notification requirements identification, qualification of information, and getting information to impacted individuals. In some cases organizations decide to wait until a full investigation is performed before notifying individuals impacted by a Breach. In other cases organizations may elect to try and ignore the fact that a Breach occurred and not notify Breach victims in fear that material financial and reputational harm will follow. Regardless of the driver, recent Breaches have seen one retailer who notified its payment processors but not the customers whose information was disclosed. On the other side we have seen some organizations that suffer a Breach, delay

notification for two to three weeks and have been met with negative perceptions within the industry as well as lawsuits from customers and merchants. In contrast two retailers notified customers within a few days of the Breach and have been well regarded. We will discuss notification later in this book and get into specific details and guidance on Breach notification

2. **Staffing an incident response team with solely technical experts**
   Cyber security is a whole-business issue, not just a technology issue. A proper cyber security strategy includes embedding security throughout and engaging various areas of the business. Despite this holistic approach to proactively protecting an organization, many organization's staff response teams have primarily technical security and forensics personnel. A Breach response team of IT subject matter experts is helpful, however will have very little effectiveness in managing the nontechnical aspects of Breaches such as developing plans to communicate with internal and external stakeholders and identifying the legal requirements associated with different types of data that may have been exposed and making decisions in the best interest of the business

3. **Ineffective operationalization of an incident response plan**
   Developing an incident response plan is a good measure in proactively preparing for a Breach. Equally as important as developing the plan is ensuring it is effectively operationalized to ensure awareness, and proper testing and execution. Common challenge areas are having a plan that was not regularly updated to align with changes to business such as the development or consolidation of business lines, the changes in response team members and contact details, or simply having a plan that various stakeholders are not clear on their roles and responsibilities. Minute details such as the procurement process to bring in third party response assistance is critical as is ensuring the team has appropriate authority to carry out the roles and responsibilities that they are assigned

4. **Demonstrating a lack of support and empathy for Breach victims**
   Breaches can be a traumatic event for organizations as well as their customers. In the event of a Breach that impacts its customers, the organization suffering the Breach will be looking for timely information on the Breach, known or potential impact to them, and what they can do to protect themselves
   As with any issue that can impact an organization's reputation, it is imperative that no less consideration is given to communication planning than would be given in the event of a fire, natural disaster, or other potential crisis. Following the counsel of communications advisors is key as is ensuring personable and empathetic spokespeople are well prepared to manage your messages throughout your Breach

investigation. Breach investigations can last a long period of time—organizations have been criticized for changing spokespeople throughout the course of the Breach and being ill-prepared to communicate with Breach victims, customers, employees, shareholders, and the media

One retailer who was Breached posted a notice of the Breach on their website however the notice was very difficult to locate on the website which frustrated victims who couldn't find it. The same retailer also experienced challenges in managing the volume of inquiries they received from victims who quickly overwhelmed the retailer's telephone support lines and social media channels again resulting in frustration

As discussed earlier in this chapter there is a systemic impact to data Breaches and in some cases financial institutions who issued cards that were compromised in a Breach capitalized on the Breach events to help further build trust and credibility with victims. Measures such as working extended hours to replace compromised cards and reducing daily cash limit to suspect accounts helped limit the potential impact to victims

SUMMARY

Earlier in my career data Breaches were taboo, they just weren't mentioned in the business world. They did not dominate the media headlines and weren't on the radar of the Boards of directors and organizational executives. There was some visibility at an operational level, and one of my core performance objectives was to ensure the organization did not experience any data security Breaches. This objective naturally was passed down to my team to also strive toward. Looking back with the benefit of hindsight, I can now wonder how a security team could possibly be tasked with ensuring the data security of an entire organization? Well security was not seen as a whole business issue, and alternatively, the organization viewed a data Breach as an event (and consequence) arising as a result of the security team not doing their jobs effectively. This view as we know now was incorrect, however at that time was the norm. Today, data Breaches are seen by many organizations as an inevitable event and just "a part of doing business." Organizations are understanding that you can't prevent Breaches from occurring; however, the earlier you can detect them, the greater likelihood you can limit the associated impact. Stemming from this view, I have observed on countless occasions that the objectives of today's organizational security teams have extended from just trying to prevent Breaches to also trying to detect them quicker. Objectives are actually created with the goal of having security teams partner with organizational stakeholders to proactively be prepared for Breaches, improve protection mechanisms, and security awareness training and other controls to help the organization identify, manage, and recover from Breaches quicker than they have been able to in the past.

Accomplishing this new objective requires a true understanding of data Breaches. Granted most people in the corporate world today have heard about Breaches in one form or another; however, they are unclear on which aspects of the Breach are relevant to them and their organization. This chapter has provided you the overview of what a data Breach is, the motivations and actors behind them, the impact of a Breach, and—more importantly—context around this information, so you can apply it to your both personal and business environments and improve your cyber awareness.

CHAPTER 2

Preparing to Develop a Computer Security Incident Response Plan

Kevvie Fowler, George Takach, Greg Markell

INTRODUCTION

In the May 2015 edition of Forbes magazine[1] the CEO of one of the largest banks in the United States is quoted as admitting that there are only three things that he fears could destroy his bank over-night: "meteors, nuclear weapons, and cyber security."

This quote is an interesting one, however not unexpected as there is no shortage of stories capturing television, online, print, and social media headlines by exposing organizations impacted by data Breaches. Some of these stories are projected to carry losses of over a billion dollars. Not only are these losses a result of hard business costs of managing a data Breach, but as a result of lawsuits resulting from perceived negligence leading up to a Breach as well as how well the organization is perceived to have responded to an incident.

With this awareness, it is shocking to many that organizations continually seem to be caught off-guard when they are faced with a data Breach. They feel they are proactively prepared in advance and when faced with a material Breach often find that their Breach response program is ineffective in properly managing the incident at-hand.

This chapter will review critical activities that should be completed in advance of developing a Breach response program. These activities will ensure the plan you will eventually develop will identify, respond, and help your organization recover from a Breach.

CSIR PLAN PLANNING

Most organizations understand the importance of having a CSIR Plan. The challenge is ensuring that the plan is tailored to navigate the departments, cultures, politics, and environments that exist across the enterprise. Fuelling this challenge

---

[1]Forbes May 4, 2015 "Next Billion-Dollar Startups."

Data Breach Preparation and Response. http://dx.doi.org/10.1016/B978-0-12-803451-4.00002-2

is the reality that Breach planning can be viewed differently by different people, different organizations, and by different people within one organization.

Some organizations view Breach plan development as a check-box exercise, they understand the need to have one but do the bare minimum in their perspective to comply with the requirement. From personal experience I have observed an organization which obtained a Breach response plan template that was downloaded from the internet, changed a few references and contact information and adopted the plan as their own. When they were faced with a material incident the plan led to confusion and mishandled response that placed them in noncompliance with legislative and regulatory requirements. The check-box driven approach to plan development seemed to be a quick solution however ultimately cost this organization in the long run.

I have also observed an organization that had good intentions and wanted to develop an effective Breach response plan. They leveraged their existing Business Continuity Program (BCP) assuming it would adequately also cover them for cyber incidents. Proper Breach response scenarios were never tested and during a material incident involving the disclosure of sensitive data realized they were ill-equipped to manage it. In this case the organization suffered a Breach involving criminals who infiltrated the network and stole client data. The organization leveraged the BCP to the best of their ability to manage the cyber incident including individuals who they deemed as forensic investigators however had not been formally trained. The investigation team concluded that they understood the scope of the Breach and had identified the root cause which was successfully mitigated. This statement was made to the media to publicly reassure the organization's clients of the effectiveness of their response. The criminals responsible for the original incident were able to demonstrate that they still had access to the network by stealing and disclosing additional data and posting it on the internet. The public nature of these events and the associated media attention resulted in the organization loosing creditably with clients, peers, and partners who were reassured that the root issue was addressed only to find their personal and business information continued to leak out of the Breached organization. Looking at both of these examples, one organization took short-cuts to develop the CSIR Plan, the other organization unknowingly did the same, and both organizations achieved the same result—ineffective incident response that increased the impact of the incident. Not knowing how to develop and maintain an effective CSIR Plan can carry the same impact as not having one at all.

Developing a Breach response plan and right-sizing it for your organization is a critical task but what does it involve? Well it starts long before you begin drafting the plan documentation. In this chapter we will step through the critical steps that should be performed to drive future plan development.

CSIR Plan Development Prerequisites

There are no two organizations alike. Each organization has fundamental differences, from their culture, management expectations, and business units to their processes and technology. In some cases a single organization may experience these fundamental differences across business units which are most frequent if the organization has undergone a recent acquisition and both entities are operating independently of each other. These key differences serve as prerequisites that should be identified in advance of developing the CSIR Plan to ensure the plan is tailored to navigate them effectively. A four-phased methodology, which can be used to identify CSIR Plan dependencies and requirements, is illustrated in Fig. 2.1.

FIGURE 2.1 Four-phased methodology to prepare for CSIR Plan development.

Gaining Executive Support

The first step in defining a Breach response program has nothing to do with actually writing a policy document. It involves reaching out to key organizational executives to gain alignment on the scope of the program as well as the support and authority you will need to develop and execute the program. Key CSIR Plan areas to discuss and gain executive alignment on are:

- *Scope of the program.* Organizations often abide by multiple overlapping programs, policies, and governance frameworks. Even organizations that follow a centralized policy and governance framework commonly have outlier areas of their organization that follow alternative policies and programs. These outlier areas commonly exist within business unit(s) that may be part of a new acquisition or perhaps are located in a geography that follows a separate governance and management regime. Defining a single holistic program without considering these outlier areas typically result in a program that will fail due to duplication of CSIR Plans or the lack of authority over people and systems needed when managing an incident which can waste valuable time in the management of an incident that will ultimately increase the cost and impact of the incident. Gaining alignment with executives on how the CSIR Plan should deal with outlier areas of an organization and associated protocols needed to fast-track system and process changes needed to secure and recover the organization is essential. These protocols and decisions should be incorporated into the CSIR Plan document and in the event of incident will save time and frustration for all parties involved

- *Allocation of personnel.* Development of a CSIR Plan will not be a localized activity that can be done in isolation. Stakeholders from key teams and business units across an organization will need to provide input and assistance in developing the response plan. Clarity around the anticipated assistance needed from resources should be discussed and aligned on before engaging stakeholders for assistance. These stakeholders will typically be very busy in their normal job roles and it may be difficult to gain their time as appropriate to assist with CSIR Plan development. Communication from the executives down to stakeholders advising them of the program and the assistance they are expected to provide is typically the most efficient way to successfully secure required personnel for CSIR Plan development
- *Capital expenditures and operational expenses.* In addition to assistance from internal resources there will be a number of expenses that are associated with the development of a CSIR Plan. There will be capital costs associated with the development of the program including consultant time, equipments such as printers and dedicated computers for use by the CSIR Team and other costs to ensure adequate facilities for war room activities. Operational costs should also be considered. These costs may include price of maintaining the program by defining an owner, governance structure, and ensuring the program is updated and socialized in response to changes internal and external to the organization. The effort required for the CSIR Team to execute and test the program should also be factored into cost estimates. Endorsement of capital and operational expenditures are often overlooked when engaging the executive team. This oversight can result in developing a CSIR Plan that cannot be adequately maintained and can quickly become out-of-date and ineffective within the organization

As we step through this chapter, as well as Chapter 3, the various areas of resource and investment required for CSIR Plan development and execution will become clearer, however not exact. Gaining executive endorsement for the development and execution of a CSIR Plan rarely requires a formal business case however discussing and gaining alignment on the scope, costs, and support that will be needed to develop and execute the CSIR Plan can be an indispensable step in right-sizing the CSIR Plan to your organization.

Building a CSIR Team

The first CSIR Team was established in 1988 in response to the Morris worm,[2] an automated threat that exploited vulnerabilities and spread over the internet. This CSIR Team comprised of technical experts who together helped manage

---

[2]http://ieeexplore.ieee.org/xpls/icp.jsp?reload=true&arnumber=6924687.

the incident. Since 1988 our use of technology has changed and the complexity, frequency, and threats that we face today are also vastly different from those 15 years ago. Today cyber security is a whole business issue which, to be effective, needs to be embedded within teams and lines-of-business across an organization. With this in mind it is trivial to see that a failure in cyber security resulting in a Breach is also best managed by stakeholders from across the organization. These organizational contacts will make up key personnel within a CSIR Team who will be a core team essential in the management of incidents and communicating to internal and external stakeholders. CSIR Teams within most organizations rely on key internal personnel as well as external stakeholders such as business partners, third party service providers, and law enforcement agencies as an extension of their CSIR Team. CSIR Teams at small organizations can contain a handful of people and at large organizations can exceed 50 members. When considering a CSIR Team for your organization there are factors that can influence the size of the team:

- Number of divisions, systems, and environments across your organization
- Anticipated security incident load to be managed via the CSIR Plan
- Response service level agreements and expectations (9×5 or $7/24$ support, etc.)
- Geographical locations that the CSIR Team will have authority to operate within
- Expected complexity of incidents
- Degree of reliance on third party providers
- Anticipated regulatory, legislative, and contract requirements which dictate response and notification actions and timelines to be adhered to
- Funding allocated for the CSIR Plan

One uniform principal that defines a CSIR Team is that, regardless of the size, the team needs a defined operational model and clearly defined roles and responsibilities to effectively lead an organization through the management of security incidents. Depending on the scope of an incident and the anticipated stakeholders that need to be involved in its management, there are several possible CSIR Team operational models that can be used:

Centralized model. Utilizes a single team that manages execution of the CSIR Plan to manage a detected incident.
Decentralized model. Involves multiple CSIR Teams working concurrently in the management of a large or complex incident. In these cases CSIR Teams are typically defined at a specific regional/geographical or business unit level and overseen by a centralized individual or team to ensure consistent response execution and management.

Fig. 2.2 illustrates a sample centralized CSIR Team organizational model used to manage an incident involving external legal counsel and other third party service providers in the management of an incident.

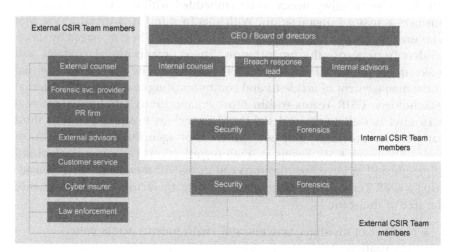

FIGURE 2.2 Sample centralized CSIR Team operational model.

CSIR Team roles captured in Fig. 2.2 are explained in further details within Table 2.1.

Table 2.1 Example CSIR Team Roles and Responsibilities

CSIR Team Role	Roles Within an Organization	Duties
CEO/Board of Directors	CEO, Board of Directors, or Audit Committee depending on who is tasked with cyber security oversight within the organization	■ Endorse budget, scope, and CSIR Team staffing ■ Approve containment and recovery measures as appropriate ■ Approve internal and external communication messages
Breach response lead	Sr. Manager, Director within Information Security or Forensics teams	■ Lead the internal response team in the efficient and effective management of an incident
Internal counsel	Internal legal counsel with knowledge of regulatory, legislative, and contract requirements of the organization	■ Validate that the CSIR Plan and related procedures and processes are compliant with legal requirements ■ Advise the CSIR Team on the legal obligations and ramifications of response actions during testing and in the management of an incident ■ Serve as the liaison between the organization and third party CSIR Team members
Internal advisors	Business service line executives, Senior HR, Privacy, Security, and other C-Suite leaders of functional areas for the organization	■ Advise the CSIR Team as required in support of CSIR Plan testing and the management of an incident

Table 2.1 Example CSIR Team Roles and Responsibilities—cont'd

CSIR Team Role	Roles Within an Organization	Duties
Security	In-house information security responders	■ Approve technological and process related changes within the advisor's respective area of authority ■ Assist in the detection, investigation, management, and recovery of an incident ■ Serve as advisors to the CSIR Team incident leader as appropriate
Forensics	In-house forensic responders	■ Acquire and preserve digital evidence ■ Analyze collected evidence ■ Serve as advisors to the CSIR Team incident leader as appropriate
External counsel	External lawyer	■ Serve as the single communication channel between third parties and legal counsel of the victim organization ■ Serve as advisors to the CSIR Team incident leader as appropriate
Third party providers	Various specialized service providers to augment in-house delivery capabilities or maintain independent requirements	■ Provide specialized services and advice including: – Breach advisory and coaching services – Customer service helpdesk services to manage victim inquiries – Cyber insurers to manage claims and help determine the financial impact of the Breach – Public relations firms to manage Breach communication to the public – Law enforcement to assist in the investigation and legal recourse stemming from the incident ■ Assist in the detection, investigation, management, and recovery of an incident ■ Serve as advisors to the CSIR Team incident leader as appropriate

As seen in the sample CSIR Team organizational model there is a reliance on third party service providers. This is common for specialized areas of expertise such as forensic responders and credit monitoring providers. A few sample third party service providers were captured in Table 2.1. However, there are also some commonly overlooked third party service providers that are beneficial to develop and maintain relationships with in advance of an incident.

It is best to identify and get agreements in place with third parties in advance of an incident which will put your organization in the best possible position to:

Select the right vendor. The time to look for and select a vendor to assist your CSIR Team in incident response is in advance of an incident. Doing so during the time of an incident introduces delays in managing the incident. This delay is twofold, it could take weeks to identify the right vendor who can support your needs and response requirements delaying the start of the investigation and during this vendor identification period who do you think will be interviewing the various response providers? The in-house people that likely should have been assisting in response activities however have had their focus redirected to screening vendors. When evaluating vendors ensure to look at the role they will play in relation to the type of insurance coverage that they have. Vendors, like anyone else, can be the source of errors and omissions that can introduce new or increase Breach related harm to your organization. Ensuring your vendor has adequate insurance coverage to protect your organization in event of mistakes that they make during the course of the investigation should be a factor in the decision-making process.

Align on rates and response timeframes. Soliciting and signing agreements with third parties in the heat of an incident with urgent timeframes will usually result in a higher hourly rate, a response timeframe that may not meet your needs and agreeing to terms and conditions that may not align to your organizational requirements.

Agree on terms and conditions that minimize risk. Terms and conditions (also known as the fine print or T&Cs) are there to protect engaged and engaging parties in an agreement. There is normally back and forth between legal departments as T&Cs are finalized. This back and forth can delay beginning a key aspect of the investigation or worst yet result in your organization signing off on T&Cs that are misaligned with your requirements as in the middle of an investigation the pressure associated with the Breach will usually trump the need for legal review and alignment.

Each CSIR Team member, regardless of being internal or external to your organization should have contact details (phone, e-mail), backup contacts as well as escalation paths to be used in time of unavailability, issue, or conflict. Common details obtained for CSIR Team members include:

- Contact Name
- Role
- Email
- Work, mobile, and home phone
- Supervisor/Manager contact information and escalation process to use in order to engage them
- Threshold (As applicable some third parties such as Law Enforcement may not get involved in an incident under a set financial impact amount)

Identifying Critical Assets and Breach Scenarios

The sole goal of a CSIR Plan is to effectively and efficiently manage security incidents when they occur. In order to develop a tailored response plan for your organization, forethought into the type of assets that you have and the nature of the Breach scenarios you will be faced with are required in advance.

Critical Asset Identification

In many organizations IT departments are tasked with defining sensitive data in the company and where it resides within their systems. This approach places IT departments in a difficult position as they seldom know enough about the regulatory, legislative, or contract requirements to define information as sensitive nor enough about the various lines-of-businesses across the organization to properly classify sensitive data for each line-of-business. Furthermore they are often tasked with keeping systems available and not tasked with identifying what systems store, process, or transmit sensitive data. Tasking IT to define sensitive data more often than not will result in sensitive data being incorrectly classified as nonsensitive and the whereabouts of the data internal and external to the organization being incorrectly scoped. Proper identification of critical assets should involve stakeholders from across the organization, including key operational teams and business unit leaders. Each business unit owner should be tasked with reviewing their business unit in search of critical data assets using a two-staged approach, the first is identifying what is important to the organization and the other is data that is likely to be targeted by cyber criminals.

Defining What Is Important to Your Organization

The information typically deemed sensitive by organizations are a combination of data sets critical to the sustainability of the organization such as intellectual property, client lists, and information that is directly protected by regulatory, legislative, and contract commercial requirements such as client data or Personally Identifiable Information (PII). Examples of PII are as follows:

- Usernames and passwords
- Name or alias
- Social security/insurance number
- Driver's license and other identifiers
- Citizenship, legal status, citizenship, gender, race/ethnicity
- Date of birth
- Home and personal cell/telephone numbers
- Personal e-mail and home mailing address
- Religious belief
- Mother's middle and maiden names
- Spousal information, child information, marital status, emergency contact information
- Financial information, medical information, disability information
- Educational information

The identification of sensitive information should be completed on a one-time basis as well as on an ongoing basis to ensure that changes within a business unit that may dispose of or take on additional forms of sensitive data can be factored into the plan accordingly. This should be done in response to organizational changes such as mergers and acquisition activity as well as the divesting of a business unit.

Organizations can experience Breaches not only due to sensitive information that is modified or stolen but also due to disclosure of information that the organization does not see as sensitive at all.

Defining What Is Important to Cyber Criminals

There have been several recent examples of organizations that have been Breached for information that they likely did not view as mission-critical or sensitive within their organizations. One example is a large e-commerce organization that suffered a Breach which disclosed a reported 145 million usernames and passwords[3] belonging to their clients. As discussed in Chapter 1 usernames and passwords are typically reused across multiple systems and applications, many of them being high-value targets for criminals such as banking application, funds transfer, or healthcare related sites. A security incident experienced within an organization often carries the same media attention and damage to brand reputation regardless of whether it involved sensitive information critical to the organization's sustainability or not. A Breach involving data desirable to cyber criminals can still result in negative publicity of your organization in the media and with your clients. Ensuring that your organization augments a sensitive data listing with information that cyber criminals find desirable will help ensure that detection, protection, and management can be planned accordingly.

Please refer to Table 1.2 within Chapter 1 for the types of data that are frequently traded within the underground economy and targeted by cyber criminals. After identification of sensitive information the next step is to identify how you perceive the information can be exposed via a Breach within your organization.

Breach Scenarios

Years ago many organizations developed a generic Breach response plan and assumed this would effectively manage their response and recovery for any conceivable cyber related Breach. Threats and the nature of Breaches however have changed and can often require different methods to detect, respond, and recover from. An example of this is DDoS attacks which involve a coordinated attack by one or several external machines designed to overwhelm network infrastructure and servers to deny access to services by legitimate users. Response and recovery from DDoS attacks can involve leveraging specialized third party technologies and service providers such as internet service providers. This is very different from isolating and removing a compromised system from the network which is under your complete control. Without this understanding ahead of time an organization facing a DDoS attack can find itself scrambling to

---

[3]https://www.washingtonpost.com/news/the-switch/wp/2014/05/21/ebay-asks-145-million-users-to-change-passwords-after-data-breach/.

identify possible mitigation steps and ensure they have processes in place to invoke them. The expectation when identifying Breach scenarios is not to identify every conceivable Breach scenario that may be experienced, in contrast it is to identify the most likely Breach scenarios that you will experience and tailor your CSIR Plan accordingly to increase its effectiveness. Table 2.2 contains examples of some commonly used Breach scenarios, the anticipated likelihood of the scenario being experienced and anticipated challenges for each, which again, will allow for the proactive identification and preparation to overcome them in advance of a Breach.

Table 2.2 Example Breach Scenarios

Breach Scenarios	Description	Likelihood	Key Anticipated Challenges
DDoS attack	DDoS conditions that disrupts online services	Medium	■ Mitigating an attack affecting your organization's infrastructure as well as third party telecommunications equipment
Insider attack	Sensitive information presumed stolen by an internal employee	High	■ Determining if sensitive information was accessed, modified, or exfiltrated from the environment
Malware incident	Custom Remote Access Trojan (RAT) detected on multiple workstations	High	■ Detecting other compromised systems ■ Determining the traits and impact of the custom malware ■ Determining if sensitive information was accessed, modified, or exfiltrated from the environment
Ransom-attack	Ransomware infection that has rendered sensitive information unusable or a proactive ransom threat to steal data or disrupt operations	High	■ Management's ability to decide on paying the ransom and the potential legal and cyber insurance coverage related challenges ■ Capabilities to substantiate the claims of the hackers and confirm if an incident has or is likely to occur
Social engineering/ phishing attack	Unauthorized wire transfer or system access using credentials believed to have been gathered via social engineering	High	■ Identifying how the criminals targeted and gained sensitive workflow information and the names and timeframes to staff targeted in the attack ■ Determining if sensitive information was accessed, modified, or exfiltrated from the environment
Exploitation of unpatched software/system	Compromise or defacement of a server due to unpatched vulnerability	High	■ Ability to detect other systems containing the unspecified vulnerability and how remediation should be prioritized ■ Determining if sensitive information was accessed, modified, or exfiltrated from the environment

Continued

Table 2.2 Example Breach Scenarios—cont'd

Breach Scenarios	Description	Likelihood	Key Anticipated Challenges
Attempted brute-force attack	The attempted compromise of credentials through automated brute-force attack	High	■ If successful access was gained by the attacker ■ The actions performed by the attacker
Laptop/ smartphone/ removable media theft	Loss or theft of laptops, smartphones, or removable media such as USB thumb drives	Low	■ Identifying the sensitivity of the information stored on the device ■ Determining if implemented laptop/ smartphone safeguards, such as encryption, adequately protect sensitive information from disclosure in association with the incident
Errors and omissions	Exposure of sensitive information via unintentional application or human error	Medium	■ Determining the precise scope of exposure and nature of information at risk ■ Determining successful unauthorized access of information by unauthorized customers or employees
Web application attack	Compromise of a web application resulting in the theft or manipulation of sensitive information	Medium	■ Determining what actions were performed by the attacker ■ Determining if sensitive information was accessed, modified, or exfiltrated from the environment
Cyber espionage	Targeted and covert attack that is believed to have resulted in the theft of sensitive intellectual property	Low	■ Determining if sensitive information was accessed, modified, or exfiltrated from the environment ■ Identifying the point of entry used by the attacker, the duration, and the scope of unauthorized access
Cloud provider Breach	The suspected compromise of sensitive information hosted within a cloud-based environment	Medium	■ Accessibility to cloud systems to allow organizational or third party response and investigation ■ Determining if sensitive information was accessed, modified, or exfiltrated from the cloud environment
Third party partner Breach	Loss of sensitive information in possession of a third party service provider	High	■ Accessibility to third party hosted systems to allow organizational response and investigation ■ Determining if sensitive information was accessed, modified, or exfiltrated from the third party environment

Common examples of evidence sources are in Table 2.3 and may have differing levels of applicability, likelihood, and anticipated challenges from organization to organization.

The Breach scenarios will be very useful in the development of a CSIR Plan as they help ensure that you factor in your ability to self-detect the Breach (which we will discuss in greater detail next chapter), and plan the CSIR Plan testing strategy which can leverage the scenarios and likelihood of experiencing them in CSIR Plan testing regime. Knowing the type of incidents you will likely face and the anticipated challenges associated with the incidents is necessary to ensure you factor in effective response. A challenge commonly overlooked when developing a CSIR Plan is understanding the type of evidence you expect to encounter and ensuring you or your forensic provider can preserve and analyze it during the course of an investigation.

Identifying Potential Evidence Sources and the Types of Evidence

Whether you have trained in-house forensic responders or you will rely on a third party forensic services provider, it is important to understand what sources of evidence you likely will face during the management of a Breach and ensure the tasked forensic team has the required skills, tools, and processes. A little earlier in my career I lived in a subdivision where neighbors knew each other and would not shy away from asking for assistance when needed. My neighbors understood I was in IT and saw me as the "IT guy" who knew everything about IT related subjects. With this they contacted me every time they had computer issues—with some of the most frequent requests being to install printers, modems, and set up wireless networks within their homes. My professional career at the time was enterprise security, and with this I knew very little about the desktop support related tasks my neighbors were coming to me with. Through trial and error I would fumble through their requests, eventually succeeding but requiring substantially more time than someone with the correct skills would have needed to complete the same task. In the grand scheme of things assisting neighbors is relatively low-stake; if it takes longer than expected or if the results are not as intended there is not a material impact. When dealing with a Breach, effectiveness and efficiency is critical in minimizing impact and ensuring resources with the right training and capabilities is of paramount importance. When looking at digital forensics capabilities please keep the example of my past in mind, having an in-house or third party forensics provider does not necessarily mean they have the training, skills, and equipment to assist you in the specific areas of investigation that you may require. Understanding the sources of evidence will help ensure you can effectively identify your forensic requirements for in-house or third party forensic service providers.

Defining evidence collection requirements involves determining the technology your organization uses, where they are located, and the format of data that may serve as key evidence. For example, if sensitive data has been identified within a line-of-business that predominantly uses Macintosh computers then your forensic services team should ensure they have investigators with the necessary training, tools, and processes to manage an investigation on MAC computers. Another common area of conflict between organizational requirements and forensics capabilities are cloud providers. When dealing with investigations in the cloud, the ability to access cloud-based systems and extract relevant evidence from big data technology such as Apache Hadoop[4] can require specialized tools and training which should be factored into forensics response requirements. Table 2.3 captures some common sources of evidence that may be helpful when examining forensic requirements for your organization.

Table 2.3 Common Evidence Sources

Evidence Type	Description
Operating system evidence	Information contained within the popular operating systems (Microsoft, Unix, Macintosh) such as OS log files, file structures, memory, and restore points
Database evidence	Database (SQL Server, Oracle, MySQL, PostgreSQL) logs, metadata, and memory stored within the database structures and system memory
Mobile device evidence	Data stored within mobile devices such as IPAD, MS Surface Tablets, and Smartphones
Physical security evidence	Digital video recordings from close circuit televisions and video camera systems as well as access card system logs
Web browser	Data stored within web browser (MS Edge, Internet Explorer, Google Chrome) databases and file structures
Commercial off-the-shelf (COTS) and custom applications	Data stored within proprietary and nonproprietary application databases and file structures
Email	Data stored within corporate mail server
Virtual machines	Data contained within virtual host machine images
Network device logs	Data stored in proprietary and open source network logging formats
Cloud mail and file storage	Data stored within Cloud providers such as office 365, Gmail, Hotmail, and DropBox
Network packet captures	Previously collected log traffic

An organization's ability to acquire, preserve, and analyze various types of evidence should be considered under real-world scenarios such as working with live evidence as well as that retrieved from backups and how to overcome a variety of challenges you are likely to face such as the existence of hard-drive encryption, previously deleted data, locked computers, and password protected devices. The appropriate organizational stakeholder should also proactively confirm data retention standards to help ensure the availability of key evidence (OS evidence, database evidence, etc.) at the time of an incident.

The last phase of the four-phased preparation plan to be completed prior to developing the CSIR Plan is to define key requirements that will guide the scope, processes, and execution of the CSIR Plan process.

---

[4]https://hadoop.apache.org.

Defining CSIR Plan Requirements

This far we have looked at several CSIR Plan prerequisites that will help shape the CSIR Plan while it is being developed. The majority of these prerequisites were internally focused such as gaining executive support, assembling a CSIR Team, and identifying sensitive data. CSIR Plan requirements are also driven from external sources such as industry good practices on how to manage an incident.

We will explore some key external sources of CSIR Plan requirements that should be factored into plan development beginning with legal considerations that will assist in preparing for the inevitable, a lawsuit or regulatory and contractual penalties stemming from a data security Breach.

Legal Considerations

In the current environment and particularly after the high profile data Breach incidents highlighted in Chapter 1, it is very likely that a material data Breach incident today will be followed by one or the other, or both, of the following types of litigation brought against your organization:

Class action lawsuit brought on behalf of all customers and other persons adversely affected (or potentially affected) by the Breach.

Derivative lawsuit brought on behalf of shareholders alleging that your company's disclosure of cyber risk was inadequate or misleading. This form of lawsuit will be possible if your company is listed on a stock exchange and your share price dropped on news of the data Breach.

These types of litigation are expensive, and not just in terms of settlement payouts, costs of legal counsel and experts, and the significant management time and distraction, the reputational harm can be very important as well. While preparing to develop the formal CSIR Plan, legal considerations are an important factor that will ultimately influence how your CSIR Plan will be developed and executed in the event of an incident. So, what steps can you take now—before the data Breach—to reduce the fallout from this risk? The good news is there are some practical, discrete actions you can do right away, and incorporate into the CSIR Plan in advance of an incident. They would not bring the risk to 0—but they will help materially manage the risk.

Pre-Breach Public Disclosure

If you are with a public company (ie, your company's shares trade on a stock exchange), you may be providing reasonable disclosure about data Breach risks in your prospectuses, annual information form, and other continuous disclosure documents.

In the United States, the SEC has published guidance for cyber security risk disclosure,[5] which could include: (a) aspects of your business that give rise to material risks for Breaches; (b) the degree to which you outsource those risks; (c) a description of previous Breaches; (d) particular risks if the Breach incident is undetected for a period of time; and (e) any relevant insurance coverage.

In Canada, the instructions to Form 51-102F1 (Management Discussion and Analysis) require a discussion of risks that have, or could have, impacted financial statements, which would encompass Breach situations.

As we covered earlier, CSIR Plan preparedness involves the definition of Breach scenarios and frequently the improvement of organizational Breach detection and management capabilities which should be considered for pre-Breach disclosure. In contemplating your approach to Breach risk disclosure, of course keep in mind that you do not want this disclosure to ironically assist the bad guys who are planning to unleash the cyber attack against you—so, care and judgment, and legal review, need to inform this disclosure.

In addition to exploring legal requirements associated with a Breach it is important to identify legal requirements which will need to be addressed via the CSIR Plan.

Legal Components of the CSIR Plan

With the focus on Breaches in the industry there is increased focus on regulatory and legislative cyber security requirements to protect information as well as requirements to abide by in the event of a Breach. Identifying appropriate legal requirements can efficiently be performed by developing a Breach Legal Risk Profile.

Assessing Your Organization's Breach Legal Risk Profile

The first step in addressing legal considerations in and around your CSIR Plan, is to evaluate your organization's legal risk profile regarding Breaches. Some of the key considerations are:

Factor Description

- Is the organization in an industry with a *regulatory framework* that dictates certain cyber-protection measures? For instance, for an organization in the financial services industry in Canada, your organization will have to comply with existing and emerging regulations promulgated by the Office

---

[5]SEC—CF Disclosure Guidance: Topic No. 2—Cybersecurity https://www.sec.gov/divisions/corpfin/guidance/cfguidance-topic2.htm&gt.

of the Superintendent of Financial Institutions, Investment Industry Regulatory Organization of Canada, and the Canadian Securities Administrators
- Does the organization do business in *multiple jurisdictions*? Where is it collecting, processing, and storing data?
- Is the organization a private company, or a public company with *many shareholders* and subject to exchange oversight?
- Will the organization be handling *personal information and/or personal health information*? If so, existing and evolving privacy protection laws will come into play
- If an IT solution has been contracted for, does it use a Business to Business or Business to Consumer (*B2B* or *B2C*) delivery model that is more or less likely to affect a greater number of users?
- Will the IT solution involve third party components such as *hosting or payment providers*?

In a similar vein, in order to craft a legally sound CSIR Plan, you need to understand your IT environment, and in that regard, the ecosystem you have of vendors (of IT but also other services) who have access to your own IT systems and organizational data. The following chart regarding vendors illustrates some of the key questions that should inform this stage of legal due diligence:

Inquiry

- What is the state of the vendor's *security framework*? What policies and procedures does it have in place to maintain the integrity of the framework?
- Will the vendor permit *penetration testing* and other exploration of vulnerabilities?
- Are the vendor's facilities audited for industry-recognized internal controls? Does the vendor perform *internal audits*, and is it willing to share the results with you?
- Where are the vendor's service delivery centers? What and how does it process and *store data*?
- What data Breach risk insurance does the vendor carry, and has it made *any claims* in the last 5 years?

The Data Breach Risk Profile will help determine factors that need to be considered during CSIR Plan development. However, legal requirements extend beyond just the risk profile, the following legal areas should also be included into the CSIR Plan planning process:

Mandatory (and Voluntary) Breach Notification

Various jurisdictions and certain regulations covering specific industries, have different rules requiring you to notify regulators, customers, or certain third parties, of a data Breach. Much more on this important topic is provided in Chapter 8. Suffice it to say for now, that the CSIR Plan should contain a thorough and crisp list of what notifications apply, and under what timelines and circumstances, so that when a data Breach occurs, your team is not scrambling.

Law Enforcement Management

One third party often involved in the mix of a larger type of data Breach is the police—or whatever other law enforcement group might be applicable in your jurisdiction (ranging from the Federal Bureau of Investigation (FBI), to the Royal Canadian Mounted Police (RCMP), to state and provincial police). On bigger data Breaches—particularly if they are attracting publicity in the media—you may be approached first by law enforcement, particularly if they conclude a criminal offense has taken place. In other cases, you might want to loop them in even before they call you.

One very difficult judgment call you may be confronted with if the police get involved, is that quite often they will ask you not to notify customers of the data Breach, in order to allow law enforcement officials to pursue the investigation more fruitfully (ie, without tipping off the bad guys). But this delay in notification might be contrary to a legal requirement to notify customers and others as soon as possible. This can make for a very difficult decision-making environment, and you should have legal counsel in the thick of this determination. It is best to define what position your organization will take and when law enforcement will be contacted and define it within the CSIR Plan to avoid any confusion.

Maintaining Privilege

Generally, when your organization is involved in litigation, you have to provide the other side with copies of all your relevant internal documents, including notes, reports, and the all revealing internal e-mails. The law makes an exception to this disclosure for what are called "privileged" documents; namely, those that are communications between your staff and a lawyer (whether an external legal advisor, or an "in-house" lawyer), or communications that were prepared by a lawyer, or by a nonlawyer for a lawyer, in contemplation of litigation. The importance of privileged documents is that they may not have to be disclosed to the other side in litigation, nor will they be revealed in court through some other means. Therefore, claiming privilege over certain documents can be very important, and the process for doing so should be addressed in the CSIR Plan.

It can be easy to lose privilege if you are not careful. For example, CSIR Teams include representatives from the business unit, IT, risk management, customer experience, corporate security, and in-house legal. Well, just because an in-house lawyer sits on the CSIR Team will not make e-mails circulated among members of this committee privileged.

Rather, the CSIR Plan should be clear that where a member of the CSIR Team is discussing a legal liability or similar issue, that e-mail (or report, etc.) should be sent only to the in-house lawyer as the prime recipient, and then the in-house lawyer can reach out to others as appropriate. This latter communications approach is not that much more complicated, but will stand a much better chance of claiming privilege over its related materials. Provisions for these communication paths and requirements should be factored into CSIR Team development.

Evaluating Cyber Insurance

As discussed in Chapter 1, a Breach can cause different types of costs to an organization. Insurance can be an effective way to protect the organization by transferring the risk to someone else's balance sheet. If your organization has yet to explore cyber insurance this may not be a pragmatic time to do so in conjunction with CSIR Plan development, however, if cyber insurance is being discussed at your organization there are factors that can influence the development and execution of the CSIR Plan if cyber insurance is indeed obtained. With this we will review it within this chapter.

While direct and systemic costs can be transferred to an insurer through an insurance contract with first and third party liability coverages, a portion of indirect costs can also be mitigated through the use of insurance. When discussing insurance, it is important to note that first party costs are referring to costs that your business would directly incur in the event of a Breach, and third party costs refer to financial loss sustained by others that look to recoup by suing the company. Let us examine how insurance can be used alongside existing security measures in place to manage an organization's cyber resilience. The first step in this process is: assessment.

Assess Your Cyber Risk

As is the case in any insurance conversation, the first step is to determine what you are trying to insure. Cyber and privacy liability is no different.

A valuable starting point is to evaluate the current coverages your organization is purchasing and assessing where there may be gaps. The evolution of the general liability and property policies has seen absolute "data" exclusions being included which, basically put, afford no coverage for cyber or privacy scenarios under traditional insurance policies. If your organization purchases more tailored policies to cover the professional operations, different contractual obligations, credit risk, management liability, or a variety of other types of policies—it is important to audit these policies in an effort to determine exactly where there may be coverage, if any at all. It is imperative that this exercise be performed in order to avoid duplication of coverage. Nearly every insurance contract contains language called the "Other Insurance Clause" which states that if there is coverage found in any other policy that policy would be looked at to respond in the event of a claim. This due diligence process can help avoid the situation where two different insurers are pointing fingers at each other as to who will be paying a claim, which causes legal costs to add up, coverage limits to erode, and increases the likelihood of deniability.

Further, it is important to assess what information the organization stores, and what it would cost if it went missing. Please refer to the Identifying Sensitive Information section of this chapter for additional details on this. As we discussed in Chapter 1, costs of detection and escalation, notification, and post-Breach services are not inconsequential and can have a material impact on a business. As a result, determining what insurance limit profile would fit your organization becomes important, as well as what the company can afford to retain itself in the form of a deductible. Running a probable maximum loss scenario based on the type of data housed within the systems and the cost of replacing it, or making each individual/organization affected fully is a good place to start.

Insurance companies can help run through these scenarios, and are able to use their claims data to help assess what potential first party costs might look like should your organization sustain a Breach. Additionally, given the type of information being collected and stored, it would be important to determine the implication should there be a third party lawsuit against the organization as well. Certain types of data cost more to replace than others, which could have an impact on other companies. This brings us to step two when looking to purchase insurance for cyber and privacy liability.

Managing Your Cyber and Privacy Risks

When talking in terms of cyber insurance, managing the risk involves several components including what the insurance policy requires your organization to do on a one-time, reoccurring and in event of a Breach which typically includes some type of initial risk assessment, reoccurring vulnerability assessments to identify and remediate security exposures and to notify the insurer promptly in the event of an incident which may serve as additional requirements for your CSIR plan. These requirements will be addressed in greater detail throughout the chapters of this book.

A cyber and privacy liability policy can be broken down into two different areas of coverage. There is coverage for first party costs to the organization and for financial loss your company causes to another. The sections in a policy are often broken down as can be seen in Table 2.4.

Table 2.4 Common Insurance Policy Coverage Section Inquiries

First Party Coverages	Third Party Coverages
■ System Remediation	■ Breach of Confidentiality
■ Forensic Costs	■ Invasion of Privacy Rights
■ Customer Notification/Credit Monitoring	■ Defamation, Libel, and Slander (Media)
■ Crisis Management/Public Relations	■ Misleading Advertising
■ Regulatory Actions/Awards	■ Virus Transmission
■ Loss of Business Revenue	■ Third Party Actions (Class)
■ Computer Crime	

The portion of the insurance policy that is triggered immediately is that concerning first party coverages. Because of the number of different teams that can be involved in remedying the situation, these are complex plans with clearly defined roles, which we will be exploring in greater detail in a later chapter. However, the insurance policy can help align vendors in each of these respective fields in an effort to mitigate immediate damage to the organization, and help prevent reputational harm. In doing so, this also helps prevent potential third party losses further down the line.

In the event that other individuals or businesses sue your organization as a result of having their information compromised—third party liability coverage found in a cyber and privacy policy would step in. The costs of defending the organization through a class action can be astronomical, and unless your organization has an incredibly strong balance sheet, it could prove catastrophic.

Financing Your Cyber and Privacy Risks

With the complexity of determining who internally and externally is involved during a Breach, it can be very costly when handling these events—especially if vendors are not assessed prior to a Breach occurrence. Insurance policies can dovetail with a company's disaster recovery plan, and vet the organizations involved when an event occurs. The advantage this brings is that insurance companies are able to secure highly competitive rates with legal, forensics, public relations, credit monitoring, remediation, and Breach coaching firms because of the volume they are able to drive. This is significant, because it allows the limits purchased to go further than what you would be able to achieve by paying increased rates out of pocket. Additionally, vendors that are approved by the insurers are approved because they have experience in handling Breach situations.

As is the case with any insurance policy, running a cost-benefit analysis should be done before a purchase is made. Unique to cyber and privacy liability policies is the added benefit of vendor and pre-Breach planning that need to be factored in. With Breach implications and costs being so significant, an organization should consider looking to insurance to not only transfer some of their own risk, but help them with their overall enterprise risk management, and vendor management.

SUMMARY

Data Breaches are a material risk for most organizations. The need to formalize their ability to detect, respond, and manage a Breach is a top Boardroom priority which is typically tasked to an individual or group to oversee. Proceeding directly into defining a CSIR Plan can actually be more damaging to an organization than not having a CSIR Plan at all. Developing a program that is misaligned with an organizational culture or requirements can provide a false sense of security that will not be realized until working one or more Breach scenarios through the CSIR Plan. As someone who has seen misaligned CSIR Plans, the risk organizations are unknowingly facing and the impact when a Breach does occur, I offer only one piece of advice. Whether you are the one who will assign the task of developing a CSIR Plan, the one receiving the task, or just someone curious about the process, the first step in truly developing a CSIR Plan tailored to your organization is not to do it (well at this point anyway). Put the keyboard down and start by identifying the requirements and issues that will serve as hindrances to defining the CSIR Plan. Use the guidance provided in this chapter as a starting point to identify the unique requirements and obstacles that will make your CSIR Plan less efficient and effective. It may be tempting to perform a few internet searches for CSIR Plan examples and try and apply them to your organization. When dealing with Breaches the stakes are high and preparedness is often the difference between catastrophic loss and a manageable impact.

CHAPTER 3

Developing a Computer Security Incident Response Plan

Kevvie Fowler

INTRODUCTION

It is ironic that the most time-consuming part of developing a CSIR Plan has nothing to do with actually writing the document. As we stepped through in Chapter 2 there are many prerequisites that must be performed to identify the requirements as well as the challenges to be addressed within CSIR Plan documentation. Whether your organization has an existing incident response program that you are enhancing or you are developing one for the first time, this chapter will guide you through the writing of a CSIR Plan that will leverage the outputs from Chapter 2 and incorporate them into a program tailored for your organization.

DEVELOPING THE DATA BREACH RESPONSE POLICY

A Google search for the term "Data Breach Policy" returns thousands of results linking to CSIR Plans, many from universities who typically tend to make their policy documentation public. In the deluge of CSIR Plan references there are examples of good policies however there is no shortage of links to CSIR Plans that are flawed and missing several core elements that will certainly result in failure when executed during a material incident. Trying to find one of the good CSIR Plan document examples out there on the internet and customizing a document tailored for another organization to yours can be risky and time-consuming. The safest approach is using the outputs from Chapter 2 to develop a new document or to enhance an existing policy within your organization. When executing this task a common question you may have is how high level or granular do you need to get with the policy? To answer the question some good industry frameworks actually recommend that you develop multiple

CONTENTS

Data Breach Preparation and Response. http://dx.doi.org/10.1016/B978-0-12-803451-4.00003-4

documents with varying degrees of detail. The following describes the recommended classes of CSIR Plan documents and their inter-relationships:

CSIR Policy is a high-level document outlining the goal and objective of the incident response program, the scope of the program across the organization, program roles, responsibilities, and authority and how program outputs such as incident communication and reporting will be managed.

CSIR Plan is a formal document outlining how the high-level policy document will be implemented and operationalized within the organization. Core elements of a security incident response plan include communication protocols that will be used to manage the sharing of incident updates and reports with internal and external stakeholders, metrics for measuring the effectiveness of the program, events that would trigger an update to the plan, and the strategy to improve and mature the plan over time.

Standard Operating Procedures are documents containing technical step-by-step actions that the CSIR Team will take to manage specific incidents. Standard Operating Procedures (SOPs) help minimize incident management errors and ensure a consistent and repeatable incident management capability. SOPs traditionally also include the forms and checklists that will be used by CSIR Team members in the execution of the CSIR Team.

The relationship between a CSIR Policy, plan, and SOPs are further illustrated within Fig. 3.1.

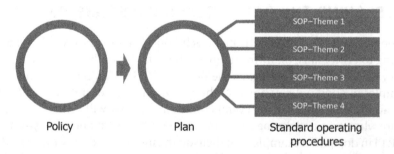

| Policy | Plan | Standard operating procedures |

FIGURE 3.1 Relationship between a CSIR Policy, Plan, and Standard Operating Procedures.

There are excellent security incident management standards which capture recommendations on how to structure a CSIR Policy, plan, and SOPs. Despite this guidance it is my experience that most organizations maintain a single hybrid CSIR Plan and policy document rather than maintaining two separate documents. In an effort to cater to the majority of the organizations who will develop CSIR Plans, I will focus the guidance of this chapter on building a hybrid policy/plan document and separate SOPs to manage specific incidents.

For organizations that would prefer to develop separate policy and plan documents, please refer to the guidance contained within the following information security frameworks referenced in Table 3.1.

Table 3.1 Popular Incident Management Frameworks

Institution	Reference
National Institute of Standards and Technology (NIST)	NIST SP 800-61 Information response guide release 2
International Organization for Standardization (ISO)	ISO 27002 13.0 Information Security Incident Management & 14.0 Business Continuity Management
IT Infrastructure Library (ITIL)	ITIL Service Operation 4.1.5
Control Objectives for Information and related Technology (COBIT)	COBIT Deliver & Support DS8 Manage Service Desk and Incidents

Regardless of whether you plan to build a hybrid plan/policy document or maintain separate documents, the structure of the documents is critical to its comprehension and ultimately how well it will be executed within the organization.

CSIR Plan Document Elements

The structure of a CSIR Plan is important because, if well-structured, your procedure ensures that the information needed during the management of an incident is available to the CSIR Team and is presented in a manner that can be absorbed efficiently. In the chaos of managing a material incident, if CSIR Team members can't find the information needed they often may make decisions that were previously agreed upon as should not be made, or waste valuable time seeking approvals to execute tasks that have already been preapproved by senior management and the CSIR Team. The content and sections of a CSIR Plan commonly differ between organizations depending on the organization's size, structure, functions, and requirements, however, core CSIR Plan elements are listed in Table 3.2.

Table 3.2 Sample CSIR Plan Document Elements

CSIR Plan Document Section	Description
Introduction	■ The purpose and goal of the document
Management commitment	■ The commitment received from management to endorse the development and execution of the program

Continued

Table 3.2 Sample CSIR Plan Document Elements—cont'd

CSIR Plan Document Section	Description
Scope and ownership	■ The scope and authority of the policy across the enterprise and any outlier business segments in which the policy will not apply. This applies in the event an organization has more than one incident response policy and identifies how the policies will intersect and if one policy will supersede another
	■ The team or individual responsible for owning and maintaining the CSIR Plan
Definitions	■ Key organizational definitions such as how sensitive information is defined, terms such as "incident" and "Breach" and incident event types and severities
Roles and responsibilities	■ CSIR Team member roles and responsibilities and the authority granted to them to execute required duties including shutting down systems, monitoring network and voice communications, and taking possession of employee systems and devices for analysis
	■ The protocol to follow to change defined roles and responsibilities
CSIR Plan Methodology	■ The methodology, supporting processes, and SOPs that are part of the CSIR Plan process
CSIR Plan Validation and Testing	■ A strategy outlining the frequency, scope, and type of testing that will be performed on the CSIR Plan and the CSIR Team members who will participate in the testing
Performance metrics	■ The metrics and calculations that will be used to gage the effectiveness of the CSIR Plan

Introduction

The introduction section should outline the objectives and intended use of the document. This will differ depending on the organization, however many good documents capture the need to qualify and manage incidents in a repeatable and efficient manner to minimize impact to the organization. Examples of specific objectives are as follows:

- Qualify and confirm whether an incident has occurred
- Outline a defined incident notification process for internal and external stakeholders
- Define the level and type of documentation that should be maintained in association with the investigation and response
- Outline proper evidence collection and handling processes
- Provide guidelines on how the incident should be contained to limit impact in an efficient and effective manner and minimize disruption to network and application operations
- Ensure accurate and measurable incident management metrics
- Reduce the likelihood of experiencing a similar incident from occurring again in the future

Management Commitment

The management commitment section of the CSIR Plan should outline the policies and or objectives defined by management to proactively protect information within the organization. This protection will include responding to incidents that threaten information availability, integrity, and confidentiality. Management policies and objectives should include how management:

- Has appointed knowledgeable individuals with the appropriate authority to develop the CSIR Plan and ensure its proper adoption and execution across the organization
- Will stay informed about the effectiveness of the CSIR Plan. Most commonly this is managed through CSIR Plan performance metrics that are presented to management on a reoccurring basis through a risk dashboard

Scope and Ownership

The scope and ownership of the CSIR Plan document is essential in establishing CSIR Plan coverage and the required authority to ensure its successful execution. The scope and ownership section is especially beneficial for organizations with multiple business units or sub-organizations that operate under a decentralized governance structure. In these organizations there may be multiple CSIR Plans or business segments that would be outliers and not within scope of the CSIR Plan. Clarifying the boundaries of a CSIR Plan in advance of an incident is an essential measure to ensure effective CSIR Plan execution. The scope and ownership section should also include:

- The scope of the incident types that will be managed by the CSIR Plan. We walked through defining the Breach scenarios in Chapter 2 and these scenarios will allow you to define the type of incidents the CSIR Plan will manage. If you recall, each Breach scenario may differ with respect to how and if your organization can detect and manage the incident and manage and analyze associated evidence. For a number of reasons you may wish to exclude certain classes of incidents from being managed by the CSIR Plan. For example in the event of an investigation involving employees you may wish a third party to conduct the investigation to ensure independence. Defining and communicating these exclusions in advance of an incident will help minimize confusion
- The relationship of the documented program to other related policies and programs within the organization. The CSIR Plan may tie into other organizational processes such as non-security related incidents, change and problem management, and Disaster Recovery (DR)/Business Continuity Program (BCP) programs. Identifying the linkages and triggers where appropriate for example when the DR/BCP or major incident process would initiate in response to a CSIR Plan investigation should be captured and communicated with all stakeholders
- The team or individual and their designated backup who has ownership and authority over the CSIR Plan document will ensure it is updated in response to changes to related organizational, legislative, regulatory, and

contractual requirements. Triggers for when the document should be updated should also be captured within

Definitions

Cultures and nomenclatures for cyber security terms, internal business units and systems will vary between organizations and acronyms that seemingly appear straight forward to some can lead to confusion with other CSIR Team members, both internal and external to your organization. Confusion with acronyms can result in delays in incident management should the CSIR Team incorrectly interpret an acronym and attempt to obtain approval from the incorrect system owner to make a change needed to contain an incident. The definition section within the CSIR Plan will help prevent confusion around terms and references. A good starting point of terms to clarify in the section begins with the Breach scenarios that we developed last chapter. The scenarios typically contain acronyms and abbreviations. Expanding this base to key business units, systems, and processes used across the organization and industry terms such as "DDoS" will help avoid confusion and laggard response.

Incident Assessment and Classification

Incidents governed by the CSIR Plan should be escalated to the CSIR Team who will provide an initial assessment of the incident severity and classification. This assessment will help ensure that the severity and type of incident is understood by all CSIR Team members and organizational stakeholders, that the appropriate communication and notification occurs, and that the incident is resolved within the timeframe agreed upon by organizational management. In the event the incident was previously assessed or classified prior to escalation to the CSIR Team, the CSIR Team should reclassify the incident to ensure accuracy. An example of this is a malware infection detected by a desktop support analyst. They may receive a problem ticket via the service desk alerting them to an issue on a user's machine. Upon investigation, the help desk support analyst determines the source to be a virus, assess a rating to ensure it gets routed to the CSIR Team. The virus infection may be part of a larger issue, attack that is best determined by the CSIR Team.

Incident Assessment

Incidents governed by the CSIR Plan should have a severity matrix that can be used to set the severity of the incident based on the information that is immediately available. As we covered previously, this severity will help ensure the incident is managed and communicated in accordance to business requirements throughout the course of its management. Most organizations will have a severity rating scheme associated with non-security related tickets, for instance identifying them as priority one through to priority four (P1–P4) which can also be leveraged by the CSIR Plan. If the recovery targets and/or notification timeframes of CSIR Plan incidents will differ greatly from non-security related incident severities it's recommended that a separate severity scheme is used to avoid confusion during management of an incident. A unique severity rating scheme such as severity 1 through 4 (S1–S4) may be used in this event. The severity rating should encompass more than just technological impact:

- Unauthorized access to critical systems
- Loss of data integrity or confidentiality
- Financial impact
- Disruption to business operations
- Loss in employee productivity
- Risk to the personal health and safety
- Negative media exposure (local or national or international coverage)
- Regulatory, legislative, and contract non-compliance

Incident Classification

The types of incidents will vary depending on the organization however the listing in Table 3.3 provides incident classification examples based on the US-CERT.[1]

Table 3.3 Example Types of Incident Classification

Type	Name	Description
0	Attempted unauthorized access	The attempted unauthorized access to networks, systems, applications, facilities, and employee or authorized contractors and third parties. This includes attempted social engineering attacks
1	Unauthorized access	An individual gains unauthorized logical or physical access to a network, system, application, or data
2	Ransom/extortion attack	The extortion of an individual or organization through cyber means to prevent, hinder, or combat the reported claim of a past security incident or threatened future security incident
3	Unconfirmed incident	The identification of malicious activity or an unconfirmed report of a suspected incident requiring further investigation
4	Malicious code	One or more installed instances of malicious software such as a virus or worm that infects an operating system or application
5	Denial of Service	The unauthorized execution of activity resulting in the denial or materially degraded performance of routine organizational or external services and functionality of networks, systems, and applications

Incident Severity

During a Breach the further the investigation progress, the more details that are uncovered which may change the severity or classification of the incident.

---

[1]https://www.us-cert.gov/government-users/reporting-requirements

For example, a Breach first detected as attempted unauthorized access may be upgraded to confirmed unauthorized access. It's important that as new details are identified, the classification of the Breach is updated to ensure proper visibility, reporting, and priority in support of organizational objectives.

How Sensitive Information is Classified

The definitions and references used to complete this step should be outlined in the sensitive information classification section of the CSIR Plan to ensure alignment by the reader as they execute the CSIR Plan. If your organization has a sensitive data classification policy currently, a reference can be inserted to the corresponding process to avoid repeating content and introducing another repository of information that will need to be maintained.

Other Terms and Events

With Personally Identifiable Information (PII); some organizations also focus on what is customer PII or student PII to define what PII belongs to clients or students in contrast to industry recognized definitions of generic PII. Many organizations also define what an incident is versus an event and the difference between a privacy and operational event versus a security event. An event of this is if a publicly facing webserver becomes unresponsive due to a perceived saturation of network traffic destined to the server, would the incident be managed via the CSIR Plan or there may be a logical explanation for it and it may be best managed through the organization's non-security incident management process. Defining what an operational incident is versus a security incident and how incidents will be transferred to another organization process such as a major incident process to manage critical business operations or a business continuity program to invoke a response requiring disaster recovery. Other terms frequently used in a CSIR Plan are compromised, unauthorized access, worm, and virus. These terms traditionally defined the severity and priority of many incidents and their definition should be used in a consistent and repeatable fashion. This can best be accomplished by defining them within the CSIR Plan.

Roles and Responsibilities

Last chapter we reviewed how to build a CSIR Team that is essential in both the development and execution of the CSIR Plan. A component of building the CSIR Team is defining roles and responsibilities. These roles and responsibilities should be explicitly defined in the CSIR Plan in addition to the authority granted to them to perform highly sensitive operations such as retrieve, gather, and analyze evidence from corporate, residential, and internet cloud and service providers of employees as well as monitor their network and voice communication. Legal requirements such as alerting users that their actions may be subject to monitoring, should also be addressed and documented in the CSIR Plan against the appropriate team role. Roles and responsibilities are important for the CSIR Team as well as other groups or teams who may not be a member of the CSIR Team but serve as first responders. Following our help desk example earlier this chapter if an employee calls the help desk to report a machine with abnormal behavior, the help desk would need to investigate. If the behavior is due to a virus infection the actions performed by the help desk may be called into scope of the investigation and even subsequent legal proceedings stemming from the incident. Ensuring first responders are clear on how and when to engage the CSIR Team and the appropriate steps they need to take, such as logging their actions, is the best way to ensure they do not hinder what can be used in the course of an investigation.

CSIR Plan Methodology

Ensuring efficient and effective response is a primary goal of the CSIR Team; however, ensuring that this response is performed in a consistent and repeatable manner is also critical in both incident management and dealing with post-incident litigation which we'll cover later in this book. Defining the incident response process, inclusive of the scope and depth of response and the order of operations is essential in achieving timely, effective, and repeatable incident management. The CSIR Plan should outline the incident response methodology that will be used by the CSIR Team to manage the incident and the methodology should consist of several phases spanning preparation activities conducted before an incident through to the actions performed after the incident is closed and business operations have been restored. CSIR Plan methodologies between organizations may differ in granularity; however typically contain the core elements illustrated in Fig. 3.2.

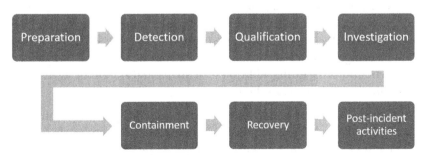

FIGURE 3.2 Sample incident response methodology.

We'll explore each phase of the sample incident response methodology in more detail providing examples of considerations for each phase.

Preparation. Many incident response methodologies I've come across have focused on the response aspect of an incident. In line with these methodologies the related preparation sections have focused on what the organization should do to prepare for responding to an incident. Effective incident management however should encompass controlling incident prevention, detection, and response. As we covered last chapter there are several dependencies such as gaining executive support, identifying sensitive data, and developing Breach scenarios prior to actually writing the CSIR Plan. One of the key steps in developing Breach scenarios is conducting a Threat Risk Assessment (TRA) to examine sensitive information, existing vulnerabilities and threats, and determining the likelihood of experiencing an incident. Organizations can leverage a number of technological, procedural, and administrative security controls to improve cyber security and limit the likelihood of experiencing an incident.

Ensuring Effective Cyber Security. Effective cyber security extends beyond purely technological controls. Effective cyber security will need to be embedded throughout multiple areas of an organization spanning procedural, technological, administrative, and awareness and education. Cyber security is a discipline that must constantly evolve in response to the threat profile of an organization and changes to the regulatory and industry threat landscape. In addition to this ongoing focus, triggers to reevaluate cyber security can occur multiple times throughout the Breach lifecycle, preparedness which we covered in Chapter 1 and Restoring trust and resuming business operations we we will discuss in Chapter 8 being two of the most notable. In this book guidance on how to effectively use cyber security to minimize cyber risk within your organization and limit the likelihood of experiencing a future incident will be covered within Chapter 8.

CSIR Plan Logistics and Planning. Earlier in this chapter we covered the core sections of a CSIR Plan document. The famous saying "the devil is in the detail" holds true with CSIR Plans. Ensuring that appropriate logistics have been identified, documented, and are communicated to CSIR Team is essential in ensuring the successful execution of the program. Table 3.4 contains recommendations regarding additional elements that should be agreed upon and outlined within the CSIR Plan.

Note: Equipment and procedures that are deemed part of a CSIR Team member's standard job role have not been captured in the supplemental CSIR Plan requirements Table 3.4. Maintaining the appropriate hardware, software, and processes to perform in a defined job role are deemed the responsibility of each CSIR Team member. For example the requirement for a forensic investigator to

Table 3.4 Supplemental CSIR Plan Requirements

Category	Element	Description
Facilities	Triage room	A temporary command center used for on-site CSIR Team members to connect, coordinate, and manage an incident. In addition to collaborating in the triage room CSIR Team members may need to perform activities with discretion such as conducting interviews and participating in confidential phone calls. These activities are best managed separately from the main triage activities. With this a main triage room and a separate meeting room are recommended. If dedicated rooms cannot be allocated establishing an approval process that would allow the CSIR Team to commandeer under short notice should be facilitated
	Evidence storage	An on-site or off-site physical location that can store digital and physical evidence that may be applicable to an incident under management. The evidence storage location should have physical access controls and support the long-term storage of evidence to support a litigation lifecycle
Technology and equipment	Dedicated printer	To be used within the triage room and support printing of evidence, incident updates, and other investigation related documents.
	Encrypted removable media	Removable media devices that will support the encryption protocol established by the CSIR Team
	Personal internet connects	Many incidents involve the degraded or loss of internet connectivity within an organization. The CSIR Team should have some mobile hotspots that will allow for the use of the internet to assist in incident verification and analysis. These hotspots are important also for key CSIR Team members who may be engaged in a location without conventional internet access
Procedures and documentation	Encrypted communication protocol	The CSIR Team may need to exchange digital information during the management of an incident which may need to be encrypted to help ensure confidentiality. The CSIR Plan should define what information should be encrypted and the types of encryption that are acceptable during an incident. This should extend beyond specifying just the algorithm that should be used. Encrypted information sent electronically or even transferred to removable media may need to be accessed long after the incident is closed for litigation and CSIR Team members may have moved on to other roles and organizations. Ensuring each file that is encrypted between CSIR Team members leverages an alternative decryption key which allows additional CSIR Team or IT employees to also view the encrypted file will help ensure its availability for future requirements
	Incident management standards	For confidentiality reasons some CSIR Plans outline special incident management guidelines that should be used during an investigation that usually limit the amount of detail captured within incident management tickets or in some cases require the use of a separate incident management system to track tickets. Some investigations may involve internal employees that may have access to ticketing systems and ensuring discretion is maintained is important in completing an impartial investigation

Continued

Table 3.4 Supplemental CSIR Plan Requirements—cont'd

Category	Element	Description
	Organizational charts, technical architectures, and data flows	During an incident the CSIR Team will need rapid access to organizational information and the CSIR Plan or a resulting SOP should have references to the locations for the documents. Some examples of key documentation needed by the CSIR Team are - Data classification policy - Sensitive data map including locations and data flows - Contact details - Standard hardening baselines and images In my experience, organizations that try to create a separate collection of documentation that is manually updated against live versions ended up with documents housing outdated information that can be a detriment to managing an incident
	CSIR Team contact information	Office, cell, home, email, and traditional mailing addresses for internal and external members of the CSIR Team
	CSIR Plan training	CSIR Team members may change or be added with changes in personnel or the scope of the program. The CSIR Plan should outline the appropriate contact and the process that can be used to provide training to new CSIR Team members, CSIR Team members who have changed roles, or remove members who are no longer part of the team
	Communication plan	Communication is essential during an investigation and ensuring you have a communication plan that will outline who should approve updates prior to sharing them and who should receive them

maintain proper forensic workstations and software needed for them to perform their duties have been omitted from Table 3.4.

Evidence Types and Sources. With the CSIR Plan scope and focus driven by the Breach scenarios defined in the previous chapter it's important to ensure that the forensic requirements outlined in the SOPs can be met by your forensic responders. Ensuring that adequate logging is in place and retained for an acceptable period of time prior to an incident, will help ensure pertinent information is present at the time of an incident. Further preparation would include ensuring that forensic responders can preserve and analyze the types of evidence anticipated to be associated with defined use cases. For example, if a Breach scenario included a compromise of sensitive data and the organization maintains sensitive data within an Apache Hadoop™ cluster, ensuring that the forensic responder is aware of the requirements and possess the tools and capabilities to extract, preserve, and analyze information from the big data platform is critical in ensuring effective response.

Detection. A good CSIR Plan doesn't start with responding to an incident, it starts with detecting one. Detecting Breaches early may involve detecting unauthorized criminals in a network before they find, access, and exfiltrate sensitive information. Alternatively, it may mean having greater control over responding to an incident which may avoid triggering the attention of traditional or social media which can force timelines to publicly respond to an incident leading to errors that can be viewed negatively by the public and impacted individuals. In either case, detecting a Breach early can increase your ability to limit financial or reputational impact. Despite the importance of detecting Breaches early, the average timeframe in the industry to detect a Breach after one occurs is 205 days.[2] There are some outliers including a telecom equipment manufacturer who didn't identify material Breaches within their organizations until 10 years after the compromise.[3] Some people believe attacks are becoming stealthier, others think organizations are still not yet placing the correct focus on incident detection versus prevention, in my opinion, it is a combination of both that are hindering Breach detection across the industry. Breach detection falls within two categories, self-detection and external detection. Ensuring your CSIR Plan deals with both is critical.

Self-detection. The minority of Breach detections occurs when an organization leverages its security controls, to purposefully—or, in some cases, by chance—detect a Breach themselves. Recent research has shown that over 8 out of 10 Breaches are discovered by third parties who bring them to the attention of the victim organization.[4] When dealing with Breaches, the stakes are high and efficiency and effectiveness are of paramount importance in minimizing financial or reputational impact. When allowing third parties to discover and alert your organization about a Breach you are placing trust in the third party to detect and notify your organization in a discrete and timely manner that would mirror the importance and focus you would place on the Breach if you had detected it yourself. Self-detecting Breaches keeps your organization in control of a timely and effective response. The following are recommendations that will help improve your ability to self-detect Breaches within your organization:

- *Employees*: Once trained and empowered, employees are a great source of incident detection. From reporting suspicious behavior by other coworkers or providing accounts of past or planned suspicious events. One great source of Breaches can be a whistle-blower program. If your

---

[2]http://investors.fireeye.com/releasedetail.cfm?ReleaseID=897918

[3]http://www.darkreading.com/attacks-and-breaches/8-lessons-from-nortels-10-year-security-breach/d/d-id/1102904?

[4]http://www.computerworlduk.com/news/security/most-data-breaches-still-discovered-by-third-parties-3615783/

organization has a whistle-blower program there is likely a telephone number or email address that will receive reports from anonymous employees. There should be a mechanism in place to ensure reports of events that would be classified via the CSIR Plan as an incident are indeed assessed by the CSIR Team and investigated. Because whistle-blowers often would like to remain anonymous it's critical to ensure that the whistle-blower line captures the appropriate level of detail during the initial report as there may not be further follow-up with the whistle-blower

■ *Security monitoring*: As cyber threats continue to evolve, more security technologies are released in the marketplace. From dedicated appliances to new security software, organizations have deployed more security controls and are generating more data than ever before. Generating the data is relatively straightforward, however, making sense of the information is a separate and common challenge faced by most organizations who struggle with the sheer volume of security events and the increased need to analyze large data sets at near real-time speeds to keep pace with the dynamic and complex nature of threats today. So what's the result of this? The security industry has come to the realization that we don't have an accurate picture of the malicious tools and techniques currently used by cyber criminals. We have the monitoring tools, the data but not the ability to analyze it to detect new attacks and identify past Breaches within our systems. Organizations ranging from small businesses to the largest Fortune 500 companies and government security agencies are continually surprised by new threats and tactics used by the criminals. When organizations do detect attacks they are sometimes shared with vendors and industry groups who can then respond with updates to security monitoring tools and techniques. This is truly a cat and mouse game that unfortunately keeps the good guys a step behind the criminals. Despite the fact that the odds are stacked against us security monitoring remains a critical element of a security program to detect threats and indicators of compromise that indicate a successful Breach. Security monitoring involves configuring network and host-based controls to log the correct data and centralize the logging for analysis. Devices typically included in security monitoring at the network level are routers, firewalls, intrusion prevention system, behavioral anomaly systems, host-based anti-virus, and intrusion prevention systems. On devices such as laptops, servers, and mobile devices security controls include device event logs, application logs, and host-based intrusion prevention clients. As we covered before there is no shortage of event sources. Factoring in the fact that there are millions of threats and activity patterns in the industry, which you can search for across multiple event sources, monitoring is a challenge for many organizations. To aid in filtering through the deluge of monitoring data and identifying the relevant information, many organizations are using Security Information and Event Monitoring (SIEM) Solutions which can receive, correlate, and help identify attacks. Doing so allows them to create scenarios that map to key threats the organization is likely to face. As well, these organizations can ensure their infrastructure and software are configured to generate the required log data so that the SIEM can correlate data to detect attacks across log data. The following are some recommended monitoring strategies to detect data security Breaches:

■ *Proactive Breach detection* involves forensic experts who will effectively perform a dry-run of a forensic investigation within an organization including forensically preserving and analyzing artifacts from systems, networks, applications, and databases analyzing them for known indicators of Compromise (IoC's). This proactive approach to Breach discovery can allow an organization to identify a Breach that may have occurred in the past and been missed by their security program. As well this approach helps to identify gaps within the environment and logging that can hinder a real forensic investigation. There are several organizations that provide these services that can be identified with a quick Google™ search

■ *Visible and invisible web monitoring* is an important element of any security program. We covered the importance of monitoring these areas of the internet to detect instances of criminals sharing information about vulnerabilities within your environment, planning future attacks targeting your organization or even selling to criminals, those previously stolen from your organization that has yet to be detected. Intelligence monitoring can be performed using Open Source Intelligence (OSINT) which is free or commercial intelligence feeds such as Norse[5] which typically have filtering capabilities that you can better target the type of intelligence you would like to receive. Regardless of OSINT or commercial intelligence feeds the following are a few recommendations that can be used to gather intelligence from the visible and invisible web that are relevant to your organization (Table 3.5)

[5]http://www.norsecorp.com

Table 3.5 Sample Intelligence Monitoring Criteria

Intelligence	Description
Global attacks	Attacks that don't target a specific organization or industry but target global infrastructure which may have an adverse effect on your organization. An example of this is if a criminal group launched an operation to take down the global DNS infrastructure this would affect all organizations who leverage the internet. If your organization had a reliance on the internet to operate, this attack would be one relevant to you
Industry attacks	Attacks that target a specific industry that your organization or key suppliers belong to. An example of this is a hacktivist group launching a cyber attack targeting the financial services sector. Organizations within financial services would be at heightened risk of attack or organizations that had a reliance on services provided by financial services organizations
Organizational attacks	Attacks targeting your specific organization or your key suppliers. These attacks may be in an effort to gain entry to or disrupt operations within your organization. Monitoring for IP addresses and URL's used within your environment, unique data elements (referred to as honey tokens) embedded within your datasets that can easily be identified on the internet, and key names of organizational executives and staff who may be targets of social engineering
Geographical-based attacks	Attacks that target key geographical locations where your organization conducts business operations. Monitoring for messages posted by criminals within key geographical areas discussing local attacks or discussing attacks targeting key locations your business operates within
Adversary intelligence	Intelligence outlining tools and techniques used by adversaries. These criminals will have been identified in the risk assessment that we reviewed last chapter

External Breach Detection

■ Research shows that most Breaches are detected by third parties[6] who identify suspicious activity and bring it to the attention of a victim organization. An example of this is a credit card payment provider who processes transactions on behalf of its clients. The payment provider runs fraud detection software against processed transactions to identify malicious activity. In the event of an incident they would alert their client and ask them to investigate. In some cases the third party may be directly targeted by a criminal who circumvents their controls and steals your information. However this source of Breach notification may not happen unless you have requirements within your third party agreement requiring them to notify you about suspected Breaches involving your information. Receiving notification is the first step, however, your organization must also ensure there is a process in place to receive the notification and act on it efficiently. Some organizations manage external Breach notification through their 7×24 service desk, some others designate primary and secondary contacts who they escalate to. Ensuring these notifications can

---

[6]https://securityintelligence.com/news/global-security-report-shows-majority-of-companies-do-not-detect-breaches-on-their-own/

be qualified and responded to is imperative. Looking back at the sample of incident categories we reviewed earlier in this chapter, a report of suspicious activity from a third party could be categorized as a severity 3 - Unconfirmed incident depending on the amount of associated details available and the source of the claims

Qualification. Whether identified by self-detection or by a third party, when an incident is reported it should undergo qualification to determine the scope, magnitude, and pertinent areas of the organization affected. This approach is similar to that taken by hospital staff when new patients are admitted to the emergency room, the first step is gaining an understanding of the extent, scope, and severity of the injuries, the second is ensuring they prioritize and have the right medical expertise to assist. Looking back at our Breach lifecycle, the qualification phase occurs early on and is squarely focused on learning the scope and potential impact so the incident can be prioritized correctly and the organization can appropriately engage the correct stakeholders to successfully manage it. This phase is not to perform the investigation (which will come later), it's just to gather the pertinent details that will allow the organization to ensure notification and management of the incident is properly aligned to the scope and potential impact of the incident.

There may be SOPs established to guide the appropriate responder through this. For example if a mobile device was reported stolen there may be a SOP in place for the IT department to remotely erase the device.

Most CSIR Teams will have seen their fair share of reported "major" incidents which after investigation were determined to be false or nonexistent and these are referred to as false positives. Another benefit of qualification is that it serves as a gatekeeper activity, allowing the CSIR Team to identify false positives early in the lifecycle. The further an incident goes in the lifecycle the more costly it is and the more resources that are diverted away from managing actual security incidents.

Incidents, whether self-detected or detected by a third party should be referred to as a potential incident or Breach (depending on which term you use within your organization) until it can be investigated by the CSIR Team. After investigation, the CSIR Team can confirm that the incident does indeed match the definition used within the CSIR Plan. Terms matter during incident response and forensics and using terms incorrectly, for example stating that "a compromise has occurred" rather than stating "the CSIR Team is investigating a suspected compromise," can lead to confusion and cause people within the organization to believe that the issue is smaller or much bigger than it is in reality.

Investigation. Using the investigation scope identified in the qualification phase, the investigation phase is where the CSIR Team reassembles the pieces of the puzzle and determines the past actions of the attacker. This phase is not a trivial task and can be the equivalent of finding the proverbial needle in a haystack. With typical investigations spanning multiple systems which can have hard drives in excess of a 1TB—the crime scene of today can be one large haystack! CSIR Plan documents should reference SOPs which will guide the CSIR Team through the steps they should follow when responding to specific incidents. In Chapter 2 we identified that Breach scenarios and SOPs should be developed to step the CSIR Team through each Breach scenario to ensure consistent incident qualification and analysis.

A key objective of the investigation phase is determining the correct scope of the incident. When dealing with cyber incidents size matters and the cost and impact of a Breach is largely influenced by the type of data and number of records involved. Being able to determine which information was specially accessed, modified, deleted, or affected in an incident limits impact to the affected organization. For example tracking a criminal's actions to a data store but not being able to determine what information was accessed can force the victim organization to disclose that all information may have been involved and set the scope of the investigation at the entire data store. Once this scope is incorrectly gaged the impact may rise in proportion. An organization may unnecessarily incur financial costs to notify affected clients and provide credit and fraud monitoring services for affected victims as well as reputational costs with industry or media perceptions about the magnitude of the incident further damaging brand. Advanced investigation techniques can be used to help ensure the correct scope of an incident is established and investigated accordingly. We will cover some detailed investigation and analysis techniques within Chapter 6 of this book.

Containment. The scope set during the investigation phase is used by CSIR Team members during containment and recovery to effectively "stop the bleeding" and preventing the scope of the incident from growing and increasing impact to the organization. Common steps taken by CSIR Team members to contain incidents include isolating and containing compromised systems or eliminating unauthorized access within an environment. Similar to the actions performed during the investigation phase, actions taken by forensic responders can also greatly influence the impact and intrusiveness of the investigation on business operations. Being able to pinpoint the source and scope of an incident will allow you to properly contain it without unnecessarily disrupting business operations. For example if there was a vulnerability within a web application an easy containment step could be to disconnect the web server from the network, however, this would be intrusive to business if other services were located on the web server. Containing the incident by disabling just the affected web page or section of the web application could allow you to contain the incident without unnecessarily impacting other business operations.

Recovery. Once containment has occurred, focus can shift to recovery including closing exposures and vulnerabilities associated with the incident and restoring business operations to normal. Referring back to our earlier example of the web application containing the vulnerability, containment, and recovery of this incident could involve patching the code to fix the vulnerability and restoring functionality to the affected area of the application. Other typical recovery steps include rebuilding customized systems from trusted images and backups. Attention is required to ensure compromised systems are truly clean and protected before being returned to production use. Some organizations have a team, other than the forensic responders, to verify the scope of the incident as well as the containment and recovery steps taken. This ensures alignment from an independent organization or team prior to determining the environment as clean and resuming business operations.

Post Incident Activities. The incident has been investigated, you have identified the source of the intrusion and implemented additional controls to help prevent a repeat occurrence. You have also restored untrusted systems to resume business operations. To use a baseball analogy, the CSIR Team may feel like they are rounding third base and heading home, however, there are several activities that should be considered after the incident in order to continue to minimize impact and prevent a repeat incident in the future.

Post-Mortem Reviews. Performing a post-mortem review after an incident allows the CSIR Team to identify what went well as well as key weaknesses that led to the incident and hindered detection or response. This knowledge can improve future response activities. A few key areas examined during a post-mortem review include:

1. A listing of all steps taken during response to an attack
2. Root cause of the incident as well as the steps taken to identify root cause
3. Recommendations to improve detection and management of similar incidents in the future
4. The engagement and performance of CSIR Team personnel

The silver lining associated with dealing with a Breach is the ability to learn and improve organizational incident prevention, detection, and response. Each opportunity for improvement should be identified and assigned to a specific individual or team for action. It's a good practice to formally track post-mortem results within a database which can be leveraged for the development of incident and forensic responders, risk metrics as well as situational awareness during future incidents.

Use of Evidence and Evidence Retention. Organizations will have standard information retention and lifecycle policies. This is no different within forensics. However, with any policies there are exceptions and these exceptions should be formally documented to ensure evidence is retained appropriately. Response procedures should include a standard timeframe that evidence will be maintained, the intended use of collected evidence as well as the process to follow to record exceptions to the policy and who should be notified and approve the exceptions.

Improving Cyber Security. Cyber security is a dynamic discipline that requires constant focus and alignment to industry threats and regulatory and legislative requirements that are growing with increased complexity. Security leaders within many organizations try to keep their organizations in pace with industry good cyber security practices; however do fall short, whether due to lack of executive support for investment or resources to work on activities or simply because they don't think their organization is a target. After a Breach most organizations make additional investments into cyber security to help prevent a repeat occurrence and to rebuild the trust of key organizational partners, regulators, and clients. As mentioned earlier a silver lining of a Breach is gaining the visibility and support needed to make immediate investments into the improvement of cyber security across an organization. In the aftermath of a Breach, albeit tempting, it's important to refrain from focusing in on the sole exposure that resulted in the Breach. Security should be approached holistically and in addition to addressing the exposure that resulted in the recent Breach, your organization should also focus on identifying the assets requiring protection with a mind to having aligned protection, detection, and response capabilities. There is no guarantee that the Breach detected is the only one within your organization and that the immediate root cause for the known Breach is the greatest risk for your organization. This approach will help proactively address key areas of risk that are likely to result in a future Breach. The CSIR Plan should outline the team responsible for examining the incident to determine areas of failure across the existing security program and defining and approving security fixes to improve cyber security across the organization. We will cover recommendations on improving cyber security in Chapter 8 of this book.

Documentation and Reporting. This section of the CSIR Plan should outline a documentation and reporting protocol that will be followed by CSIR Team members in both the management and follow-up after a Breach. This protocol should be inclusive of:

- Documentation and templates that should be filled out by the CSIR Team during the management of a Breach such as chain of custody and evidence related documentation
- The level of detail that should be contained within investigation updates, the frequency of updates, and who should receive the updates
- The target delivery time after an incident is contained that the full incident report will be delivered to appropriate stakeholders. This may vary depending on incident classification such as low-impact incidents may receive a report with fewer details in contrast to incidents of greater severity which may require a more detailed report and may be associated with a longer delivery timeframe
- Who the incident report will be sent to and the protocol that should be followed to share it with both internal and external parties

CSIR PLAN VALIDATION AND TESTING

A well-developed CSIR Plan is created and tailored to successfully navigate the culture, technology, and Breach scenarios of a specific organization. Proper awareness of this program, once developed, will ensure CSIR Team members are knowledgeable of it and their specific role in its execution. However, many organizations make it to this point but when they actually need the CSIR Plan they realize they have an outdated document that is not effective for the organization to efficiently and effectively manage a Breach. Changes within the external threat landscape or internally within the organization can quickly outdate a CSIR Plan which will be hindered in its execution when managing a Breach unless it is properly validated and tested on an ongoing basis.

CSIR Plan Document Validation

As we discussed during the selection of the CSIR Team and defining the roles and responsibilities, one important responsibility is leading the review of the CSIR Plan documentation across internal and external stakeholders. This review should happen at least once per year and focus on identifying changes, internal and external to the organization that need to be reflected within the CSIR Plan. This can include organizational changes that will affect contact and communication workflows, areas in-scope versus out-of-scope in which the CSIR Plan will apply, and even new business units that introduce new data sets and technology that will need to be investigated in the event of a Breach. External changes with client contracts, expectations, and regulatory and legislative requirements can also change the manner in which the CSIR Plan is executed. Table 3.6 outlines some of these key elements that should be reviewed when validating the CSIR Plan.

Table 3.6 Key CSIR Plan Validation Areas

(#)	Goal	Description
1	CSIR Plan scope	The scope of the CSIR Plan including types of data, third parties, or areas of the organization which are or are not in scope of authority of the CSIR Plan\Team
2	CSIR Team roles and responsibilities	Have CSIR Team members review and validate the roles and responsibilities assigned to them. Note any differences and CSIR Team members should follow the defined process to make changes accordingly
3	Regulatory, legislative, and contract requirement review	Review any changes to CSIR Plan requirements. These requirements can stem from changes to corporate expectations, contract requirements, industry good practices, and regulatory and legislative requirements
4	Asset identification and classification	Record changes to the manner in which assets are identified or classified. Some changes to asset classification may require revisiting the classifications of assets assessed prior to the change. This can affect the severity and prioritization of incidents which include these data types
5	Critical assets and Breach scenarios	Identify the applicability of identified Breach scenarios and scenarios that should be removed from the scope of CSIR Plan response or new ones for incorporation
6	Standard Operating Procedures	Examine any changes to SOPs and the need to remove or add SOPs to support updated Breach scenarios, experience in managing past incidents and experience gained since the last document review. This includes keeping up-to-date with the tools and the techniques used by criminals to compromise systems and hide their actions. Updating SOPs to remain effective against the evolution of criminal cyber activity is essential in detecting, analyzing, and containing incidents
7	Evidence types and sources	Identify the type and nature of evidence that will need to be preserved in association with the anticipated Breach scenarios. This includes verifying that previously identified evidence stores such as logging continue to be maintained and retained for the defined period of time
8	Communication strategy	Identify changes to the communication workflows, message templates, or individuals who should be notified. Reviewing the pre-developed guidelines used for public notification of a Breach via web, print, mail, and social media should be reviewed as well as the communication vehicle intended to be used
9	Metrics	In response to third party audits or experienced incidents, the metrics tracked and the insight gathered from past incidents can frequently change. Ensuring that these changes are captured is critical in continuing to track the progress and the success of the CSIR Plan

CSIR Plan Testing

Periodic testing of a CSIR Plan is one of the best investments in time and resources that an organization can make. At this point the organization will understand the importance of having a CSIR Plan and will have spent significant resources on developing one. Ensuring the proper periodic testing of the CSIR Plan should be viewed as mandatory rather than optional in order to get the benefit of the organization's investment into the plan.

Let's look at the different types of CSIR Plan testing that can be performed to ensure CSIR Team members are intimate with the CSIR Plan and their specific role in its execution. Table 3.7 outlines some of the most common forms of testing.

Table 3.7 Types of CSIR Plan Testing

Test	Description	Achievements	Limitations	Difficulty
Paper-based test	A mental step-by-step review of the CSIR Plan in search for process, contact, or other errors	Identify procedural issues within the CSIR Plan	No actual review of the CSIR Plan\Team's ability to manage a cyber incident	Easy
Table top test	A non-intrusive discussion-based exercise focusing on CSIR Team roles and responsibilities and how the team would respond in specific scenarios to manage an incident	Determine the CSIR Team's ability to verbally articulate their roles and responsibilities and the actions that they would take to manage a specific incident	Only provides a high-level view into the CSIR Plan\Team's ability to manage a cyber security incident. CSIR Team skills, required resources, and organizational capabilities required for the successful execution of the plan are not tested	Moderate
Simulated test	An actual role-playing test of the CSIR Team/Plan's in response to pre-developed testing scenarios. This simulation requires internal and external CSIR Team members who will execute the tests within test/lab or production environment	An end-to-end walk through of the CSIR Plan by CSIR Team members	Requires internal and external stakeholder participation which has a demand on resources and typically requires executive sponsorship	Advanced

It is recommended that organizations begin testing the CSIR Plan with easier testing methods to gage capabilities and maturity before moving on to more advanced forms of testing.

Planning for a CSIR Plan Test

Knowing that a CSIR Plan test needs to be performed is a great start, knowing the best way to test it is another challenge in itself. Most organizations will have multiple Breach scenarios and limited resources and time to participate in the testing. How best can you ensure you are testing the right Breach scenarios and elements of the CSIR Plan? By using a holistic and coordinated approach to relate testing elements to specific objectives. This objective-driven testing approach uses CSIR Plan test scenarios to ensure selected Breach scenarios and hindrance events (both of which we'll discuss later in this chapter) can be woven together into a scenario developed to achieve the defined test objectives. Fig. 3.3 illustrates the relationship of testing elements in greater detail.

FIGURE 3.3 Relationships between CSIR Plan test scenarios, objectives, Breach scenarios, and hindrance events.

Each of the elements captured in Fig. 3.3 is described in greater detail below.

Test Objectives

CSIR Plan test objectives are specific areas of focus within the CSIR Plan. As basic as these objectives sounds they are essential in ensuring a successful CSIR Plan testing outcome. It is common for CSIR Plan test participants to independently attempt to steer the exercise in a direction of their choosing based on their perceived view of what they think the test should evaluate. This view often encounters conflicting objectives and dysfunctional testing that jumps between scenarios and can lead to spending too much time focusing on areas of the CSIR Plan that do not need to be assessed. Developing CSIR Plan test objectives are essential in focusing the test execution and participants in pursuit of specific previously agreed upon outcomes that are in the best interest of the organization. The following are a few examples of CSIR Plan test objectives:

- Ensure the accurate scoping and classification of cyber events
- Ensure the appropriate selection of CSIR Team members assist in the response to a specific cyber event
- Ensure that the defined CSIR Team roles, responsibilities, and authority are sufficient for the effective execution of the CSIR Plan to manage a specific incident
- Ensure the effective management of dynamic events that may occur concurrently with the primary incident
- Ensure the effective management of a specific cyber event in a manner that minimizes business disruption
- Ensure effective information sharing between internal and external CSIR Team, organizational, and partner stakeholders

With test objectives defined, you can now develop the test scenarios that will ultimately allow you to achieve them.

CSIR Plan Test Scenarios

Most organizations will have several Breach scenarios that they developed which can individually serve as good test. You however can't test everything and the previously defined test objectives will allow you to ensure you are testing the appropriate scenario based on risk. An example of a test scenario would be the disclosure of sensitive information by a hacktivist group. It would factor in the outcome or impact which is the disclosure of sensitive information and the threat in this example is the hacktivist group. A timeline associated with this test scenario is captured in Table 3.8.

Table 3.8 Sample Test Scenario	
Time	**Activity**
11:30 AM	A client calls into your service desk and advises them that their information has been posted on the internet by a hacker who is claiming that the information was taken from your systems due to political statements recently made by your CEO
12:15 AM	Two other clients call reporting similar events of their information identified on the web pointing back to your organization
12:45 PM	Your IT team begins to investigate
1:30 PM	Your internal IT team reports that there is suspicious activity originating from internal servers and destined to unknown origins
2:22 PM	A blog by an investigative journalist discusses the incident and that a hacktivist group that claims they have hacked your organization due to the political and social beliefs of your CEO. The group claims they have compromised your network and posted 5 GB of information publicly and is currently in possession of an additional 90GB of data including corporate email that they will post unless your CEO recants his recent comments publicly

Organizational cyber response may differ depending on the threat and it's good to incorporate this into your test scenarios. For example some organizations have policies that restrict them from adhering to extortion demands such as those associated with ransomware and will have a different response to the incident than the same incident without an extortion demand.

Table top and simulated testing include role playing the management of a cyber event and should be organized using test scenarios. CSIR Plan validation and paper-based testing do not involve actual role playing the management of a cyber incident and therefore are exempt from test scenario development. When looking at a test scenario insight into the scope and participants of the exercise should be included. Another factor to consider when planning test scenarios are those that have already been tested through live-fire testing. Live-fire testing is testing via actually managing the incident. It is common for organizations to perform live-fire testing of malware and phishing attacks routinely between formal tests of the CSIR Plan. If a scenario has been tested via live-fire testing to a good depth and the results have been positive it may be more beneficial for your organization to perform test management of other Breach scenarios which we've covered in depth in the previous chapter.

Hindrance Events

Few investigations are managed without a hitch and allow the CSIR Team to execute from beginning to end without experiencing an issue. To help prepare the CSIR Team for the dynamic nature of incident management, scenario testing should also include multiple hindrance events that are designed to frustrate execution of the CSIR Plan. For example during an incident simulation a hindrance event could be the inability to contact a key member of the CSIR Team to provide approval needed to contain the incident. Some additional examples of hindrance events that can be used during incident testing are:

- Encountering encrypted files believed to contain relevant evidence
- A media interview is published regarding the Breach with inaccuracies that were provided by someone within your organization who wasn't authorized to speak publicly about the case
- A sudden large volume of calls directed to your reception desk from concerned clients and partners asking about the Breach
- A dump of data presumably your own has been posted to the internet and contains far more records than what you have publicly reported
- You receive a ransom demand from criminals who threaten to disclose data or disrupt business operations if you do not shut down operations or pay an online ransom

Establishing CSIR Plan Testing Roles

Roles and responsibilities are critical in the execution of the CSIR Plan, however they are equally important in the testing of the CSIR Plan also. Ensuring in advance that there is a defined leadership during the test and someone who will capture observations, both good and bad, throughout the session is achieving the test objectives. The testing captured in Table 3.9 are examples of testing roles and recommended testing materials to be developed prior to a test.

Table 3.9 Sample CSIR Plan Testing Roles and Required Exercise Materials

Role	Role Description	Recommended Exercise Materials
Facilitator	<ul><li>Leads the testing sessions and presents the scenario(s) to be executed</li><li>Periodically asks questions to participants to understand roles and responsibilities and decision-making</li><li>Manages the direction of the test towards the defined objectives inclusive of focusing participants in the event they steer off-course during the test</li><li>Capture notes and observations during test</li></ul>	A facilitator guide that will serve as a structured approach to executing and soliciting responses from test participants. The facilitator guide should include the scope and objectives of the test as well as the scenarios to be exercised. Another essential element is a list of questions targeting each phase of the CSIR Plan that will extract mindset and thoughts from the participants to gage their thought and decision-making process. Questions should be asked at each phase of the CSIR Plans. An example of a question for the Detection and Analysis phase would be "How would the incident response team prioritize the handling of this incident?"

Table 3.9 Sample CSIR Plan Testing Roles and Required Exercise Materials—cont'd

Role	Role Description	Recommended Exercise Materials
Data Collector	■ Formally documents actions, issues, and success during test execution	Exercise template that will be used to capture observations, challenges, and successes associated with the test
Participant	■ Execute roles and responsibilities defined within the CSIR Plan	A participant guide will help educate CSIR Team members about the factors and issues that will be encountered during the test. This guide can mirror that of the facilitator with the exclusion of the facilitator questions and wild card events to help maintain a dynamic flow of the test

In the absence of defined testing roles, participants tend to provide an unbiased view of how they view their area executed during the test resulting in missed opportunities for independent evaluation and improvement both within specific CSIR Team member areas as well as how multiple members work together. These missed areas are critical and come back to haunt you when managing an actual Breach.

CSIR Plan Testing Facilities

The facility locations such as "war rooms" and tele- and video-conference equipment that will be used in a real incident should themselves be tested under these circumstances. In my experience I have seen conference bridges without international dial-in numbers for CSIR Team members in other countries or limitations in the number of tele-conference attendees that can concurrently join the line and temporary "war room" offices that can't be used in short notice due to higher priority bookings by other operational and executive teams. These challenges can be overcome however they slow the team down and lead to distractions that take the CSIR Team's attention away from managing the actual incident. Testing facilities may not be possible for every drill however testing should occur a minimum of at least once per year to ensure failures in essential equipment and resources don't hinder the execution of the CSIR Plan.

Executing a CSIR Plan Test

The facilitator leads the testing and should take control during the execution of the CSIR Plan test. Depending on the nature of testing, some CSIR Team members may not be familiar with others in the room and it's recommended to begin with introductions where each participant outlines who they are and their role in the testing, for the facilitator to review the test objectives and scenario to be covered. When this is completed executing the exercise is as simple as executing the defined test scenario. Participants should step through the CSIR Plan methodology, phase by phase to manage the incident with each team member leading their respective area. The facilitator will periodically ask questions to gage the mindset of the test participants as well as interject some hindrance events as appropriate.

Evaluating the Testing

All effort and steps taken thus far from preparing to executing the CSIR Plan test will have resulted in several observations by the facilitator, data collectors, and participants of what worked well and areas for improvement. It's important that immediately following the test that the facilitator, data collector, and participants should debrief to discuss success, failures, and possible improvements to the CSIR Plan. This can be verbal however the data collector should capture minutes of the meeting and leverage feedback for the formal post-test report.

Following the post-test debrief, a report with an evaluation of the test's ability to achieve the defined objectives and the CSIR Team's ability to execute the CSIR Plan to manage the simulated incidents is provided. This report should be followed up with specific action items and owners to ensure the findings are evaluated and acted accordingly.

CSIR Plan Performance Metrics

CSIR Plan performance metrics measure the effectiveness and efficiency of the design and effectiveness of the CSIR Plan. Collecting and reviewing incident metrics can allow for the identification of trends and issues such as resource constraints, the lack of authority to efficiently manage incidents or even the need to provide additional training and tools to existing team members. Table 3.10 contain sample metrics organized by category that can be used to measure CSIR Plan effectiveness

Table 3.10 Sample CSIR Plan Performance Metrics

Metric Category	Metric
General	# of total incidents
	# of incidents by type
	# of incidents by category
Damage	# of personnel hours spent resolving incident
	# of days taken to contain an incident
	# of hours of system down-time per incident
	Estimated costs per incident
	# of systems affected per incident
	# of records disclosed per incident
Magnitude	# of incidents requiring forensics (collection and analysis) per year
	# of system images analyzed per incident
	# of system memory dumps examined per incident

Identifying metrics and documenting the calculations associated with the metrics will allow you to develop repeatable metrics on the efficiency and effectiveness of your CSIR Plan. As maturity grows organizations often tailor metrics to be more granular and also introduce new metrics to track additional performance data and gain further insight into CSIR Plan performance and effectiveness. Due to the importance performance metrics play in the overall health of the CSIR Plan it is essential that performance metrics are collected after each incident and should be delivered to senior executives within the organization. As we discussed in Chapter 2, obtaining support from senior executives is critical prior to developing the CSIR Plan, it is equally critical to ensure reporting on the effectiveness of the CSIR Plan make it back to the senior executives to ensure they have proper visibility into the strengths and weaknesses of the CSIR Plan and plan to address them.

SUMMARY

A popular Japanese proverb is "Tomorrow's battle is won during today's practice." This proverb is fitting when looking at Breach response, however, takes on a new meaning. Several research reports have shown that Breaches may go undetected for quite some time—a few months, years and in some cases even decades. Factoring this in and revisiting our proverb I would like to amend it to "Tomorrow's battle is won using today's practice to manage yesterday's Breach." Convoluted? Absolutely! However it is highly applicable based on the present state of the security industry.

Breaches happen. I can say with authority that they happen to all organizations and will continue to happen for the foreseeable future. Developing security strategies and implementing security controls will help reduce the frequency and number of Breaches an organization endures. They however will continue to occur. This chapter outlined the considerations and guidance needed to actually write the CSIR Plan for your organization and to effectively operationalize it to ensure its successful execution. We also looked at the importance of monitoring and measurement and how CSIR Plan metrics can be used to identify current challenges and future trends that threaten the success of the CSIR Plan.

Often what's critical in an incident is not the incident itself but how you respond to it. The guidance in this chapter will aid you in continually testing your response capabilities, identifying areas for improvement, and adapting your efforts based on gathered experience and advancements within the security community to help ensure effective Breach response.

CHAPTER 4

Qualifying and Investigating a Breach

Chris Pogue, Kevvie Fowler, Greg Markell

INTRODUCTION

Early in my career as an investigator, I investigated a Breach at a large insurance provider. Their CEO had received a ransom letter from the alleged attacker indicating that he was in possession of thousands of electronic healthcare records belonging to the CEO's customers. The letter provided a screenshot of a dozen or so examples of the data as proof that he was not bluffing. At the end of the letter, the seemingly legitimate attacker demanded one million dollars for the safe return of this information; otherwise he would make it publicly available on the internet.

The first logical step in the investigation was to ask the CEO, where does this data reside, and which systems contain this specific data in the same format as laid out in the letter? So, being a logical sort of guy, that's exactly what I did. Much to my surprise (remember, this was *EARLY* in my career; if presented with the same case today, I would sadly not be surprised at all) nobody had any idea where this information resided. There were no less than two dozen systems that "should" contain this data, and easily two dozen more that "could" contain the data. My response to the CEO was something to the effect of, "Well, if you want us to figure out how the data was stolen, we really need to know where the data could have been stolen from. Narrowing down to those systems that have this data in this format is sort of important for us to get started." So, my team and I spent three weeks just trying to identify if a Breach had actually taken place, or if the letter was a bold, well-crafted social engineering attempt.

After a great deal of hunting, searching, looking, foraging, and divining, we eventually confirmed the Breach, identified the systems pertinent to the incident, and solved the case. But the three weeks we spent hunting down potential Indicators of Compromise (IOCs) was the best example I have witnessed to date, of how *NOT* to respond to a data Breach. This organization was unprepared, driven by the all too common misconception that things like this only happen to other people. After 18 years in the field, and having worked on

79

Data Breach Preparation and Response. http://dx.doi.org/10.1016/B978-0-12-803451-4.00004-6

literally thousands of cases, I have found a pervasive mentality that spans victim type, size, and vertical. My work with local, state, and federal law enforcement has confirmed this, since countless officers, detectives, and federal agents have identified this constant as well. This is the sentiment that, "I never thought it would happen to me." Assume a Breach is going to take place and prepare accordingly.

INVOKING THE CSIR TEAM

We discussed building a CSIR Team in Chapter 2, including a range of team members across the various lines of business. These internal stakeholders and external experts in concert with security and forensics SME's are best to qualify an incident and its associated severity. Ensuring these crucial determinations are performed by a central team that is trained, knowledgeable, and abiding by a set criteria is essential in ensuring incidents are correctly identified, assessed, and managed according to severity rating. So, this begs the question—who are the right CSIR Team members to make this determination? Since you cannot predict what aspects of the business will be impacted by an incident, you need to try as best as you can to cover all of the areas that have the highest likelihood of either being targeted or having a role to play in any response. This is part of what makes Breach preparedness so critical; you simply cannot afford to wait until something bad happens to figure out what you are going to do. In my experience, Breaches are usually more complicated than they initially appear to be, so having a dedicated team that is educated, trained, and focused on responding can make the difference between your organization readily handling the incident, and ending up on the six o'clock news.

As a responder, these will be the people you ask specific technical questions to regarding the specifics of the evidence you identify and analyze. Having access to individuals that possess this level of insight into what "normal" is plays a huge role in keeping you as the responder from chasing leads (commonly referred to as rabbit trails) only to end up discovering later that the specific behavior you thought was attacker activity is normal within the company's infrastructure.

CRITICAL FIRST RESPONDER STEPS

I have written and delivered a number of different *First Responder* courses over the years to corporate investigation teams, law enforcement agencies, and university students. Regardless of who the content was being delivered to, the first few modules always focused on the same thing; knowing what you are, and what you are not. As a first responder, you are supposed to gather data, take copious notes, and prepare an initial report for the incident response team. You are not to make decisions about what is important and what is not, perform any sort of data reduction, make any assumptions about what is going on, or try to "solve the case." I know that sounds harsh, and I apologize, but this is really important; much of the subsequent response capabilities hinge on actions of the first responders. There is only one chance to gather much of the necessary data; success will aid the investigation, failure will hinder it. This is a very important step in the investigation process, and not to be taken lightly.

No organization should expect members of their first responder team to memorize all of the steps they need to perform during the initial stages of an investigation. There are far too many things to remember, and far too many potential variables to set this sort of unrealistic expectation (however, if you fail to document first responder activities, this is precisely what you are doing). Thus there is the need for a clear, concise, and well-documented CSIR Plan. This should be the *Red Binder* that is easily accessible, kept current, and contains the step-by-step processes that need to be followed once an incident has been detected.

In all of the CSIR Plans that I have written, the first responder actions are outlined in an Incident Triage Checklist. An example "Incident Triage Checklist" is included within the appendix of this book. This checklist should be easy to read, easy to follow, and contain the critical actions that need to be performed for each and every incident. Having a checklist also reduces the chances of mistakes by junior staff members and helps to eliminate tribal knowledge. Something else to consider is that now that post-Breach litigation has become "standard operating procedure," you should anticipate that your CSIR Plan will be requested by opposing counsel or investigating government agency. This means that it will end up in the hands of nontechnical people who are going to make a judgment call with regards to the thoroughness of your plan, how easy or hard it is to read and understand, and if it was followed during the incident response. Make sure your plan takes into account this potential and is written in such a manner that even the most junior staff member can readily understand and explain what actions he is supposed to take.

Evidence Acquisition

Acquiring evidence is without question, the most tedious, boring yet incredibly important phase of any response. If done properly, it provides the data necessary to conduct a thorough investigation that will stand up in a court of law (whether that's necessary or not is totally irrelevant). When acquisition is done improperly, post incident litigation or criminal prosecution becomes exponentially more difficult, if not impossible. Not to mention the data you need to "solve the case" will be gone, which can also have a negative impact on your mental health.

Let me share a story with you from the archives of my early adventures in incident response. I was on a case with a senior member of my team. This individual, who shall remain nameless, boasted close to 20 years' experience in digital forensics to my three months. In my estimation, he had forgotten more about forensics than I would ever know, so I listened to him intently, took notes, and tried to learn as much as I could from this sage master.

Okay so, we go onsite to a client location and we start to acquire images from several different systems. Once we have confirmed that data is being written, and the "images are cooking," the client Point-of-contact (POC) exits the server room leaving us to our duties. Much to my amazement, this guy pulls out a book and starts reading. Not a forensic book or a study guide for a certification test, but a Mack Bolan novel. I was stunned. I seriously asked him, "what are you doing?" He said, and I will never forget this, "There is nothing we can do until the images finish. So you should find something to do. This is going to take a while."

This guy with 20 plus years of experience wanted me to sit there and do nothing until images were finished. I was dumbfounded. I decided right then and there that if this was the way IR was being done for the past 20 years, then things have been inefficient for a very long time. It was then that I sat down and started penning the *Sniper Forensics* methodology[1] which better utilized responder time during image collection. While taking images is still SOP during an investigation, there are a ton of other things that can be done while "images are cooking." A few good examples are for first responders to begin writing your investigation plan, gather the various log files, network packet captures, memory, and volatile data from potentially impacted systems, and even start to build the shell of your preliminary report. There are loads of things that can be done before image acquisition is complete apart from reading Mack Bolan. Please don't be "that guy."

Having been an expert witness multiple times, I have noticed something about the attorneys who try cases involving digital evidence. The defense tries to get the evidence thrown out. I'm sure there are several reasons for this, but the ones I have seen the most frequently have to do with the complexity introduced into the case with the admission of this evidence. While lawyers are smart, many struggle to understand deeply technical content. Additionally, this type of evidence is not subject to interpretation. It's cold hard fact. Either

---

[1] https://www.google.com/webhp?sourceid=chrome-instant&ion=1&espv=2&ie=UTF-8#q=sniper+forensics

a login took place or it didn't. Either an IP address is present in the logs, or it's not. There is no room for interpretation; it's either a 1 or a 0 (hurray for binary truths). Now, that's not to say there is no room to argue whose fingers were on the keyboard at the time of a login, or during the time a specific IP address appears in the logs, that is debated all the time. I am specifically referring to the existence of the evidence and what it indicates. To avoid the complexities of this sort of litigation, it's just easier for them from a defense perspective to get as much of the evidence declared inadmissible as they can.

The two most common reasons why digital evidence is declared inadmissible are improper data acquisition, and broken chain of custody. To ensure proper acquisition, first responders should follow some very simple steps to include documentation of the systems from which the evidence is being acquired, such as:

- Time of day (local and system time) the evidence was acquired
- The name of the individual acquiring the evidence
- Hostname and IP address of the system(s)
- Geographical location of the system(s)
- System Information
  - Operating System
  - Serial Numbers
  - Status of the system (live or post mortem)
- The type of evidence being gathered (image, memory, volatile data)
  - Hash values of the evidence (MD5 and/or SHA2)
- A photo of the system (although I have rarely used the photos, there have been occasions that I was happy I had them)
- Target drive the evidence is being gathered to
  - Serial number of that drive

As a guide, a sample "Evidence Collection and Processing Worksheet" is provided within the appendix of this book.

After the evidence has been acquired and the evidence acquisition has been completed for each evidence item, the first responder should then fill out a Chain of Custody form. This form is used to track each time the evidence changes hands. Without this form, opposing counsel can challenge the fact that positive control of the evidence has been lost and that the potential exists that the evidence has been tampered with or altered in some way. He doesn't have to be right, he just has to raise the possibility. You may have never even taken your eyes off the hard drives; however, he just needs the Judge to think that the integrity of the evidence is in question, and that the sample can no longer be trusted as "Best Evidence." So, to keep this from happening, you should ensure to fill out the Chain of Custody form. A sample Chain of Custody form is available within the appendix of this book.

Initial Reporting

OK, so the first responders have gathered the evidence, and properly filled out the data acquisition worksheets and chain of custody forms—now what? Well, now they get to prepare an initial incident report that will be submitted to their client or manager, and read by his manager (and likely all the way up to the executive leadership team), the incident response team, the company's general counsel, and likely law enforcement. This is not the full forensic report, it's just the "prelim," so only state what has been done, and what you know right now; it's not the time for conjecture or speculation, and it's not the place to put your grammatical prowess on display. This initial report is a down and dirty, "this is what happened." This report should contain short, but detailed descriptions of the following:

- The name of the individual filling out the report
- The date and time of the report
- A brief chronology of events
  - When was the incident identified
  - Who noticed it
  - How
  - What actions were taken by the First Responders to date
- Which systems were impacted
  - What was the visible impact
- What data was gathered and where from
- What is current location of that data
- What forms have been filled out
  - The current location of those forms
- Who has been notified
  - Management
  - General Counsel
  - Law Enforcement
  - Human Resources
  - Public Relations

In some instances, there might be a need for protective markings, as well as how and to whom the evidence has been disseminated. It is important to remember that legal counsel has been properly consulted prior to any evidence distribution.

Remember, keep your report concise; don't leave information out, but don't embellish either. This is a technical report, not creative writing class. Be as stoic and factual as you possibly can. This report will be used by the IR team to begin their investigation. If it's done well, you will provide them with a tremendous advantage as they begin their investigation. If it's done poorly, or not at all, the investigation can be delayed, potentially for weeks, as the IR team is forced to redo the initial triage and evidence acquisition process.

Something else to keep in mind is that in today's world of post-Breach litigation, the initial report will undoubtedly end up in the hands of legal counsel as they prepare for Breach-related litigation. As such, the accuracy of the report coupled with the evidence that has contributed to the conclusions being drawn is of utmost importance. At this stage of the reporting, it is also acceptable to indicate that there are certain aspects of the investigation that are ongoing and still require additional information before the working hypothesis can be confirmed. This is perfectly OK and legal counsel will likely appreciate your candor. Not knowing something, and stating that you don't know is far better than not knowing, pretending like you do (in an effort to appease some premature demand for answers) and being wrong. In post-Breach litigation, being wrong can have a significant negative impact to your credibility as an expert, which can seriously damage your company's ability to withstand the scrutiny of opposing counsel or government regulators. Recent Breaches have underscored this point several times over making the old saying, "you can't un-ring the bell" ever more important and appropriate.

ENGAGING AND MANAGING THIRD PARTIES

In Chapter 2 we discussed that few organizations are able to staff a CSIR Team entirely with internal resources who are subject matter experts across all disciplines related to an incident. Most organizations identify Breach scenarios, the roles they feel their internal resources can satisfy and then identify appropriate third-party responders that have the skills, experience, and capabilities that will assemble and support them effectively and efficiently during their time of need—nice and simple right? You wish. Over my career I have seen countless Breaches where the victim organization retained third parties who were experts in their respective disciplines, pointed them at the incident and let the experts do their thing. I refer to this as the "set and forget" approach, and the result? Bloated investigation timeframes, excessive fees, and several investigations that ended up chasing answers to questions that were irrelevant to the organization and differed from the objective in which the third party was originally retained. I have also seen organizations that leveraged third parties to assist in an investigation which resulted in achieving the objective in a fraction of the anticipated timeframe. The obvious question is what is the core reason for the difference in outcome between cases? It comes down to the need to effectively managing third parties during an investigation.

Third parties may be experts in their respective fields, however not necessarily in working together with other internal or third-party responders and being able to respond to discoveries and challenges in the best interest of a victim organization during an investigation.

Effective management of third parties during an incident can be achieved using the third-party management criteria outlined in Table 4.1.

The third-party management criteria outlined in Table 4.1 will be helpful in keeping the investigation on-the-rails during management. There however are additional factors that should be considered when dealing with specific

Table 4.1 Sample Third-Party Management Criteria

Criteria	Description
Direction	Each task or objective you provide to a third party should involve the explicit documentation of what you need the third party to do for you and within what timeframe. An example of this can be as simple as, "look for instances of unauthorized access within the environment" and, "do this for a week before reevaluating progress." Clear direction is essential in ensuring that the responder focuses effort in the right area associated with the investigation
Context	Each task or objective you provide a third party should be accompanied with the reasoning as to why you need the third party to execute the task you've requested. At the end of the day the third party will likely be more skilled within their respective discipline and simply put will know more than you in this area. Letting them know why you are providing them specific objectives can provide them the opportunity to suggest alternative objectives or courses of action that can get you the answers to the questions you need in a more efficient manner. Don't play in the weeds here and request all changes to an approach be verified with you. However, material changes that will affect agreed upon timelines and effort estimates or require the involvement of other organizational stakeholders should be raised to you for alignment. Allowing third parties full control over making these decisions without consulting you more often than not, results in confusion, frustration, and missed objectives
Management expectations	There are lots of moving pieces during an incident. Establish how frequently and detailed you would like communication and updates on the investigation as well as how you would like communication, approval, and purchases to be managed ■ Establish a leader or Breach coach (normally an attorney) as the focal point that all resources should report to ■ You will need to provide frequent updates to senior management. As such, all down-stream CSIR Team members must be aware of when updates are needed, what format they need to be in, and to whom to send them. This process is essential in managing expectations as well as ensuring proper dissemination of sensitive Breach related information ■ Administrative duties such as timesheet submission may seem trivial however can lead to frustration and the halting of service delivery. Ensuring resources are clear on whom the timesheets should be directed to and expectations around payment should be established especially if the payroll department has been affected by the Breach there may be extended payment terms that will need to be established

third-party response groups. We will cover five of the most common beginning with managing the Data Breach Coach.

Data Breach Coach

By now it is probably clear that when a major data Breach occurs, a lot of moving parts quickly come into play, and you do not have the luxury of time. What you do—or fail to do—in the first 48–72 hours can often be critical to how well, or how poorly the situation is managed. Moreover, if there is a high risk of post-Breach litigation (particularly if a material amount of personal information is involved, such as ePHI, PII, or PCI data) then even the first 24 hours can make a big difference.

It is for these reasons, companies often retain a "data Breach coach" at the first sign of an incident; to be more precise, the "retainer" happens much earlier, when the organization is putting together its CSIR Plan; but the actual "activation" of the data Breach coach is triggered when the organization gets its first inkling that a data Breach *may* have occurred.

The coach is typically someone from outside the organization, though sometimes it can be an internal person if they've had sufficient experience with material data Breach incidents. If you are leaning towards using someone for this critical job who is internal, or is at one of your sister companies, take a good, long look in the mirror—and ask, honestly, does this person have the requisite experience? Not simply in drafting a data privacy policy, or even data Breach planning, but in actual, hands on, live, data Breach management. This is not an entry level job or one that you learn by doing, and eventually "get it." You need a seasoned veteran (a beneficial irony, though, of the large volume of data Breaches recently, is that, there are now enough data Breaches occurring that data Breach coaches with real live experience are not that hard to find) who understands the multitude of requirements such as Breach disclosure notification laws and compliance obligations, has a strong grasp on communications strategies such as who do you tell, how much, and when, and can guide you around the pitfalls identified over hundreds of response scenarios.

Think of the coach like an orchestra conductor. His or her job is to make sure all the various players on your team work well together. Sometimes, in a musical orchestra, the violins might be able to play beautifully but if they are drowned out by an all too loud—and off key—brass section, then the experience for the audience is not optimal. Such is the case with a major data Breach. It is indeed useful if the IT department knows what to do on the forensics side but the anticipated benefit of this fine effort might be compromised or lost altogether if the public relations department fails to get timely and appropriate messaging out to impacted customers. Hence the critical role of the data Breach coach is to make sure all the different subgroups and subspecialists on the data Breach response team are coordinated and working harmoniously towards a coordinated goal that is in alignment with the CSIR Plan, local, state, and federal law, contractual obligations, and industry regulators.

With this role it is easy for an organization to treat the Breach coach as a single point-of-contact to answer executive questions and to manage the internal and external response teams. That however is where the issue lies, funneling communication through the Breach coach can break attorney-client privilege (unless of course the Breach coach is an attorney—which is the case with a large percentage of coaches) and open the information and communication surrounding the Breach during future legal proceedings. The Breach coach should indeed call the shots; however, communication around the Breach should still be managed by legal counsel to provide the protection of privilege.

Early in my career, an executive at my organization would repeatedly state that he needs "one throat to choke" in the event of an issue. The meaning behind this is if he was directly dealing with multiple people on an activity or task and it failed he'd have to follow up with each person one by one to choke their throats if things didn't go as expected. This seemed odd to me however observing the benefits first hand of having one person manage the requests across many and how it provided a level of control and simplicity across incident management was invaluable. Also, yes, in the event of an issue it was far easier to choke one throat (and your hands are less tired). Unfortunately on numerous occasions it was my throat that was choked; however, this experience again was invaluable in my personal and professional development.

Data Breach Legal Counsel

By now it should be apparent that numerous legal and regulatory issues are triggered by your data Breach, especially if it is a material one (ie, contains or is suspected to contain material losses). Simply stated, anticipate post-Breach litigation. In order to adequately prepare, you will need experienced legal counsel to assist you, in order to determine:

- What is your legal risk profile, given all the facts coming to light about the incident? (and often the full story only unfolds in dribs and drabs)
- Given what you know at the particular time, which external entities need to be notified, and which ones might make sense to notify (even though not legally required)?
- What can and should be said to the customer base, whether in a Business to Consumer (B2C) or Business to Business (B2B) Breach situation; in each case the tone, content, and communication channels might be very

different, and what would be folly to communicate, particularly from a litigation risk perspective?

- What should you do (and say) when (or if) your insurance carrier denies coverage under your relevant insurance policy?

If these emails (including memos, reports, etc.) are created and then circulated by and between nonlegal staff at the company, then they will not acquire any quality of "privilege", even if they eventually find their way into the email box of a legal counsel. Therefore, they will be able to be searched and read by anyone ultimately involved in the litigation flowing from the incident, including parties adverse to your interests. It is important to note that only communication with an attorney can invoke attorney-client privilege, with and for the purposes of obtaining legal advice. Simply putting, "Privileged and Confidential" on an email will not preclude it from discovery. You have to be seeking legal advice or counsel on a matter of compliance, legal risk, or obligation. So, it is a very good idea to speak with your legal counsel before you actually have the need to send any such communications, and work out the details needed to ensure the greatest measure of protection for your organization. By contrast, if the emails with sensitive messages and data are sent to legal counsel, then typically solicitor-client privilege can be claimed over such materials, such that they cannot be released or shared with the plaintiffs or their legal counsel bringing the litigation. The rationale for this "privilege rule" is to allow company representatives to talk freely to the lawyers of the company, without being worried that their own words might come back to bite them during litigation.

The important role of legal counsel to serve as the conduit between CSIR Team members in order to maintain attorney-client privilege and advisor to legal aspects of the Breach response is not a 9×5 job. Communication between the CSIR Team will be occurring around the clock, weekends, and often throughout holidays. Ensure to set expectations with legal counsel as early in an investigation to ensure there is coverage to ensure the protection of Breach-related communication. The last thing a response effort needs is having communication between the CSIR Team come to a screeching halt due to the unavailability of a lawyer to manage communication across the team.

Recent developments in post-Breach litigation and legislation has created an elusive, and as of the writing of this book, largely undefined, standard called, "reasonableness." While the premise seems simple, Did the impacted organization have security controls in place, and conduct post-Breach response and remediation efforts in a manner that is "reasonable"? It's not. From what I have witnessed to date, the term "reasonable" has proven to be tremendously problematic, provided its subjective nature. Reasonable according to whom? Me? You? Your lawyer? A judge? A jury? Each of these parties can and will have their own opinions; and should your incident wind up in litigation, opposing counsel will undoubtedly have their own expert that will testify that your steps to meet this standard were inadequate. As is clearly apparent, for your organization to establish a defensible position regarding what is "reasonable," you will need the expert advice of outside counsel.

Forensics, Security, and Technical Consultants

Whether your CSIR Team requires the assistance of specialized forensics consultants to investigate the incident, or security consultants to assist in identifying weaknesses within the environment and to devise security controls to remediate, or technical consultants to implement remediation measures and make system changes, maintaining control of consultants is essential during an incident. Consultants are common during Breach response and mid-to-large size Breaches can require the use of dozens of consultants executing multiple work streams simultaneously. Proper oversight is critical in ensuring consultants are working towards established objectives in an efficient and effective manner. The following are some key areas to ensure and establish at the onset of a Breach:

- How often to update you on progress and challenges experienced during their investigation. Each objective you provide, a third party may take days, weeks, or months to satisfy. Outlining to them when and how you would like to be communicated, will help you ensure the course of the investigation is towards the objectives you set. It is easier for a response provider to get distracted on areas of response that lead away from the investigation objective, sometimes this is to work on the "sexy" area of the investigation such as reconstructing malware that is not relevant in the objective you've set or may be better managed by another third party or automated solution provider online. However, keep in mind that an excessive update schedule will redirect precious time resources that should be assisting in the investigation to administrative update duties. Three people from the third party who may be involved in providing two 1-hour updates each day will lose the equivalent of one day of effort each day in delivering and preparing for the updates. The update frequency doesn't have to be set in stone so ensure to monitor the progress of the investigation and the materiality of the updates. Getting routine updates that provide little value can be an indicator that updates are occurring too frequently
- How often to update you on the burn rate which tracks how much resources they have invested into the investigation-to-date, and equally as important, how much you will need to pay them for their assistance-to-date. During Breach investigations the engaging organization will inevitably ask the question "how much should this cost" the engaged provider will respond with something along the lines of, "you can't

estimate until they get more information about the case." This is fine, but ask them when they will know or what objective they will set to ensure they can provide you a rough estimate. You can use this estimate as your first block of resources you will purchase with the organization. It's best not to provide a blank check to the response provider, alternatively set thresholds based on their feedback on each objective within the investigation and track progress to these thresholds using the burn rate calculation that you request on a periodic basis

- Ensure to know and discuss the logistics around the work-day for the course of the investigation. This includes what work will be done onsite vs off-site, the frequency of fly-backs for out-of-town responders and if work will occur during weekend and holiday periods. You may have a role to provide resources to assist the third parties late nights, weekends, and holidays as well to arrange travel and accommodations. Identifying the work-day logistics up front will help avoid delays in the investigation such as third-party resources waiting for a client contact to provide information or access off hours, which will bring the investigation to a screeching halt

Law Enforcement

When your company is the victim of a data Breach incident, you will usually have to consider when and how you will interact with law enforcement. By "law enforcement," we mean a number of potential different police and related organizations. It might be the "local" municipal police service, such as the New York Police Department or Toronto Police Services. For certain situations, it might be the state or provincial police organization such as the Oklahoma State Bureau of Investigation or the Ontario Provincial Police. Depending on the seriousness of the situation, it may also be the federal law enforcement bodies, in the United States, the Secret Service or the Federal Bureau of Investigation and in Canada the Royal Canadian Mounted Police (RCMP). Additionally, if the circumstances indicate international criminal activity, particularly if it might be state sponsored, then the federal government's intelligence agencies might get involved as well.

In some cases, you will not have a choice whether to involve law enforcement, because they will simply insert themselves into the situation. This is likely to happen if the data Breach is related to a criminal event where a material fraud or theft (including identity theft) is facilitated by the Breach. Indeed, in such a scenario, the first indication you may have of the incident is a phone call or visit from law enforcement, informing you of the Breach, which in turn was reported to law enforcement by a bank, an online payment company, or one or more of your customers.

In other circumstances, it may well be that you learn of the data Breach first, coupled with an IT security penetration, and it may be that you decide the matter is serious enough to warrant the involvement of law enforcement. Or, it might be that when you review your insurance policy, it actually requires you—in the case of cyber-related fraud or theft—to report the matter to the police (so, again, you may in fact have no other option but to reach out to law enforcement).

It often happens that the police do not find your incident significant enough to warrant their attention; after all, law enforcement is usually strapped for resources, and therefore a "run of the mill" small size data Breach (however much you might feel "violated" by it) may simply not get onto the police's radar screen (ha…no pun intended). That being said, sometimes getting law enforcement to engage on your behalf is quite a struggle. In these cases, you can help your case if you prepare a well-stocked binder of material—or USB drive—that contains the relevant evidence compiled to that point, and includes examples of the harm caused by the perpetrators of the incident. Put another way, you may have to do some (and sometimes a great deal) of the preparatory leg work for the police (including forensic reviews), because their resources are stretched thin.

Be prepared to have law enforcement tell you to maintain the confidentiality of the data Breach for some period of time, to allow them to conduct the initial portion of their investigation without "tipping off the bad guys." Where law enforcement only asks this of you for a few days, it is easier to accommodate; where, however, they ask for a "black out period" of some weeks, you may have a significant problem on your hands, particularly if your analysis concludes that you should (or in some cases *must*) notify a relevant government authority, or perhaps you have concluded it is imperative that you tell your customer base of an incident that impacts their personal information. These situations can develop into very finicky problems, requiring skillful, and careful management; and of course, as you approach these challenges, you are always asking yourself—"how will this impact our organization's insurance coverage, and our legal liability?"

Another risk with law enforcement is that they may want to "seize the evidence," and might decide they want to impound a number of computers or servers hosting the relevant data. If this is a possibility, then make sure you've created backups of the relevant data before the police arrive, so you are not left high and dry, from either an operations perspective, or even if it's simply not being able to continue your own forensic investigation. Keep in mind with the police that, fundamentally, while their role is "to serve and protect," they tend to think about those goals in a big picture, societal sense—"to serve and protect *the public*"; that is, your specific concerns and worries may not be uppermost in their mind. So, you have to look out for your own interests when dealing with law enforcement—remember this at all times. In terms of operationalizing this, it's probably a good idea that your staff never meet one-on-one with police—always have a second person from your organization in the room. And ideally that second person will be a lawyer, at least early on when the preliminary "rules of engagement" are being worked out between you and them.

Both of the previous scenarios point to a general risk factor when you interface with law enforcement—namely, that you will of course be unable to control the extent of their investigation, and so you need to be ready for whatever likely action they might take. The old scout's motto is useful here: "Be Prepared!" For example, if the police do take possession of some of your laptop computers, they will be able to see all the material on the machine's hard drive. Ideally they will not find any problematic content, whether it be bootleg software, or child pornography. It's at times like these when you hope that everyone in the organization has complied with your organization's ethical computer use policy. Now, you won't have time once the data Breach incident hits, to review your computers for digital contraband—so, please make sure this agenda item gets proper coverage at your organization's annual general staff training session, etc.

For these reasons it is a good idea to reach out to your local police force, and whichever federal agencies have a field office in your area. Each of these agencies will have detectives or agents assigned to a "Cyber Crimes Squad" that would be the ones assigned to your case should something bad happen. Call them, introduce yourself, or meet them for lunch. Making that connection before an incident occurs as opposed to cold calling them can have a dramatic impact on the speed and intrusiveness of their response. Also, many of these agencies have public/private working ground such as the US Secret Service Electronic Crimes Task Force,[2] or the FBI Infragard.[3] Join these groups, attend the meetings, and become familiar with the other members, officers, constables, and agents. You may find this to be an effort very well spent when an incident occurs.

Cyber Insurer

As if dealing with law enforcement, technical experts, forensic consultants, a Breach coach, and cyber security legal counsel weren't enough, we'll add one more function to your already busy data Breach agenda; liaising with your internal and external risk management/insurance people.

---

[2]https://www.dhs.gov/sites/default/files/publications/USSS%20Electronic%20Crimes%20Task%20Force.pdf

[3]https://www.infragard.org/

No matter what the size of your organization, a Breach can leave you unable to conduct business and can jeopardize profitability causing loss of customer confidence, loss of market share, and shareholder dissidence. When looking at things from an enterprise risk management perspective, one option is always that of transferring the risk you are worried about as a business off the balance sheet. Commonly, this is achieved through the use of insurance, and cyber risk is no different.

The insurance market has evolved to offer stand-alone policies that achieve risk transfer mechanisms exclusive to cyber risk. These policies involve a number of post-Breach mitigation factors that help limit the damage to the organization, as well as the cost to the insurer for covered loss. As we've discussed throughout the chapter, there are a number of service providers involved in post-Breach mitigation for the organization. The insurance policy can help in not just aligning these service providers, but also doing so at a lower cost than the company would incur should they have to go through a Breach response on their own. This is due to the fact that the insurers have prenegotiated rates with these service providers based on volume discounts (the vendors on these lists are referred to as "panels"). This can be powerful for a company, because not only do they get reputable service providers to handle these situations (not to mention predefined Service Level Agreements (SLAs)), but the overall amount of the insurance that they purchase, in terms of policy limits, goes even further to mitigate loss.

What must not be forgotten is that the insurers are in the business of paying claims (albeit sometimes begrudgingly). With cyber policies being as complex as they are, it is important to understand that the traditional concept of a "claim" as being a written demand or a suit is one dimensional under the policy. While it is true that these two items (amongst several others) would trigger a claim under the third party (loss caused by your organization to another organization) section of the policy, in situations of Breaches it is important that mitigation techniques are employed. These techniques, or triage process, form part of the first-party coverage section (costs incurred by your company in the event of a incident) of a cyber and privacy liability policy. These would be items such as forensics, public relations, legal, credit monitoring, and remediation costs— to name a few; basically, the cost of outside vendors that are involved in a security or privacy event.

Not unlike other insurance products, once it is understood what can be transferred, next is to understand the implications surrounding how the insurance company is alerted when a claim does arise. Insurance policies have reporting provisions as to when you must notify the insurer of a claim, or a potential claim. There is also the importance of *who* can report, and when they report. For example, if the IT department knows about a situation occurring, but wants to try to fix it before escalating it up the ranks within the organization, when would management have known, or ought to have known about the issue in order to report it? This is an important factor in how situations are handled. Often times, an incident response plan will identify key personnel involved in these situations. The insurers will want to know that there are dedicated employees that will handle these situations, and will assign notice provisions accordingly. That way, it is clear as to who needs to be aware of the situation and report it to the insurer.

With this in mind, it is important to have the discussions with your insurer and plan for these types of situations. Establishing who will report a claim is simply the first step in what would begin the triage process. Insurers will work with the company to help establish this process, and align service providers that are going to be involved. Fig. 4.1 provides a typical flow of events that unfold during the claims handling process.

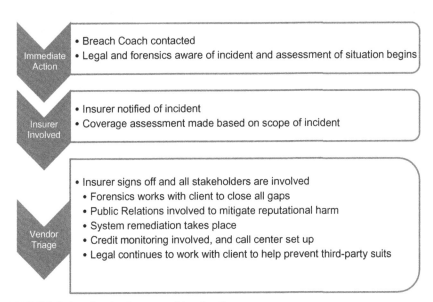

FIGURE 4.1 Sample cyber insurance claims handling process.

When a Breach is detected, it is a good practice for someone in your risk management group, with your cyber insurance policy firmly tucked under their arm, to begin tracking events, and most importantly, costs in real time. You will have a range of first-party costs that need to be recorded, such as costs for external legal and Breach coach services, all the various expenses related to notifications (of third-party suppliers, and especially customers, but also regulators), public relations efforts, including ad buys for large public relations campaigns where required, business interruption costs, various fines you may have to pay, including to credit card payment associations, and then fees associated with identity theft monitoring (typically through the credit reporting services), and other credit monitoring services, including call center expenses.

Specifics on what to do will be contained within your specific cyber security insurance policy language, the notification section will clearly outlay what is required of the client in the event of a claim. Often, cyber & privacy liability policies will define what the insured's obligations are in the event of a claim as well. This would include the provision of documents, demand letters, suit papers, and other documents pursuant to the Breach as soon as practicable. Additionally, from the time that an event occurs, it is imperative that the actions of the organization and the specifics of the situation be recorded, so the insurer can review. These policies usually contain the terminology "as soon as practicable," which means that the company should report as soon as any member of the Breach/privacy management team becomes aware of a situation. Again, having a predetermined incident response plan in place helps ease any confusion as to when the insurer is contacted. This is especially true if a Breach coach exists; guiding members of the organization in terms of when notice should be given based on the language contained in the policy.

When developing your CSIR Plan the specific steps the insurance policy requires should have been factored into your response protocol. At the time of an incident insurers will have a set order of operations they would like you to follow, and your organization may have a slightly separate order of operations outlined within the CSIR Plan. You will need to rely on management advice to resolve any conflicts. For example, during a Breach your insurance policy may mandate that you publicly disclose a Breach in order for the cyber insurance policy to be honored. This decision (and when it should occur) will need to be made by senior executives within your organization, not the insurer. Damages associated with following an insurance policy versus the CSIR Plan developed and endorsed by your organization may be greater than the benefits associated with the cyber insurance coverage.

Lastly, it is important to remember that whatever steps your organization had to take to obtain its data Breach policy, must be maintained so as to not invalidate that policy. As of the writing of this book, there have been several instances in which the Breached entity, pursuant to a forensics investigation, was found to have invalidated their policy by not maintaining the technical security controls that were demanded by the provider. In these cases the provider has brought suit against their policy holder for reimbursement of the utilized funds.

INVESTIGATING THE SUSPECTED BREACH

When you are investigating a Breach, as complex as it may seem, and regardless of how many systems are involved, you are really only answering four questions. This concept is frequently referred to as the *Breach Breakdown* and it is comprised of the following elements:

Infiltration How did the bad guys gain access to the target environment?

Propagation How did the bad guys move from the point of entry, to the location of the targeted data or system?

Aggregation How did the bad guys access and harvest the targeted data or gain control of the targeted system?

Exfiltration How did the bad guys move the harvested data from a system controlled by the victim to a system controlled by the attacker(s)?

The Breach Breakdown is most applicable when the goal of the attack is to steal data. Attacks carrying a Denial of Service (DoS) condition may have the sole objective of disrupting systems and therefore not involve the exfiltration of data. As the investigation unfolds you can simplify your efforts and reporting by breaking everything down and placing it under one of these four headings (Fig. 4.2).

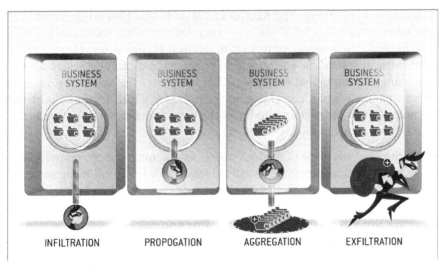

FIGURE 4.2 The Breach breakdown.

You will always be well served by introducing logic and consistency into a situation dominated by complexity. The most challenging aspect of data Breach investigations is not what takes place at the keyboard, it is not in the acquisition or analysis of evidence, and it is not in maintaining current technical knowledge; rather, what takes place in your mind as you logically work through the various stages of the investigation.

There are only so many ways for an intruder to gain access to a system. There are so many ways for that intruder to move laterally to other targets. There are so many ways for him or her to harvest data, and so many ways to move that data to a location of their control. The hard part is keeping all of these components clear in your mind and stringing them together to tell the story of the Breach. It is crucial that you understand this as you move forward with this book, and in your career as an incident responder because you are also a story teller. The degree to which you can succinctly tell the story of each Breach you investigate, in a manner that your target audience can understand, will play a significant role in your being an average investigator, or an exceptional one.

When an investigation first begins, the investigator will be presented with a laundry list of questions and a tremendous amount of information. It is very easy to get overwhelmed with confusion and feelings of hopelessness. The overwhelming feelings of confusion you are facing, has been labeled, "Analysis Paralysis," and the concept is precisely how it sounds, being paralyzed to inaction by the sheer volume of pending analysis. The panic of "where do I even begin" *will* come flooding into your mind followed closely by a deluge of technical information (books and forensics blog posts you have read, classes you have taken, conference talks you have attended, etc.) that you think is going to be helpful. The majority of this information is totally useless to you at this point in the investigation, and should be either ignored entirely (at least for the time being), or annotated for later (much later) use. The key to get through analysis paralysis is understanding where to begin; which logically, is at the beginning—with the people who know the most at this point and time about the case, the organizational personnel.

Some intro and overview of the four phases in the investigation: Interviewing, Hypothesis, Investigation Plan, Execution are covered in the following sections.

Interviewing Key Organizational Personnel

One of the most challenging questions to answer early on in a Breach investigation is determining how bad things really are. Many victims in the news recently have made the mistake of communicating externally what they presumably believe to be the full extent of the Breach, only to have to issue subsequent statements recanting or modifying their position, and in most cases indicating that the Breach is worse than they originally believed. Simply stated, they overstate the complexity of the Breach, while understating (sometimes grossly) the impact. They either didn't take their time to make certain they understood all of the facts, didn't have the time to make sure they have fully understood all of the facts, made the decisions to communicate based on incomplete information, or intentionally misled the public. Whatever the case may be, these very public missteps underscore the challenges faced when determining initial scope and highlight the importance of being accurate. We used to have a saying in the Army, "You can have it right, or you can have it fast. Pick one." This saying holds true in the context of Breach investigations as much as it does in the military.

10 Core Interview Questions to Ask in Each Breach Investigation

As an incident responder, when you walk into an incident you should have a set of previously thought out questions that you ask the victim. As you are provided answers to these questions, you can begin to formulate an investigation strategy so that you can begin the response process in a very targeted, deliberate manner. Ten core questions that should be asked during an investigation are:

1. *Explain to me what has led you to believe there has been a data Breach.*
   - There will be some reason why you have been called in to assist; somebody saw something, there was an alert, or perhaps a third party (like the USSS or the FBI) informed them. Whatever the reason may be, it's important for you to understand how the victim went from conducting business as usual, to believing something bad has happened
2. *Who came to the conclusion that a Breach had occurred and what data do they have that led them there?*
   - Who made the decision to escalate the anomaly to a potential incident and engage the IR team? Was it someone technical? Was it a SOC analyst, a help desk employee, or an engineer? Their level of technical acumen could lend credence to their assessment, or detract from it. Do they have the specific log entries, alerts, or report that led them to decide this was not simply an anomaly
3. *What data is believed to have been targeted, and where does that data reside?*
   - Some more mature organizations have both identified and segregated their most valuable data (very few). They may even have a network diagram that illustrates how this data is accessed and how it is utilized in normal business operations. Having this information is a tremendous, albeit uncommon asset. A huge percentage of companies that suffer data Breaches simply don't know what data they have or where it's located
4. *If so, where? If not, do you know all possible locations?*
   - Again, some companies will have a handle on this, but most won't. It's an important question to ask, but don't expect much

5. *Has there been any third-party validation that a Breach has taken place?*
   - Sometimes victim organizations are informed of their Breach by the USSS, FBI, payment card brands, merchant bank, or even the attackers themselves. If such a communication has taken place, it's important for you to get your hands on it as it likely contains information valuable to the investigation such as what data has been stolen, when it was or may have been taken, and possibly even attacker motivation

6. *Have you taken any additional steps to further validate your initial conclusion?*
   - Some victim organizations have some very smart, technically savvy members of their IT staff who take additional steps to gather important data which they believe will aid in the investigation. Be sure to ask for this information as well as ask them why they chose to gather this specific data, and how it aided them in their conclusion

7. *What steps have you taken thus far to contain the incident?*
   - Many organizations will take some initial steps to help contain the incident such as changing passwords, disabling remote access, and removing systems from the network. It's important for you to know what has been done, when, why, and by whom so that you can establish a baseline of understanding regarding what is "good guy" activity, and what is "bad guy" activity. Some of these activities also may have contaminated, or worse, destroyed evidence, so it's important for you to know if this has happened, especially if your final report ends up in the hands of an opposing counsel, or a government regulator (which it probably will)

8. *Who have you notified of the suspected Breach?*
   - Is the knowledge of the incident still a closely guarded secret, or does the media already know? Have they spoken with outside counsel, law enforcement, or a regulatory body? If external communication has taken place, what were they told and by whom? Knowing who knows what will help you advise the victim on how to proceed with further communications. Also, ask that you be privy to all such communications throughout the course of the response

9. *What are your goals for the investigation?*
   - Do they want to pursue those responsible criminally or civilly, or are they just interested in business resumption? Is there a governing body that will have to be informed and who could potentially launch an inquiry of their own? Best for you, as the responder, to be prepared for the worst. Assume this case is going to trial, that the SEC is going to launch a post-Breach inquiry, and that your actions will show up on the six o'clock news, and proceed. No pressure

10. *Is there anything else you think I should be aware of?*
    - I have been in many investigations where the victim just keeps talking about things they think are strange, weird, or "just off." To quote my pastor, Dr. Alex Himaya,[4] "Never pass up an opportunity to shut your mouth and open your ears" (smart man). If the members of the victim organization want to talk, let them. Take copious notes; you never know what tidbit of information may prove to be useful later on in the investigation

After meeting with key organizational personnel you will have their thoughts and observations on the facts to date. At this point as an investigator you should factor in your own thoughts and experience into the investigation.

Developing a Hypothesis

In Chapter 1 we reviewed the type of information and access criminals are looking to gain. Applying this information during an investigation can make it relatively trivial to hypothesize the criminal's objectives in conjunction with a Breach. Like so many other aspects of data Breach investigations, having a healthy dose of common sense can take you a long way. Some investigators call this the "gut feeling," while others call it their "Spidey Sense." Whatever name you want to give it, making logical assumptions of what data or system access is being targeted is smart, and can help you reduce the potential data set in the early stages of the investigation.

The foundational principles necessary to conduct a clearly defined, comprehensive investigation have been in place, in some instances, for more than 700 years. Investigations, regardless of the type follow a logical progression. This progression has evolved over time through repetition, the fine tuning of the procedures, and the integration of technology. The inclusion and adaptation of these linear, logical processes into digital forensics and incident response has improved the speed, efficiency, and effectiveness of investigators all over the world.

Logic based investigative methodologies, such as Chris Pogue's *Sniper Forensics*, are typically founded in older theories which by combining them can provide investigators with the framework needed to successfully investigate even the most complex data Breaches. These theories include:

Locard's Exchange Principle
Dr. Edmund Locard (13 December 1877–4 May 1966) was a medical examiner in France's Lyon in the early 1900s. Dr. Locard became the founder of the

---

[4]http://thechurch.at/about/our-pastor/

concept of forensic science and introduced his theory that "every contact leaves a trace." This later became known as *Locard's Exchange Principle*.

> The absence of evidence is not the evidence of absence.
>
> **Dr. Carl Sagan**

Occam's Razor

William of Occam (sometimes spelled Ockham—c. 1287–1347) was a 14th century Franciscan friar, philosopher, and along with Thomas Acquinas and John Duns Scotus, was one of the most influential minds of the middle ages. His theory which was labeled *"Occam's Razor"* stated that the answer to which the least number of assumptions are required has the highest likelihood of being correct.

The Alexiou Principle

Created by Mike Alexiou (Former Georgia State Trooper and Current CTO at CyTech Services, Inc. in Washington, DC), the principle outlines the four stages of evidence analysis which are:

1. What question are you trying to answer?
2. What data do you need to answer that question?
3. How do you extract and analyze that data?
4. What does the data tell you?

By integrating these three principles into the *Sniper Forensics* methodology, the investigator can focus on the logical evidence, what that analysis of that evidence either proves or disproves, and how those results effect the overall investigation.

Now, that's not to say that all data Breaches are going to be this linear. Many will be multifaceted and have the potential to involve multiple data types, but most won't. They will be straight up data thefts. No smoke, no mirrors, no level 9 mages; just bad guys stealing data. Remember to apply Occam's Razor, the solution that requires the least number of assumptions has the highest likelihood of being correct. For example, if you store, process, or transmit payment card data, chances are a data Breach is going to target payment card data. Or, if you are a healthcare provider that retains the ePHI of your customers, it's not a leap to assume that an attacker would target that ePHI.

Once you have established what data is being targeted, either through empirical evidence, third-party information, or Occam's Razor, you will need to start gathering information from the systems that store, process, and transmit that data. Be very careful at this stage of the investigation not to become singularly focused on your initial working theory. Many responders formulate a hypothesis of what they think happened based on the information they have been able to gather during the initial stages of the investigation. This is normal and is something that should be part of the investigation plan. However, where the danger lies, and the reason for my caution is that there is a pervasive tendency to stick with the initial hypothesis regardless of what the evidence indicates. I'm not entirely sure if it's ego, arrogance, or pride, but so many people in this industry (veterans and rookies alike) just don't want to be wrong. It is this desire to be right where serious mistakes are made and evidence that contradicts the working theory is ignored, and only supporting evidence is included or worse yet, misinterpreted (so seriously, check your ego at the door). Here's the truth…investigating data Breaches is a very complicated, fluid process that can change direction in an instant. As an investigator, your job is to formulate a working hypothesis based on the evidence that is available to you at the time. If evidence is found that proves your hypothesis, great, you are on the right track! However, if you find evidence that disproves your hypothesis, that is also great, since it tells you that you are on the wrong track! Remember, the goal should be to disprove your hypothesis, not to prove it (there will always be sufficient evidence for you to "prove" something took place).

The goal of any investigation is to finish up in a place where you can tell the full story of the Breach. You should not care how many twists and turns you have to make to get there; it's all about the destination rather than the journey. Evidence should be followed in the same way that a bloodhound follows footprints. One step at a time. An indispensable method of ensuring your investigation is focused on getting to the intended destination is with an investigation plan.

Developing an Investigation Plan

When responding to a Breach, you as the investigator have been brought in to answer a question or series of questions. Some of these questions may be

- How did the attacker Breach the perimeter defenses?
- How did the attacker gain access to the sensitive data?
- How were the contents of the database extracted?

Whatever the case may be, there is something specific that is being asked, and logically there is a specific answer.

The more you can break the Breach down through question(s) into smaller, more manageable chunks, the easier it will be for you to narrow your focus and address one portion at a time. This focus will help keep evidence that is not necessary for that particular portion of the Breach out of your field of view. Limiting scope in this manner, and subsequently the evidence you are looking at will go a long way in helping you avoid getting analysis paralysis. A great approach at managing this is by creating an investigation plan.

Research has shown that an alarming number of professional incident responders and digital forensic investigators do not take this first, critical step. Whether born out of laziness, arrogance, or a lack of knowledge, failing to create an investigation plan is a mistake. Benjamin Franklin is quoted as saying, "By failing to prepare, you are preparing to fail."

The creation of the investigation plan should include something called "success indicators." Put simply, success indicators are the answers to the questions that prompted the investigation (ie, how will you know when you have found the thing you have been asked to look for). For example, based on the questions laid out in the beginning of this section:

1. How did the attacker Breach the perimeter defenses?
   a. Success Indicator—Evidence showing point of entry. Will likely be found in log files (access, security, third-party remote access application log, VPN; system dependent). Also look for evidence of the utilization of legitimate access controls: open remote access, weak/default passwords, or no authentication
   In this question, the success indicator would be to identify the point of entry in the applicable log files, which based on the operating system, application, or type of networking appliance, will logically change. The identification of this piece of evidence will answer this question and will set the stop point for the investigator indicating that no further action is needed for this specific portion of the investigation
2. How did the attacker gain access to the target data?
   a. Success Indicator—Access to the targeted data means that the attacker needed a set of permissions sufficient to perform lateral movement from the point of entry to the location of that data. This means that the attacker needed a set level of permissions to access the data as well as performing lateral movement from the point of entry to the location of Breached data (remember the Breach Breakdown discussed earlier in this chapter (Fig. 4.2)). This activity would be required and should be logged by the targeted systems, and on any network appliances used for segregation. If the means of infiltration was identified, logically that should be the starting point for identifying lateral movement
   Showing lateral movement is a bit more complicated and requires knowledge of the target network as well as the connection to other evidence items. Knowing what level of access is required is important and will permit for data reduction of any user accounts that do not have that level of access. Additionally, looking back to the method of entry can provide valuable leads that can make tracking lateral

movement easier. By being able to determine which user ID was used to access the target environment, these questions can be answered, and this portion of the investigation can be closed out

3. How were the contents of the database extracted?

    a. Success Indicator—Identifying if the database data was accessed while stored within the database or an export or backup of the data stored separately. Staring with identifying the information that was accessed and identifying if the data flows external to the database to a file share or other system. Identifying the data flow will allow you to investigate and confirm or discount a Breach of database data through a primary channel, while it resided in the database, or a secondary channel, when it was legitimately exported from the database. We will take a closer look at database forensics and how it can be used to better investigate Breaches, within Chapter 6

While these examples are by no means exhaustive, they illustrate the importance of both, creating an investigation plan, and generating success indicators. They don't have to be formal, and they don't have to be verbose, rather they can be (and should be) clear, concise, and relevant to each question you have been asked to answer. By reading these examples you may think taking this step is too simple, unimportant, and/or unnecessary. Having gone through this process literally thousands of times, I can assure you that nothing is further from the truth. Know what you are doing, why you are doing it, and what it's going to look like when you are done is absolutely critical if you ever hope to solve Breach investigations in a timely manner. With experience and repetition this process will get easier, your success indictors will become more precise, and your ability to solve Breaches will be greatly improved.

Now that your investigation plan has been established, it should be reviewed by legal counsel in anticipation of litigation. Remember, your plan and its execution will be scrutinized at some level up to and including in a court of law. On the witness stand during cross examination is not the time you want to be trying to justify why you didn't think it was a good idea to review your investigation plan with legal counsel. We operate in an increasingly litigious sector of business, so you need to be prepared to justify your actions with confidence and resolve.

Executing Your Plan and Following the Facts

A statement I like to use is "people lie, data doesn't." Some of the statements taken during interviews conducted at the early stage of the investigation may not match the data. There are two reasons for such discrepancies, innocent mistakes and deceit. Innocent mistakes happen when people unaccustomed to high pressure situations such as an incident response are pressed for answers they may not have or fully understand, coupled with the fact that senior management is very likely looking to them for answers (and likely for someone to blame). These misstatements are not an intentional effort to deceive, but rather attempts to cover for the incomplete understanding of the situation or to embellish that individual's perceived level of technical competence (remember, their job may very well be at stake). So when this happens (and it will), don't be surprised and don't take offense. They are just people who are scared and are trying to do their best in the middle of a terrible situation.

Incident response investigations are stressful events. Our team regularly tells our customers that, "your worst day is our everyday." Being an experienced responder means that you will eventually become comfortable in these types of high stress situations, and may even find you enjoy and thrive in them. Don't make the mistake in thinking that the victims you are working with share your level of comfort. Use your experience to become the voice of calm and reason that brings sanity to an otherwise insane situation.

The other reason for a misstatement, as I have indicated, is an intentional effort to deceive. In my experience, the reason for these situations is that the individual feels threatened by the situation in that their façade of professional and technical competence is going to be destroyed. Like other animals, when human beings are backed into a corner and feel threatened, they will take whatever steps they deem necessary for self-preservation. During an incident response investigation, that means doing whatever they have to do to ensure that the blame for the situation does not fall on them. Whatever the circumstances may be, if you have reason to believe an insider within the victim organization is being intentionally deceptive, legal counsel should be notified immediately.

In either situation, the best way to address the problem is by being direct; ask a lot of direct questions, take copious notes, and conduct follow-up interviews or send summary emails. Let the interviewee know that you appreciate their time and insight into the situation, and that since their statement will become part of the investigation report you want to make sure you have all the facts correct (ergo the reason for the follow-ups). When people know that what they are saying is going to be written down, and will become part of an "official report" (whether that's true or not) they are less likely to lie or embellish. Those that insist on maintaining their "throne of lies" will eventually be found out during the investigation. In such situations remain stoic and stick to the facts. Let the victim's HR and management teams handle it. Remember, your notes and any emails you send can be discoverable; make sure that they are fact based and devoid of emotion.

CONFIRMING OR DENYING A SUSPECTED BREACH

Many organizations that have suffered data Breaches have indicated that the impact of the Breach is limited in the number of records that were impacted; only later to announce that the Breach was bigger than they originally suspected. While this is not a position you ever want to find yourself in, there are several reasons why Breached organizations incorrectly scope Breaches.

First, when an organization suffers a data Breach, they are under a tremendous amount of pressure and scrutiny. The Board of directors, investors, executive staff, rank and file employees, and now the media are very interested in what happened, and all of them want answers. This is not unexpected and is totally understandable. Where mistakes are made is when someone within the chain of command commits information that will be provided in a status update without fully understanding the ramifications of making such a statement. They want to appear to the world as if they are on top of things, that they are in control, and that the Breach really isn't all that bad. However, as was stated previously in this chapter, you cannot "un-ring the bell." Once a statement is made it is out there forever, so unless you want to be walking back your statement and explaining why you were wrong, your best course of action is to be right the first time. In our profession, being accurate is far better than being fast.

Next, I have found in my tenure as an investigator that things are seldom as easy as you would like them to be. Investigations take time to unravel and will include complexities that you wish were not there. However, "Murphy's Law" usually holds true in our world, and as technology continues to march forward introducing new and diverse data types that must be included and reviewed as evidence, it will continue to hold true…expect when things go wrong, expect unforeseen twists and turns, and expect the worst case scenario. We discussed the importance of identifying and preparing for these complexities when identifying evidence sources and types within Chapter 2. One of the best quotes of incident responders comes from an unknown origin, "Hope for the best, anticipate the worst, and deal with what you get."

CONCLUSION

Hopefully you have come to the place where you have a solid understanding of the core elements of investigating a suspected Breach. There is a very logical, succinct process that can be followed that will guide you through the various stages of the investigation and allow you to be comprehensive, efficient, and effective. The recommended actions which have been covered in this chapter are the result of literally thousands of Breach investigations and have been refined, fine-tuned, over and over again. Regardless of where you are in your career, putting them into practice will help you to become a better investigator by introducing clarity and consistency in a career where uncertainty and confusion reign supreme.

Remember to be inquisitive, relentless, and above all, pliable. As data Breaches become more and more complex, the demands on incident responders likewise increase. The level of technical acumen required to be effective is greater today than it has ever been, and it will be greater still tomorrow. Make sure you are following new and emerging technologies, putting in the "chair time" to familiarize yourself with new operating systems, and consulting with your fellow forensicators. Those that are responsible for data Breaches are working together; we put ourselves at a tremendous disadvantage if we are not doing the same.

One final recommendation is to find yourself a few penetration testers that you know and trust (knowing a great number of these folks, I use the word "trust" with a grain of salt). They are basically professional hackers who spend their days researching vulnerabilities, fine tuning their skills of exploitation and subterfuge, and Breaching targets. Establishing a relationship with a few select individuals can provide you with a wealth of information regarding intruder activity to include how reconnaissance is performed, how specific attacks are carried out, what tools are used, and the residual trace evidence that is left behind from their actions. I strongly recommend standing up a series of virtual machines that represent any number of potential scenarios, operating systems, and data types and asking your pentest buddies to hack them. When they are done, ask them to explain what they did, how, and why and then match up the forensic evidence to what you know to be the actions they took. Doing so will deepen your understanding of data Breaches from the hacker's perspective, and give you a distinct advantage in your subsequent Breach response investigations.

CHAPTER 5

Containing a Breach

Chris Pogue

INTRODUCTION

OK, so … now what? At this phase of the Breach, you are more than likely past the worst of it. I say, "more than likely" due to the fact that many Breach investigators make the mistake of myopically focusing on the Breach that they were brought in to investigate, discounting entirely that this particular compromise may be one of many. There may even be multiple attackers that have exploited multiple vulnerabilities to gain access to the target systems. In these instances, the respective investigation and remediation becomes exponentially more complex. Experience has afforded me the wisdom to confidently state that things are almost always much worse that they initially appear; so don't jump to conclusions too quickly. Research shows that it takes the average organization over 200 days to detect a Breach. That's a long window of time and considering organizations can be Breached multiple times within a close timeframe (I have seen this several times in my career), you could be brought investigating one Breach not knowing there's another one yet to be discovered that occurred months prior. An analogy I will draw is taking your car to the mechanic, paying a large bill to fix a problem with your engine, and a week later realizing something is wrong with your car again, you take it to the mechanic and they inform you something else has gone wrong in the engine, unrelated to what you fixed prior, and that it should be fixed. Sure it could be something completely unrelated but try explaining that to the angry customer. When dealing with Breaches the statements made by the victim organization will be scrutinized ad nauseam in the court of public opinion, by industry and government regulators, and potentially by opposing counsel. As their trusted advisor your guidance needs to be candid, technically sound, underpinned by the wisdom of your experience. The impact of a data Breach is staggering on many levels that include the loss of customer confidence, loss of market share, loss of company valuation; and are tremendously expensive as the victim will dole out potentially tens or hundreds of

CONTENTS

Data Breach Preparation and Response. http://dx.doi.org/10.1016/B978-0-12-803451-4.00005-8

millions of dollars in violations and fines, legal fees, and forensics fees. As the client marshals their collective efforts recovering from one incident, imagine the initial impact amplified exponentially should they be compelled to announce that "it happened again." However, presuming that you don't fall into that category, your organization or your client now needs to take steps to stop the bleeding.

The time frame from the initial Breach to containment of the Breach, is called the *Window of Compromise*. Now let's be careful with our terminology here, because this is important to understand. The *Window of Compromise* tends to get confused with the *Window of Intrusion*, which is the time frame from the initial Breach to final eradication of the attacker beach head. The important take away here is that you can contain a Breach while the attackers or malware are still present. Think back to the final stage of the Breach Breakdown introduced in Chapter 4—Exfiltration. If the bad guys lose communication with the target, and no longer have the capability to move data from the victim system(s) to their systems, the Breach is contained. Fig. 5.1 illustrates the window of intrusion versus the window of compromise.

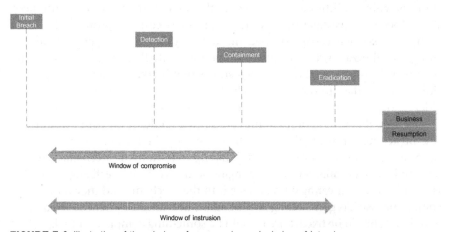

FIGURE 5.1 Illustration of the window of compromise and window of intrusion.

In our world of social media, security blogs, and "up to the minute news," the victim's ability to contain the security Breach is big news, and will travel fast. To say that you'd better be right is something of an understatement. I have said many times that during the *fog of compromise* and the push to make a statement, a large percentage of organizations have the propensity of overstating the complexity of the attack, while understating the impact. Pick an incident that has taken place over the past couple of years and read some of the media coverage in chronological order for an illustration of precisely what I am talking about. The lesson learned from these misstatements is that any statement made by the victim can be syndicated to a global audience, and will, not may, end up in the hands of opposing counsel should the incident ever go to litigation, which it probably will. It is important to balance accuracy and speed when it comes to this type of communication which we discuss in further detail within Chapter 7. There is no room for error and there is no unringing the bell.

Finally, and arguably most importantly, the Breach actually has to be contained. Regardless of what you call it, or when it's communicated, it has to be done, and it has to be done right. There are two important aspects to this notion of "done right" that are important to introduce, implementation and validation. Very simply put, you have to fix what's broken, and make sure the fixes have their intended impact (these are frequently called *countermeasures*). I have witnessed many organizations either totally fail to remediate the vulnerabilities that the investigation identified to have been the cause of the Breach (remember, there may be multiple Breaches with multiple vulnerabilities), or implement a flawed plan with a road map that focuses on the wrong vulnerabilities (not the ones associated with the Breach or Breaches), in the wrong order (having no order of criticality), and at a later time that never arrives (daily business gets in the way). There are dozens of example of organizations that have been Breached multiple times over a one or two year period via the same vulnerabilities. Do not let your company or your customer be "that organization."

Now, assuming that you are, in fact, not "that organization," and the fixes or countermeasures after a Breach were deployed as planned, they have to be tested to make sure they are having their intended impact. This is a critical step that many victims fail to take, thereby providing them with a false sense of security. An external pentest team (yes, external—lots of reasons why, which will be covered later) should be engaged to try to exploit or circumvent the countermeasures, as well as help to identify any other potential attack vectors that may be present, and have been used in another Breach yet to be discovered.

Getting Breached is increasingly and sadly becoming commonplace. It's understood for the most part that defending every possible attack vector to include human beings, all day, every day, without ever missing a single one, is a bit of an unrealistic expectation. Therefore and rightfully so, there is a heightened emphasis on how an organization responds, and how quickly they can contain the Breach. Even if the Breach was not detected until 200+ days after the intrusion initially occurred, there will be a significant focused place on the speed of response, ie…once you knew about it, how quickly did you act to stop the bleeding? Success here can very literally save the business millions of dollars; failure can mean closing the doors for good.

BREACH CONTAINMENT

The concept of the *Window of Compromise* was first introduced in the "Introduction" section to this chapter and will serve as the primary focus of the remainder of this chapter. Again, this window spans the time from the initial Breach, when a bad guy gains access to the target environment, to the victim containing the Breach and preventing further external communication with the attackers. To visualize this concept, think of a bank robber, if the measure of a successful bank robbery is getting away with the money and the bank robber gets trapped in the bank, he fails. Same concept here—if the attackers and any other malware or the malicious tools they brought with them are present yet their mechanism of communicating with those tools and/or exfiltrating data is disrupted or terminated, then the Breach has been successfully contained. It is important that you understand this concept and how it differs from the *Window of Intrusion*.

While the *Window of Compromise* can be achieved while the attackers and their malicious tools are still present, the *Window of Intrusion* cannot. The Window of Intrusion is the time frame from the initial Breach to complete eradication of the attacker. Understand that "closing the window" may (and in all likelihood will) take the form of a temporary fix that focuses on the prevention of further external communication and will not provide a long term solution. To completely remove this infiltration vector the associated vulnerabilities need to be identified and remediated, and the countermeasures tested to ensure that the attackers will not simply reenter the target using this same vector. At the conclusion of this window, the bad guys are gone, their tools are gone, the malware has been removed, and you are ready to resume business. These are two different windows with two different criteria which communicate two different things. It is important for you as the investigator to understand this, and be able to adequately explain it to a nontechnical audience. The example of the bank robbery is my favorite, and one I have used over and over in offices, Board room, and court rooms many times.

1. *Window of compromise*
   a. Bank robber has broken into the bank
   b. Stolen the money
   c. Failed to make a getaway

2. *Window of intrusion*
   a. Bank robber has broken into the bank
   b. Stolen the money
   c. Arrested by the police, he and his entire set of bank robbery tools have been hauled away, and possibly (under the best of circumstances) some or all of the money has been recovered

Now that you hopefully have a better understanding of the various windows present during this stage of the Breach, it's important to understand what "containment" does and doesn't mean.

What Are You Containing?

For an attacker to have gained access into the target environment he had to have taken advantage of a vulnerability or misconfiguration that provided him with that access. Potential attack vectors can include an unpatched server, a vulnerable plugin on a website, an improperly configured firewall, a default password, or human error. Whatever the case may be, something let the bad guys in and has been identified during the course of the investigation. There is where the focus of the initial containment steps should be.

It is a good practice to map out what you believe to be the Breach Breakdown in some sort of visual manner so that you can more clearly define your working hypothesis. You should also include a timeline of events that represents the chronological progression of the attack. This will be of particular interest to executives and general counsel as they prepare statements regarding what happened and when. In addition, you should also maintain a partner list of the impacted systems represented in the diagram. This list should include additional system details such as IP address, hostname, OS, system function (ie, webserver, database, workstation), and method of compromise. This diagram should depict which system the attacker initially used to gain access to the target environment, the systems that were used as he moved from the point of entry to the ultimate location of the targeted data, and the systems involved in harvesting and exfiltrating that data. In some instances, this process will be very short, as the Breach only involved a small number of systems, while in others you may have very large numbers. This is not entirely unlike Peter Chen's Entity Relationship Model,[1] or the string models used on police television shows. Whatever the case, you will benefit greatly from maintaining this diagram and partnering list as it provides a mechanism for you to track which systems were involved in the incident, and how. Trust me, while this may sound somewhat banal, it works (Fig. 5.2).

---

[1]https://en.wikipedia.org/wiki/Entity%E2%80%93relationship_model

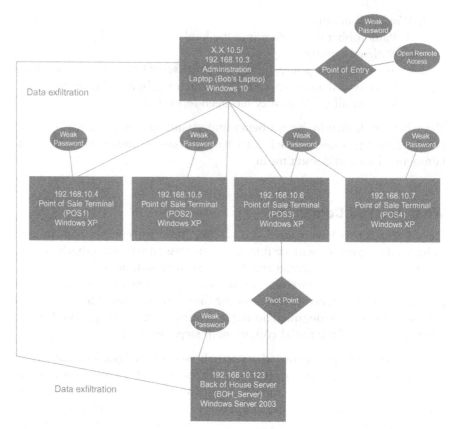

FIGURE 5.2 Sample Breach breakdown.

To effectively cut off the attacker's infiltration and exfiltration vectors (how the bad guys got in, and how they either got data out, or are maintaining communications with the target) it is critical that you fully understand how the Breach took place (hence the diagram). Many organizations that have been Breached are so overwhelmed by the gravity of what just happened that they panic (understandably so) and either lose focus or fail to gain it entirely. Their actions are erratic and disjointed instead of being coordinated and tactical. Senior management or the executives would want to fix every possible vulnerability and attack vector under the assumption that doing so will help them to save face with the Board, the customers, and the court of public opinion (movement for the sake of moving). However, the reality of the situation is that by not taking the time to formulate a logical response strategy based on the nature of the vulnerabilities that were present during the attack, they themselves are becoming the primary obstacle that will prevent them from achieving the very thing they are trying to accomplish. It's also important to mention if the Breach ends up in litigation, they will want to be able to establish a defensible position of reasonableness; the foundation of which will be predicated on how they both planned to respond, and how they actually responded to the Breach. This is completely normal and to be expected especially considering the current post-Breach, litigation-infested landscape. However, this sort of "knee jerk" reaction creates the tendency to address symptoms rather than the root cause of the issues. It's haphazard, ineffective and should be strongly discouraged inasmuch as you are able to influence your organization. This is where being a seasoned investigator can be of tremendous value, having likely watched this play out literally hundreds or even thousands of times. You need to be that voice of reason and confidence. Remind them to take a deep breath, calm down, and proceed with forethought and logic.

The message that needs to be communicated is that while there may be multiple issues that have been identified, *only a very small subset (usually just one or two) needs to be addressed immediately in order to contain the Breach.* The focus of remediation efforts should be on these specific vulnerabilities, nothing more. That's not to say that fixing the other identified issues is not important; quite the contrary—it is vital that all of the vulnerabilities get addressed or they run the risk of being right back in the same mess in a couple of months. However, under the present circumstances, a more myopic approach is what's needed to effectively contain the incident. Additional vulnerabilities that were not part of the Breach should be noted, triaged based on criticality, prioritized, and put on a roadmap to be addressed later (so long as they are actually addressed). Many organizations actually do this during a Breach, and while I'm sure they have every intention of following through later, they become distracted by some other business driver and never actually complete the process. These are the ones that end up in the news several months later announcing that they have been Breached again.

Remediating Your Exposures

Once a thorough understanding of the components of the Breach Breakdown, the systems that were involved, and the vulnerabilities that were exploited have been established, remediation steps can begin. These steps should be prioritized based on their positioning within the network, the criticality of the vulnerability, and the complexity of the fix. Externally facing systems should be addressed first since they have the highest likelihood of being compromised again, followed by internal systems in and around the location of the targeted data. Using the diagram you presumably created that includes all of the systems involved in the Breach is a great mechanism for tracking system vulnerabilities, and determining the order of remediation. This is also true for deploying new countermeasures such as firewalls, encryption, or user-based access control mechanisms.

There is a common misconception that once the vulnerabilities on the affected systems have been addressed, they are now "safe" from attackers. Well, how do you know that the fixes and countermeasures that have been deployed are having the desired impact? Short answer is, "you don't." In many of the cases I have worked when I bring this exact point up, I get the "deer in the headlights" look. So, I happily (it's sort of fun at this point in my career) repeat my question, this time a bit more slowly, emphasizing every few words, "How do you know, that the steps that you have taken to secure the affected systems are having the desired impact?". The overwhelming majority of the time, the answer has been, "We don't."

Imagine the logic in that? There is a significant data Breach that is going to be expensive to investigate, will have a presently unquantifiable negative impact on the brand and company valuation to include stock price, and may very well end up being litigated for the next few years. You figure out how the Breach took place and focus all available resources on remediating the vulnerabilities that were exploited by the attackers. But, you don't see the need to get an external team of experts to VALIDATE that those fixes are actually doing what you think they are going to do. Why? I said they would work, and they will! That's good enough, right? Yet as crazy as that sounds, it is very much a reality in organizations all over the world.

Funny how in so many other aspects of life this is simply assumed but in computer security it's like a pink fluffy unicorn dancing on a rainbow. Would you let your plumber fix a water leak without testing it to make sure the pipe is not still leaking? Would you expect your mechanic to fix the air conditioning on your car without turning it on to make sure it's blowing cold air? Would you want your doctor remove a cast from a broken bone without taking an X-ray to determine if the bone had healed properly? No, no, and no. So why in the world, after suffering an expensive, damaging, data Breach would you not expect to test the remediation steps to make sure they are functioning properly? Hint: you shouldn't.

For this process, I recommend retaining external penetration test or "Red Team" services, which we discuss further in Chapter 8, to ensure that the specific vulnerabilities exploited by the attackers have been remediated, and to confirm that any countermeasures that have been deployed are having their intended impact. There are a few reasons for my recommendation to use an external team, rather than internal resources. One, they are experts in identifying and exploiting system, configuration, and application weaknesses. They will look at your systems from the *eyes of an attacker* and provide you with a candid view of your security posture; something you may not be willing or able to do. Two, they are not beholden to anyone within your organization and can therefore remain unbiased. Political pressures will exist from the executives, or IT manager (likely both) to provide a "clean bill of health" so that business can resume. These pressures can also surface from individuals within the organization whose responsibility was to maintain the security of the impacted systems, who may very well be in jeopardy of losing that job. These pressures and the desire to get back to normal operations can lead to a premature or imprecise decision making that could very well do more harm to the organization than good.

An external tester that is not beholden to anyone within the organization is free (for the most part albeit not entirely) from these pressures. Three, they can also help to identify vulnerabilities that you may or may not have known about and help prioritize them based on their exploitability. Not all vulnerabilities are exploitable in the context of the current environment and its security controls. Understanding the impact of known vulnerabilities can help direct your remediation priorities. In addition, the likelihood of exploitability, due to its complexity, knowledge requirements, or the vector of attack also plays into this prioritization.

Are There More of You?

In many cases, malware and attacker tools play a significant role in a data Breach. Once initial access by the attacker has been achieved, these tools are utilized for everything from reconnaissance, privilege escalation, and lateral movement, to data harvesting and exfiltration. The good news about the presence of these utilities (if there has to be a silver lining) is that most of them have a signature and leave evidence of their existence or execution. There are some more advanced malware packages that live in memory and attack techniques that literally leave zero trace. In those cases, what is being outlined in this section would be of diminished value.

The hackers know they will probably at some point lose contact using their primary communication method with the installed malware. As such, there are typically at least one or more alternate "backup" command, control and communications mechanisms present. Some of the less technically advanced mechanisms can be as simple as installing a secondary remote access application (such as Bomgar, Logmein, VNC, or pcAnywhere), or they can be as advanced as having "phone home" activation triggers due to inactivity of the primary method. I mention this as Breach containment can't focus on the one tool, as many may exist. True containment and remediation can't occur until all potential infiltration and exfiltration vectors are analyzed and understood.

At one time, taking an MD5 hash of a binary and searching for a match within a corpus of evidence such as a forensic image was considered "advanced analysis." However, as forensic methodologies, technologies, and utilities have evolved in an effort to keep pace with attack vectors, this sort of activity now falls into the category of "basic analysis." Today, we have other hashing algorithms that unlike simple hash comparisons that provide a strictly binary conclusion (the thing is either a 100% match or a 0% match), provide a percentage to which two files are similar; this is known as *Content Piecewise Hashing* or *Fuzzy Hashing*.[2] Using Jessie Kornblum's SSDEEP utility, you can compute fuzzy hash values for files, set a target percentage (eg, show all files that are 80% similar), and search other systems for potential matches. This is obviously exponentially more effective when searching for files that may not be an exact match for the known sample file.

Conversely, many types of malware are modified using a runtime compression program, yielding a file that is known as being "packed". Content piecewise hashing focuses on common sections in executable binaries such as malware (in this type of situation). Malware that has been "repacked" (reencrypted or repacked using the same or other packer) will of course change the sample file. While this is still an extremely valuable investigative tool, like any other tool in your toolbox, don't rely on it 100%.

There are also several mechanisms to track indicators of compromise such as OpenIOC,[3] STIX/TAXII,[4] CybOX,[5] and CRTIS[6] which we look at further in Chapter 8. The important thing to remember here is that you understand that the incidents have the potential, and even the likelihood, of being larger than they initially appear. Be flexible with your working hypothesis and make sure that the evidence remains the primary driver rather than the other way around. *Many investigators get into the bad habit of allowing their theory drive what evidence they choose to include and exclude any evidence that does not fit their theory.* Conducting a comprehensive investigation is not about being right or wrong the first time. It's perfectly normal to adjust your working hypothesis multiple times prior to completing the investigation. Your job is to be thorough and tell the full story of the Breach, so check your ego at the door.

REMOVING POSTED INFORMATION FROM THE INTERNET

In some Breach investigations, you may run into sensitive information that has been posted to the Internet on sites such as Pastebin and Github, as well as any number of Dark Web sites.[7] When this happens, the executive staff and legal

---

[2]http://ssdeep.sourceforge.net/

[3]http://www.openioc.org/

[4]https://stixproject.github.io/

[5]https://cyboxproject.github.io/

[6]https://crits.github.io/

[7]https://github.com/

counsel of the impacted organization need to discuss how they want to handle the situation. There will always be an impact to the brand that will have to be dealt with either through internal or external communication. For this reason, it is a good idea to retain a crisis communication firm that is experienced in handing these types of issues (see Chapter 7 for guidance on this). An improper response here, seeming aloof, or providing artificial value to the posted data (either too serious or not serious enough) can also have a negative impact on customer perception. There are literally scores of examples of Breached companies that have made statements regarding the status of an incident or the importance of the data that was compromised only to have to retract those statements at a later time. So, needless to say, allowing internal resources who may or may not have experience in such matters to handle them on their own, may not be the best option. Misstatements, or in some cases outright false-hoods about the incident, can absolutely crush executive, Board, customer, and shareholder confidence and should be avoided as much as possible⋯ and by "as much as possible," I mean never. Ever.

If the decision is made to attempt to have the posted data taken down, it is critical to engage both the appropriate law enforcement body and legal counsel. For the same reasons an organization would want to retain outside crisis management experts, Breached organizations should also look to retain outside counsel who specialize in data Breach litigation. While inside counsel may be tempted to handle these sorts of problems on their own, the likelihood is that they lack the knowledge and experience to handle the situation efficiently and effectively. There are many law firms that specialize in post-Breach activities that know what steps need to be taken to remove data from such public forums. Under such circumstances, these types of firms should be engaged early. Doing so will give the victim the greatest potential for success in removing their data. Similarly, law enforcement, based on the geographic region of the Breach as well as the geographic location of the site containing the posted data, may have the ability to demand the data be removed pursuant to criminal activity, or based on an ongoing criminal investigation. That being said if you are successful in removing posted information from the Internet, the success may be short-lived. The criminal who posted the information may learn the data has been removed and can repost it on the site or to an alternative site requiring your organization, legal team, and law enforcement to repeat the process. This in essence can resemble a game of whack-a-mole and continue until the good guys or the bad guys grow tired of the back and forth and stand down.

The key takeaway here is to engage the experts early on in the process. Their knowledge, like your own knowledge of incident response, is critical in positioning the victim organization in the best possible manner so that they can withstand the aftermath of the Breach. If left to their own internal capabilities they run the risk of making mistakes that would otherwise be avoidable; mistakes that could prove to be extremely costly, and have a potentially devastating impact on the brand.

CONTAINING COMPROMISED SYSTEMS

There may be times, particularly in the instances where law enforcement is involved in the incident investigation, when the request is made to leave impacted systems alone so that attacker activity can be monitored. Requests of this nature are normally made by law enforcement agencies when the Breach may be part of an ongoing investigation involving other Breached entities. When this happens it is important that you engage the executive staff and legal counsel immediately. The business may have conflicting priorities with law enforcement that would prohibit such a request from being granted. This may include, but is certainly not limited to, Breach disclosure notification legislation, contractual obligations, industry specific compliance standards, international business requirements, and cyber security insurance policies. As badly as you may want to assist law enforcement, do not agree or commit to anything. This is decision that needs to be made by the executive staff and the attorneys, with the full understanding that under a worst case scenario, critical data that was not initially compromised becomes compromised while cooperating with law enforcement.

In other instances, you may be presented with the request to immediately contain the systems that are known to be compromised. There are four primary approaches in containing compromised systems, shutting them down, removing them from the network, patching them, or rebuilding them.

Shutting Systems Down

You will be involved in cases in which the victim may be compelled to shut down the systems affected by the Breach. Some examples of this include the theft of payment card information, the compromise and defacement of a webpage or the presence of malware with command and control (C2) capabilities on internal systems. Requests of this nature should also be fielded by the executive team and legal counsel as there will undoubtedly be significant business ramifications that will have to be carefully considered. Services being off-line could violate customer service level agreements (SLAs) or other contractual obligations, could halt the sale of goods or services resulting in significant revenue loss, or prevent customer payments from being processed.

In every Breach investigation you will face a myriad of complexities that will require input from a wide range of stakeholders. This underscores the point we have made multiple times within this book that incident response is no longer strictly an "IT problem"; it is a business problem and needs to be recognized as such. The presence of data Breach legislation, the increased popularity of post-Breach litigation, cybercrime investigations, media attention, and cyber liability insurance have all added to the complexity of incident response. The seemingly simple decision to shut systems down, or leave them up can have a far reaching impact on multiple facets of the business. These decisions should not be taken lightly or made arbitrarily; rather they should be swiftly escalated to the appropriate parties so that a decision can be made that will hold the greatest value. It's important to note that this is not a "good choice" versus "bad choice" thing. In many if not most cases it will be more a matter of which decision will suck less.

Removing Systems From the Network

This option requires the least amount of technical capability—remove network cable—but also poses the greatest impact on the environment, since whatever function the system is performing is no longer going to be present.

Removing the system also can immediately prevent the incident from getting worse either by preventing the propagation of the attack, or abruptly halting exfiltration. This is a common decision made by smaller brick and mortar merchants whose cardholder data environment has been compromised. Pulling the network cable immediately "stops the bleeding" of credit and debit card numbers, and allows an investigation to begin without ongoing data loss. While this solution is easy to execute and only takes a couple of seconds, a much larger business impact exists that needs to be considered.

The challenge with this option is pretty obvious—the affected system is no longer going to be able to perform whatever function it was previously performing. So the business will either need to have an alternative solution in place, like rolling those services to a secondary or backup system, or they have to be able to absorb the loss of that functionality until a rebuilt system can come online. If the affected system is performing noncritical functions not associated with SLAs or other business critical capabilities, the impact should be relatively low. However, the more likely scenario is that the impacted system is doing something important, like processing payment card transactions, or allowing employees to send and receive email. In these cases, a business decision needs to be made in order to quantify the projected business impact in relation to the time it will take to transfer functionality to another system or deploy a temporary solution.

Patching Systems

Patching the affected systems is the least intrusive, so it will have the least likelihood of negatively impacting functionality and interoperability. I say least because making changes on a system, even something seemingly positive like patching the OS or out-of-date applications and protocols will create the potential for something to stop functioning. I have seen this play out many times; an update is made and suddenly a dependent process stops working and everybody wonders, "What happened?" The responsible IT party or even the vendor will say something to the effect of, "The patch should have nothing to do with that"; which of course doesn't change the fact that everything was working properly prior to the patch, and after the patch was put in place, things are no longer working.

Patching also requires that you have a complete understanding of any tools or malware what were part of the incident and what their impact was on the targeted systems. While some binaries have very basic persistence mechanisms and are simple to remove, others can be much more complex making removal exponentially more difficult to the point of being time restrictive. It's important to make sure you precisely understand and execute proper removal steps or the threat will remain present. It is for this reason that the decision to patch requires the highest skill and greatest level of technical acumen.

Rebuilding Systems

There will be times when there is so much malware present that it's not time or cost effective to attempt to remove it all. In instances like this it's going to be easier and less expensive from an employee utilization perspective to simply rebuild the system from a gold standard image (provided one exists). Rebuilding the system will have an impact on business capability, but hopefully to a very limited extent (more to come on that). Also, the technical capability to do this is much lower than it is to remove malware and patch a system.

I have worked cases in the past where the target systems had literally hundreds of unique malware packages installed on it. When I was asked by the client which of the malicious binaries could have been responsible for data exfiltration, I was like, "Pick one. There are at least 50 here that could have been the culprit!" It wasn't funny at the time (well, it sort of was), but looking back on that situation, it underscores the point I am making here.

Now, rebuilding from a gold standard image presupposes a few things. First, that you actually have a gold standard image, second that the image is both up-to-date and is not going to introduce additional vulnerabilities or reintroduce old vulnerabilities (like the one that allowed the Breach to happen in the first place), and third, that it does not contain any malware (ie, the most recent image was taken *after* the Breach had occurred). Being able to say, "yes, yes, and no" is ideal, but in reality that likely won't be the case. Murphy's law is alive and well in the world of IR.

Gold standard images are only present is relatively mature organizations that are accustomed to frequent provisioning of systems. If that is the case, multiple images should exist based on functionality, such as basic end-user laptop, developer laptop, executive laptop, webserver, mail server, or backup server. Assuming that appropriate type of image is present, it's important to verify when that image was created as it could contain out-of-date applications or protocols that potentially could introduce additional attack vectors into the environment. Now it's not difficult to allow updates, but based on when the image was created and the volume of updates that have been published since that time, this process could take a significant amount of time, which is a luxury you may not have.

Also, based on when the image was created in relation to the incident, it may contain the same malicious programs or applications that currently are present. Likewise, the vulnerabilities or misconfigurations that allowed the Breach take place may also be present. If either of these possibilities is present, restoring from the image may actually do more harm than good.

The important thing to remember with any of the four options that have been covered is that they all have the potential of improving the situation as well as making it worse. I wish I could tell you that's going to be a cut and dry situation where there will be a clear right and clear wrong path, but there won't be. Like so many other aspects of a Breach response, decisions like these are more a case of which is going to suck less. This is why they need to be made with the key stakeholders, management, executives, and legal counsel. Your technical expertise should guide them, as well as provide them with an overview of the pros and cons of each option, but the final call is theirs. Just make sure they understand the potential impact of whatever choice they make. It's also a good idea to document your recommendations, and admonitions in an email. That way, if your advice is not taken, and things go horribly wrong, you can't be blamed. Bear in mind that unless your services have been retained by legal counsel thereby being protected as privileged, anything you put down in writing can become part of a post Breach E-Discovery request. It is a misconception to think that simply putting "Privileged and Confidential" on an email, or copying an attorney suddenly covers the entirety of that thread under privilege; it does not. While this concept is explained further in Chapter 9, you should always consult with legal counsel if you have any questions regarding legal matters. Sadly, I have learned these lessons from experience, so please take my advice, and make sure you cover your six.

SUMMARY

During the early stages of an incident you will almost always be asked, "What can we do to contain the Breach?" By now you should understand that providing an answer to this question is not as easy as one might think. In the middle of a Breach most of the decisions you will have to make or will be called upon to advise on will be challenging both in terms of technology and the impact on the business, this one is no different. Solving one problem may end up creating another one, so there will almost always be competing priorities. For this reason, it is important that you engage the key stakeholders and legal counsel early and often when decisions need to be made that will impact the operations of the business.

Containing the incident may negatively impact a law enforcement investigation or the victim's ability to perform their core competency, therefore alternatives would need to be explored. Doing so may introduce the need for a phased or fragmented approach—containing certain aspects of the Breach immediately, while leaving others in place for a period of time, and addressing them later. This can be effective for short-term containment which may appear financially attractive, still requires a holistic, long-term solution. If post Breach remediation is not carried out effectively, and the lure of "good enough" being "good enough" overrides the wisdom of experience, this sort of corner cutting can lead to prolonged litigation, regulatory fines and violations, and loss of customer confidence and market share.

If the choice is made to implement short-term fixes (and it's more than likely will in some fashion), ensure that you make the recommendation that an external team of penetration testers is engaged to assess whether or not the deployed countermeasures are having the desired impact. Few things are worse during a Breach response than thinking or communicating that things have been "fixed," only to find out later that the "fixes" didn't work properly and the attack either continued or became worse.

In addition to business concerns, the victim organization needs to consider their legal and contractual obligations. Based on their geographic region and contract verbiage certain options may be off the table entirely, so make sure that legal counsel is updated regularly. If they don't have a firm grasp on the myriad of legal issues that emerge during a Breach make the recommendation that they retain outside counsel that specialize in Breach coaching and litigation.

Responding to and containing a Breach is tremendously complex. This fact necessitates a cross-functional team of experts representing multiple disciplines. As part of that team, it is your responsibility to have an understanding of how each unique skill fits together, what decisions will need to be made, the potential consequences, and how they are going to play into the overall Breach response. This is why good incident responders are in such high demand! So be thankful that you have chosen wisely, and keep reading!

CHAPTER 6

Precisely Determining the Scope of a Breach

Kevvie Fowler

INTRODUCTION

During a high-speed chase, two police officers follow a couple of robbers into a bank; the pursuit takes the criminals and the officers around the main floor and then downstairs to the bank vault. The criminals have a head start and round the corner until they enter the bank vault. The police catch up round the corner and notice that the criminals have run through the bank vault and out a back door (assuming for the sake of this story, there was a backdoor in a bank vault!). The bank manager arrives on the scene shortly after and asks—what was taken? The police officers look to each other and shrug their shoulders. The bank manager asks again and the police officers state that they have no idea what was taken but when this has happened before they just assume all valuables were taken. The bank manager looks at the two officers in a puzzled yet concerning manner.

Stepping back from this traditional bank robbery scenario into the cyber realm, as comical as this story sounds, it is a common occurrence that organizations facing incidents involving criminals who access a database and are unable to determine what information was accessed or modified, therefore assume all of it was increasing the associated impact. The guidance in this chapter will help you better investigate and discount suspected Breaches or confirm and more precisely scope them and minimize the associated impact.

DATABASE FORENSICS OVERVIEW

In the world today, organizations are desperately focusing on innovation. We are making products smarter, smaller, and faster, and ensuring that services are more accessible than ever before. The result? Devices ranging from computer servers to refrigerators and from energy meters to pace makers having embedded computers. Most of these computers need to store and retrieve data that is managed within databases. Databases have been, and will increasingly be, part of cyber investigations.

Data Breach Preparation and Response. http://dx.doi.org/10.1016/B978-0-12-803451-4.00006-X

The problem? Well, many forensic tools and even the training investigators undergo focus very little on databases. Going back to the story we stepped through to open the chapter, tracking the criminals to the crown jewels is a great start. However, not knowing what the criminals did when they got there can negate the value of an investigation and force the organization to assume that all information was involved, when in reality a small subset of it may have been.

Database forensics is a subset of forensic science focusing on the preservation and analysis of relational and nonrelational database platform artifacts to:

1. Retrace past activity within database systems
2. Recover previously deleted data
3. Determine the pre- and poststate of information

Simply put, database forensics allows you to better investigate Breaches and discount a suspected intrusion or confirm and precisely scope a Breach to limit its impact. As you can imagine this science can be a powerful tool within your Breach response toolkit and serve as your last line of defense in protecting your organization.

There are over 80 different commercial databases in existence today and are written in different languages. Investigators need to interact with each database platform and the various types and retention of artifacts scattered through the database platform. To help, we will limit the scope of database forensics within this chapter to the following popular database platforms and versions:

- Microsoft SQL Server (2005–2014)
- Oracle (10gR2–12cR1)
- MySQL (4.1–5.5)

The goal of this chapter is not to make you a database forensics expert. It is to provide you a general idea of how the science can be used to precisely scope a Breach, when it should be used within an investigation, and the associated benefits of doing so.

USING DATABASE FORENSICS IN AN INVESTIGATION

At this point, you may be thinking that database forensics seems interesting but it won't apply to many investigations, right? However, in a forensic investigation, Database very commonly contain critical evidence that can directly or indirectly benefit an investigation:

- Direct investigation benefit—when there is suspicion that information within a database has been accessed or modified by an unauthorized individual, whether by an insider abusing their granted privileges or a remote attacker exploiting a vulnerability to gain access

- Indirect investigation benefit—where data within the database is not believed to have been specifically targeted by an intruder; however, the database may contain information relevant to the investigation. An example of this is attackers have used databases as a mechanism to upload attack tools and malware to the compromise environment. Through a vulnerability such as SQL injection, an attacker can upload application executables inserted into a table and then export the table contents to the database file system, where it can be recompiled and used to extend the attackers reach and foothold within the environment. In this scenario, the attack may have involved other computers with a logical connection to the database server; forensic analysis of the database server could allow for the recovery of the actual binary used in the attack from the existing or deleted database table

Considering the discussion earlier, if an investigation involves data stored within a database or a suspected compromised system that has logical access to a database server, the database server in question should be investigated. When planning for a database investigation the first step is determining the objective of the investigation.

Defining the Objective of Your Investigation

When planning for a database investigation it's tempting to jump right into the investigation, overturning as many stones as possible to try and solve the case. When trying to confirm a suspected compromise, there may be some of this, however, the power of database forensics is being able to precisely confirm or deny specific events or the involvement of information within an incident. For example, a database objective could be assigned broadly such as confirm or discount a suspected intrusion—this objective is very vague and would require essentially kicking the tires of the database server. Going back into my high school days and shopping for my first car, I walked around an 1985 mustang that looked to be in relatively good shape. I kicked the tires and used my index and middle finger to knock the fenders of the car to try and detect patches of rust that were filled with Bondo (a filler for body repair). This is all I knew regarding checking out a car, it passed the test and I ended up buying the car. A few weeks later when driving over a bump the driver side chair fell through the floor due to a major rust issue. If I had had a specific objective—or known exactly what to look for my investigation into the car's state would have been more focused on critical safety issues (not the air pressure in the tires) and would have included checking the fenders for Bondo in addition to several other checks (and yes the floor would have likely been one of them). This is one example when having a plan would have helped prevent an incident. Jumping back to a cyber Breach realm, kicking the preverbal tires of a database server to see if something jumps out at you sometimes can have its merits but focused objectives that you base an investigation around achieving will more often than not allow you the greatest chance for success.

I have defined database investigation objectives in past as:

- Confirming or discounting if data records belonging to a specific client or resident or including sensitive data elements were included in the scope of a Breach. These objectives help limit the exposure of records protected by data notification (and protection) requirements
- Recovering previously deleted data
- Reconstructing the actions of a specified or group of database users

Each of the objectives mentioned previously can be used by an organization to minimize impact after a Breach. A key factor in ensuring reaching your objective is ensuring you have right tools at your disposal.

DATABASE FORENSIC TOOLS

The field of computer forensics has no shortage of tools, from enterprise forensic products that image computers across a network, to those that image and analyze data from system memory, mobile devices, and applications. These tools, despite their different focuses, have one thing in common; they neglect the majority of evidence within databases. Some support scripts that can be customized, however, again, access a small subset of what is available and can provide a false sense of certainty that you have assessed the database when in fact you've barely skimmed the surface. So the natural question—are there certain tools that do a better job of investigating databases? The answer is yes, well for some database platforms. There are database forensic tools that have been developed by forensic experts with one goal in mind, to gather and analyze as much database evidence as possible to aid in an investigation. These tools vary in their degree of user friendliness, however, increase the likelihood of achieving your database forensics objectives. Table 6.1 contains a listing of database forensic tools available for popular database platforms.

Table 6.1 Database Forensic Tools		
Platform	**Tool**	**Description**
SQL Server	dbInvestigator[a] dbResponder[b]	GUI-based database forensics tools supporting the identification, preservation, and analysis of artifacts across stand-alone or enterprise database servers
	OrcaMDF[c]	An off-line database file reader that can aid in an investigation
	SQL Recovery[d]	A GUI-based system administration and troubleshooting tool that can be used to aid in an database investigation of a stand-alone server

Table 6.1 Database Forensic Tools—cont'd

Platform	Tool	Description
Oracle	TNS Connection Profiler[e]	A GUI-based tool that gathers session data from Oracle servers
	Database Scalpel V3rity[f]	Tools allowing the analysis of oracle data and transaction log files. The tools were publicly released 2008–2012, however are no longer publicly released. David Litchfield[f] is the author and if contacted may be able to provide the tools
MySQL	No known tools at the time that perform data acquisition or analysis of multiple artifacts	No known MySQL database forensic tools at the time of this writing

[a]http://dbInvestigator.com.
[b]www.dbresponder.com.
[c]http://improve.dk/orcamdf-rawdatabase-a-swiss-army-knife-for-mdf-files/.
[d]http://www.dataforensics.org/sql-mdf-forensics/.
[e]http://www.databaseforensics.com/TNSConnectionProfilerforOracle.htm.
[f]http://www.davidlitchfield.com/.

CONNECTING TO THE DATABASE

Before we discuss connecting to the database, I would like to stress the importance of logging your actions while investigating a live database server.

Logging Your Actions

All actions trigger a reaction and at a later date and time you as an investigator should be clear on what you did and the consequences you may have had on the system under investigation as well as the conclusion and opinions as a result of the analysis. I recommend that the following events, at a minimum, are logged while working on a live database server:

- The date and time of your initial connection
- The commands you executed against the database server
- The results of each executed command
- Collected database data and log files and
- The date and time that you disconnected from the server

The log you maintain of your actions (assuming it's electronic) and the results received from the database server should be hashed using a secure hashing algorithm such as Secure Hash Algorithm 2 (SHA-2) to ensure the files are not altered prior to, and after analysis.

Now that we've covered the importance of logging database connections and your actions during an investigation, let's look at how to connect to a database platform to begin an investigation.

Connecting Using a Tool

As illustrated in Table 6.1, there are not many database forensic tools on the market today, however, some of the tools that do exist automate preservation and logging of your activity while on the database server and simplify the analysis of collected artifacts. An example of this is the dbInvestigator tool for Microsoft SQL Server. To connect to one or multiple database servers you,

1. Either search for databases by pressing the "Enumerate servers" button or enter the name of the database instance you would like to connect to within the "Instance name" field
2. Or press the connect button

Fig. 6.1 illustrates the preceding steps.

FIGURE 6.1 Connecting to an SQL Server instances using dbResponder.

Please consult the tool download pages for full features and instructions on how to use dbInvestigator. In addition to connecting to an instance through a tool, you can also connect through a native database client.

Connecting Using Native Clients

If there is a desire to connect to a database server using the platforms native command line or GUI-based clients tools (or unavailability of database forensic tools for the platform under investigation), you will need to do this manually and will need to ensure your actions as are logged. Table 6.2 outlines native clients and commands that can be used to echo command line text and redirect query output to a text file to facilitate activity logging.

Table 6.2 Native Database Commands and stdout Redirect Operators

Database Platform	Vendor Supported Command Line Client	Logging of Session Activity	Redirection Operator
Microsoft SQL Server	SQLCMD	e command when launching SQLCMD to echo all statements and queries sent to the server to stdout Example: SQLCMD -e	The :out output command from within the SQLCMD console will redirect stdout to the specified file. Example: :out Z:\connectionlog.txt
Oracle	SQL*Plus	ECHO ON command within SQL*Plus Example: SQL> SET ECHO ON	Spool command from within SQL Plus. Example: spool z:\connectionlog.txt
MySQL	MySQL Command Line Tool	Tee option Example: tee z:\logofactivity.txt	Will redirect stdout to the specified file. Example: tee /tmp/connectionlog.out Note: You can change the Tee output file between queries to separate the result files

Please consult vendor documentation for a full list of features and commands that can be used to connect to via a database client.

DATABASE ARTIFACTS

Database artifacts are collections of related data beneficial in an investigation. Artifacts generally apply across database platforms, however, the tools, clients, and commands used to identify and extract them will differ. Looking squarely at Microsoft SQL Server, there are 42 artifacts illustrated in Fig. 6.2.

As seen within Fig. 6.2, artifacts can be volatile or nonvolatile in nature which directly affects their retention within the database platform.

Database Artifact Volatility

Similar to other types of forensic artifacts, database artifacts are temporary and at some point will be deleted or overwritten. Microsoft SQL Server, Oracle, and MySQL have defined retention schemes that govern the retention of most database artifacts. Some platforms even have a clause that if the server encounters a state in which it is starved for resources it will evict some database artifacts from

FIGURE 6.2 Published Microsoft SQL Server database artifacts.

areas such as memory to help prevent the server from crashing. This eviction policy is good for a system availability standpoint but a hindrance during a database forensic investigation.

We will not be able to explore the preservation and analysis of all artifacts (covering how to do this for Microsoft SQL Server alone took over 480 pages within my SQL Server Forensic Analysis[1] book). In this chapter, we will take a high-level look at execution plans, transaction logs, and database objects which are three common artifacts in database investigations.

Execution Plans

A database execution plan is a generated list of steps that show a database platform the most efficient way to access or modify stored data. An example of this is if you were to look up directions to a street address. There are multiple routes you could take to get to your destination such as using highways or city streets with one route being the quickest. Looking at that analogy within the database the data to be retrieved or updated would be the destination address and the most efficient route would be using indexes (highways), city streets (manually scanning all data pages looking for specific data), or a combination of both.

[1]http://www.amazon.com/SQL-Server-Forensic-Analysis-paperback/dp/032195162X.

You may assume the highway is the fastest route, however, due to construction or an accident it may be quicker to take city streets. These are the types of questions databases ask each time a query is run in order to determine the most efficient way to satisfy them. The first time a query is sent to the database server it will be parsed, analyzed to determine which table would need to be accessed, which indexes (if any) to use, how to join or merge the results, and so on. The outcome of this analysis is stored in a structure referred to as a database execution plan. Fig. 6.3 shows an execution plan.

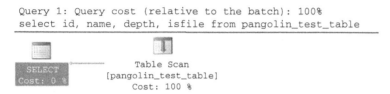

FIGURE 6.3 Graphical representation of sample SQL Server execution plan.

Execution plans are shared between internal database components during execution and stored in an area of memory, referred to as an execution plan cache store, with the hopes that it can be reused when another similar query is received. The benefit of these execution plans in the context of an investigation is that for most database platforms they contain the syntax of the actual query that forced the plans creation.

Simply put reviewing the cached execution plans will allow an investigator to obtain a record of the previous queries executed by the attacker which can be used to identify what information was viewed, modified, deleted, or extracted. Execution plan caching is done by default in many database platforms and is a good example of evidence an attacker will unknowingly leave behind after an attack, even if they try and cover their tracks. Execution plans can be a great source of evidence, they, however, like all artifacts do have some limitations.

Execution Plan Limitations
Execution plans are a great resource during an investigation, however, they are not without their limitations. A few limitations we'll cover in this chapter are eviction policies and parametrization.

Execution Plan Evictions
Database platforms retain execution plans for varying amounts of time. The amount of time is directly influenced by several factors, including:

- CPU and memory load on the database server
- Frequency of plan reuse after creation

- Modification or deletion of an object referenced within the plan
- Restart of the database services
- Manual flush of the stored plans can be performed by users with administrator privileges

Please refer to the database vendor documentation for specific execution plan eviction policies.

Paramaterization

Paramaterization is when literal values within an execution plan are substituted with variables. This process is automatically performed by the database server as needed to try and increase the number of queries the plan will satisfy. An example of this is the following query:

```
SELECT First_Name, Last_Name, Address and Social_Insurance_
Number from customers where First_Name = 'Kevvie'
```

In response to the preceding query, the database server will create a plan to efficiently retrieve the data and can store the exact query with the hopes of reusing it the next time a user repeats the same query for records with the First_Name of 'Kevvie.' 'Kevvie,' however, is not a common name and the likelihood of the database server being able to reuse the plan is low. As an alternative the database server may replace the literal value of 'Kevvie' with a variable as seen in the following program code:

```
SELECT First_Name, Last_Name, Address and Social_Insurance_
Number from customers where First_Name = @1
```

With the literal value replaced with a variable the execution plan could then be used to satisfy a future similar query for any user regardless of First_Name.

In the event an execution plan is parameterized you cannot translate the variable back to the literal value. You, however, will still be provided a glimpse of the query that was executed which can provide context into past activity within the database server.

Transaction Logs

The Structured Query Language (SQL) allows you to interact with database platforms and store, retrieve, and manipulate data. SQL consists of several statements such as SELECT * from Table1. To dig a little deeper (but not too deep), a statement can include one or more database operations. These database operations fall into two main categories which are Data Manipulation Language (DML), which typically affects data within a table such as inserting data into an existing table, and Data Definition Language (DDL) operations that affect the structure of a table or database such as creating a new table or adding a column to an existing table. A transaction log is used to record changes that are written to disk in order to recover the database back to a consistent state in event of a sever failure during the writing of information to disk.

When you look under the hood of a database server almost all statements and operations, regardless if they are DML or DDL in nature, will involve the writing or modification of information through INSERT's, UPDATE, and DELETE operations. Reversing these operations within the transaction log can allow you to identify past activity within the database.

Transaction Log Limitations

Transaction logs are enabled by default on some Relational Database Management Systems (RDBM) including Microsoft SQL Server and Oracle, however, are not enabled by default within MySQL. Table 6.3 outlines the default transaction log status and the functions that can grant access to the logs.

Table 6.3 Default Transaction Log Enablement on Popular Database Platforms

Database Platform	Enabled by Default	Access Functions
Microsoft SQL Server	Yes	fn_dblog
Oracle	Yes	v$logmnr_contents
MySQL	No	mysqlbinlog

When transaction logs are enabled they can be frequently overwritten by normal processing on busy servers or manually overwritten in response to commands and activities that can be executed on the database server. Please consult vendor documentation for additional information on the transaction log.

Database Object Timestamps

Recent databases mimic operating systems, from maintaining dedicated segments of system memory to running their own virtual operating systems which manage the database system. Similar to operating systems most database products also maintain timestamps for objects and files that have been created or modified making them an essential artifact within most investigations.

Database Object Timestamp Limitations

Database object timestamps are one of the most versatile and persistent database artifacts. Timestamp information is maintained in varying degrees depending on the type of object and the database platform. For example, on Microsoft SQL Server timestamps for some objects such as tables consist of creation and modification times whereas for schema's just the creation date is maintained. Clarity on this can be found within database product vendor documentation.

That concludes our brief look at artifacts, let's now shift gears to look at how these artifacts can be preserved.

Preserving Database Artifacts

When looking at a database investigation seldomly will you find yourself in a situation where the client has one database that needs to be investigated. Looking at SQL Server, Oracle, and MySQL, each server can have multiple instances, and each of these instances can have hundreds of databases. To further complicate matters, many organizations have several dozens of instances. What this boils down to is when performing artifact preservation manually this will likely be across several instances and multiple databases per instance. You literally may have to run a query against every database across all instances to acquire artifacts which can be a time-consuming and error-prone exercise. Leveraging tools can automate the acquisition in part of in entirety.

Using a Tool

As we have covered earlier in the chapter, there are not many database forensic tools in the market today and at the time of this writing the only database forensic tool that will log all actions, acquire artifacts, and preserve them with hashes is dbResponder and dbInvestigator. Due to this, these tools will be the primary focus of the acquisition content of this chapter. It's not self-serving but rather there are no other alternatives without diving into chapters worth of theory to discuss how and what to do.

Using dbResponder as an example, acquiring database artifacts for a single or multiple SQL Server can be performed by

1. Select (or type) the database instance names you would like to work with within the Connect tab (Fig. 6.4)
2. Select the "Acquire" tab

On the Acquire tab, complete the following steps:

1. Select the artifacts you would like to acquire and preserve
2. Specify the folder you would like to store the collected artifacts
3. Press the "Acquire" button

dbResponder will connect to each SQL Server instance and collect artifacts across all databases (Fig. 6.5). Status is provided with the progress bar in the

FIGURE 6.4 dbResponder connect tab.

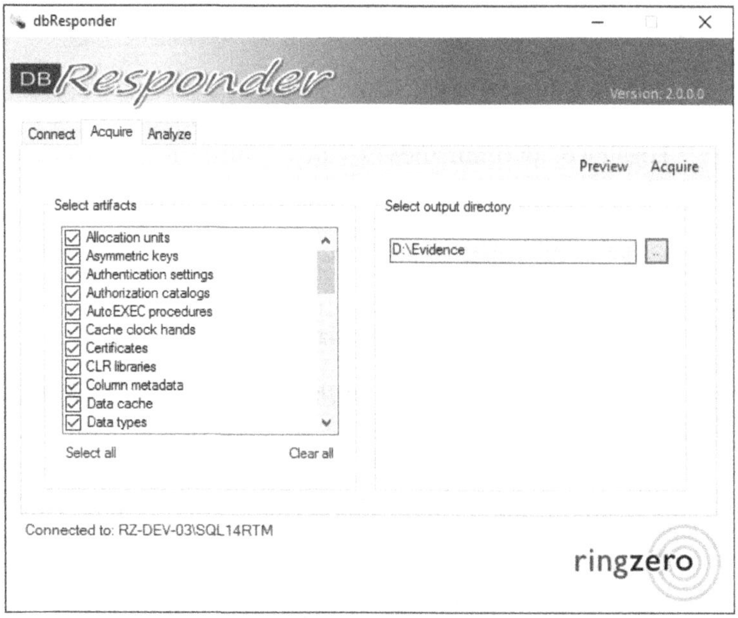

FIGURE 6.5 dbResponder acquire tab.

bottom left of the form. Full features of the application can be obtained from the official site.[2]

All artifacts preserved and the hashes for each will carry a .hal extension and reside within the folder location you specified on the Acquire tab of the tool as illustrated in Fig. 6.6. These artifacts are in plain text format.

Name ^	Date modified	Type	Size
AllocUnits	2015-11-29 1:08 AM	HAL File	79 KB
Asymmetrickeys	2015-11-29 1:08 AM	HAL File	1 KB
AuthCat	2015-11-29 1:08 AM	HAL File	292 KB
AuthenticationSettings	2015-11-29 1:08 AM	HAL File	1 KB
AutoEXEC	2015-11-29 1:08 AM	HAL File	0 KB
CacheClockHands	2015-11-29 1:08 AM	HAL File	30 KB
Certificates	2015-11-29 1:08 AM	HAL File	5 KB
CLRlibs	2015-11-29 1:08 AM	HAL File	3,823 KB
ColandDTs	2015-11-29 1:08 AM	HAL File	4,145 KB
DatabaseObjects	2015-11-29 1:08 AM	HAL File	590 KB
DataCache	2015-11-29 1:08 AM	HAL File	228 KB
DataTypes	2015-11-29 1:08 AM	HAL File	19 KB
DbJobHistory	2015-11-29 1:08 AM	HAL File	0 KB
DbJobs	2015-11-29 1:08 AM	HAL File	2 KB
DbListing	2015-11-29 1:08 AM	HAL File	3 KB
DBRoleMembership	2015-11-29 1:08 AM	HAL File	1 KB
DbServerConnections	2015-11-29 1:08 AM	HAL File	1 KB
DbServerInfo	2015-11-29 1:08 AM	HAL File	1 KB

FIGURE 6.6 Screen capture example of artifacts preserved by dbResponder.

Logging of all commands executed against each instance and database and the file names correspond to the selected artifacts that were acquired. Hashes for all collected artifacts are stored within the hash.hal file located within the same folder as the collected artifacts.

Database forensics can still be performed on database platforms without tools through the native database platform clients.

Preserving Artifacts Using the Native Database Platform Clients

Database forensics can still be practiced on database platforms that are not associated with formal tools by using ad hoc or precompiled scripts and native database platform clients to connect and obtain information.

Execution Plans

The following can be executed to extract and preserve execution plans across database platforms (Table 6.4).

---

[2]www.dbResponder.com

Table 6.4 Execution Plan Access Functions by Platform

Database Platform	Enabled by Default	Access Functions
Microsoft SQL Server	Yes	sys.dm_exec_query_stats sys.dm_exec_sql_text
Oracle	Yes	gv$sql
MySQL	No	No direct access method. Use general query log

SQL Server

The two views that can be used to access the execution plan cache are sys. dm_exec_query_stats, which provides execution information, and sys.dm_exec_sql_text, which provides the actual syntax that was executed. The following query uses the views to return the date and time the plan cache entry was created, the last time it was executed (in the case of repeat execution), the syntax executed as well as the number of times the execution plan was reused.

```
SELECT creation_time, last_execution_time, text, execution_count from sys.dm_exec_query_stats qs CROSS APPLY sys.dm_exec_sql_text(qs.sql_handle)
```

Sample results are as follows:

|Dec 9 2015 11:10 AM|Dec 9 2015 11:10 AM|select EmployeeID, FName, LName, YOB from SSFA.Employee where [fname] = 'mikaela' ;declare @z nvarchar(4000) set @z=0x43003a005c00 insert pangolin_test_table execute master..xp_dirtree @z,1,1--'|1

|Dec 9 2015 11:12 AM|Dec 9 2015 11:20 AM|USE [tempdb] SET NOCOUNT ON select '[tempdb]' COLLATE Latin1_General_CI_AS as 'Database', * from sys.asymmetric_keys|3

|Dec 9 2015 11:22 AM|Dec 9 2015 11:32 AM|select EmployeeID, FName, LName, YOB from SSFA.Employee where [fname] = 'mikaela' ;declare @z nvarchar(4000) set @z=0x43003a005c005c006b 006c006f0067005c0054003300 insert pangolin_ test_table execute master..xp_dirtree @z,1,1--'|1

|Dec 9 2015 11:29 AM|Dec 9 2015 11:49 AM|select EmployeeID, FName, LName, YOB from SSFA.Employee where [fname] = 'mikaela' ;insert pangolin_test_table exec master.dbo.xp_enumgroups;--'|1

|Dec 9 2015 11:30 AM|Dec 9 2015 11:50 AM|select EmployeeID, FName, LName, YOB from SSFA.Employee where [fname] = 'mikaela' ;insert pangolin_test_table exec master.dbo.xp_availablemedia;--'|1

Oracle

On Oracle the gv$sql view can be used to return execution plans. Please note that gv$sql is a global view that gathers execution plans from both server caches when run on an Oracle cluster but can still be executed to gather the full cache of a standalone Oracle installation. Due to this, the global view is a better choice than the v$sql view which will provide limited results when run on an Oracle cluster. The following is an example of how to use the gv$sql view:

SELECT sql_text from gv$sql;

Sample results are as follows:

```
SELECT inst_id, kmmsinam, kmmsiprp, kmmsista, kmmsinmg, kmm...
UPDATE MGMT_TARGETS SET LAST_LOAD_TIME=:B2 WHERE TARGET...
UPDATE MGMT_TARGETS SET LAST_LOAD_TIME=:B2 WHERE TARGET...
UPDATE MGMT_TARGETS SET LAST_LOAD_TIME=:B2 WHERE TARGET...
UPDATE MGMT_TARGETS SET LAST_LOAD_TIME=:B2 WHERE TARGET...
UPDATE MGMT_TARGETS SET LAST_LOAD_TIME=:B2 WHERE TARGET...
UPDATE MGMT_TARGETS SET LAST_LOAD_TIME=:B2 WHERE TARGET...
SELECT ROWID FROM EMDW_TRACE_DATA WHERE LOG_TIMESTAMP <...
SELECT /*+ no_parallel_index(t, "WRM$_SCH_VOTES_PK") ...
SELECT /*+ no_parallel_index(t, "WRM$_SCH_VOTES_PK") ...
```

MySQL

MySQL generates and stores execution plans; however, there are no vendor-issued functions developed to access the actual queries stored within. MySQL, however, does maintain a general query log that records executed queries in human-readable format. This general query log is not enabled by default, however, during an investigation you can determine its status using the "show variables" command by executing the following from within your database client.

Show variables like '%general_log%'.

The following sample results show the general log is enabled and writing to the C:\GQLog\RZ-DEV-03.log file on the server:

Variable_name | Value

——————————|————

general_log | ON

general_log_file | C:\GWLog\RZ-DEV-03.log

The status value of "ON" with the variable_name general_log means that it is enabled and will have a record of previous queries executed on the database platform.

Sample results formatted for legibility are as follows and capture the statement as well as the date and time it was executed.

8 Query   select * from user 2015-12-06 T07:14:50.940242Z

8 Query   show tables 2015-12-06 T07:14:59.174688Z

8 Query   select * from proc 2015-12-06 T07:16:58.494915Z

Transaction Logs

Transaction logs can be gathered from a database using a variety of proprietary RDBMS functions and commands. Commands will differ depending on the database you are working with and will return log data in plain text. The transaction log is relational in nature and you may need to gather additional database artifacts to fully analyze them. For example a transaction executed to insert a record into a Microsoft SQL Server database table would be logged in the transaction log under an Object ID. To determine the table where the information was inserted you would also need a listing of object names and ID's from the database. Automated tools, which we will cover later in this chapter, will gather database artifacts for direct analysis as well as the associated metadata needed to interpret them properly.

SQL Server

The transaction log within Microsoft SQL Server is enabled by default and cannot be disabled. There are a few different methods that can be used to access the transaction log. The most flexible is using the native :fn_dblog function. The following is a sample query that uses the :fn_dblog function to return all records from the transaction log of a database.

SELECT [Current LSN], Operation, [Transaction ID], [AllocUnitID], [AllocUnitName], [Page ID], [Slot ID], [Offset in Row], [Server UID], SPID, [Begin Time], [Transaction Name], [Transaction SID], [End Time], [Description], [RowLog Contents 0], [RowLog Contents 1], [RowLog Contents 2], [RowLog Contents 3], [RowLog Contents 4] from ::fn_dblog(null, null) order by [Current LSN].

Sample results are as follows:

```
[Customer]|000082d2:00000010:0025|LOP_DELETE_ROWS|
0000:00027fef|2449958261557690368|Unknown Alloc
```

```
Unit|0001:000002f1|2|1|||||||||0x3000040004000004001600
230023003B00444154413A4F464653455420544142 4C453
A3338202830783236 29202D2036323820283078 3237342920
|0x|0x|0x|0x
```

```
[Customer]|000082d2:00000010:0026|LOP_DELETE_ROWS
|0000:00027fef|2449958261557690368|Unknown Alloc
```

```
Unit|0001:000002f1|3|1|||||||||0x30000400040000040016 0023
0023003B00444154413A4F464653455420544142 4C453A3337202
83078323529202D20363134202830783236 362920|0x|0x|0x|0x
```

```
[Customer]|000082d2:0000006f:0031|LOP_INSERT_ROWS|0000:
00027ff0|24499582615 57690368|Unknown AllocUnit|0001:
0000 0077 |43|0|||||||||0x|0x|0x|0x|0x
```

```
[Customer]|000082d2:0000006f:0032|LOP_INSERT_ROWS|0000:
00027ff0|24499582615 57690368|Unknown AllocUnit|0001:
0000 0077 |44|0|||||||||0x|0x|0x|0x|0x
```

The :fn_dblog function is database-scoped meaning it's focus is just the active database. You will need to run it once per database within the scope of your investigation.

Oracle

On Oracle the transaction (archive) log is enabled by default and can't be disabled on test systems. The following query can be used within Oracle to return a list of executed INSERT, UPDATE, and DELETE operations:

```
SELECT  OPERATION,  SQL_REDO,  SQL_UNDO  FROM  V$LOGMNR_
CONTENTS WHERE OPERATION IN ('DELETE', 'INSERT', 'UPDATE ');
```

Sample results are as follows

```
DELETE from "WEBAPP"."SYNGRESS" where "A" = '80' and "B" =
'three' and "C" = TO_DATE('23-DEC-15', 'DD-MON-RR') and ROWID
= 'AAATcPAAEAAAAIuAAD';
```

```
INSERT INTO "WEBAPP"."SYNGRESS"("A","B","C") values ('80',
'three',TO_DATE('23-DEC-15', 'DD-MON-RR'));
```

MySQL

The transaction log in MySQL is not enabled by default and must be enabled in order to log transactions. To determine if the transaction log is active you can use the "show binary logs" statement:

```
SHOW BINARY LOGS;
```

If binary logging is disabled you will receive an error stating "you are not using binary logging." If it is enabled, the name of all logs will be returned as seen in the following:

```
+————————————+————+
| Log_name            | File_size |
+————————————+————+
| RZ-DEV-03-bin.000001 | 99362 |
| RZ-DEV-03-bin.000002 | 1699 |
| RZ-DEV-03-bin.000003 | 177 |
| RZ-DEV-03-bin.000004 | 177 |
| RZ-DEV-03-bin.000005 | 154 |
+————————————+————+
```

When logging is configured the first MySQL transaction logs will have the extension *. 000001 and increment each time the server restarts, the log reaches a predetermined size, or is flushed. To determine where the logs are stored you can use the following query:

SHOW VARIABLES LIKE '%HOME%';

The innodb_log_group_home_dir value within the results is the location of the log files. Within the following sample results the logs are stored within the MySQL root director (.\):

```
+————————————+————+
| Variable_name            |  Value  |
+————————————+————+
| innodb_data_home_dir      |      |
| innodb_log_group_home_dir  | .\  |
+————————————+————+
```

To dump a list of transactions from the transaction log you can use the native MySQL mysqlbinlog utility on non-windows servers, and the MySQL command line client on Windows.

The following query example shows how to return a list of all transactions recorded within the RZ-DEV-03-bin.000001 file.

mysqlbinlog 'c:\Program Files\MySQL\ RZ-DEV-03-bin.000001' > z: \transactionlog.txt.

Sample results are as follows which show the previously executed statements recorded in the logfile in human-readable form

BEGIN

/*!*/;

at 4155

#120114 0:30:34 server id 1 end_log_pos 4272 Query thread_id=16 exec_time=0 error_code=0

use world/*!*/;

SET TIMESTAMP=1326519034/*!*/;

update city set name = 'Ashburn' where name = 'Kabul'

/*!*/;

at 4272

#120114 0:30:34 server id 1 end_log_pos 4342 Query thread_id=16 exec_time=0 error_code=0

SET TIMESTAMP=1326519034/*!*/;

COMMIT

/*!*/;

at 4342

#120114 0:30:52 server id 1 end_log_pos 4411 Query thread_id=16 exec_time=0 error_code=0

SET TIMESTAMP=1326519052/*!*/;

BEGIN

/*!*/;

at 4411

#120114 0:30:52 server id 1 end_log_pos 4514 Query thread_id=16 exec_time=0 error_code=0

SET TIMESTAMP=1326519052/*!*/;

delete from city where name = 'Ashburn'

/*!*/;

at 4514

#120114 0:30:52 server id 1 end_log_pos 4584 Query thread_id=16 exec_time=0 error_code=0

SET TIMESTAMP=1326519052/*!*/;

COMMIT

/*!*/;

DELIMITER ;

End of log file

ROLLBACK /* added by mysqlbinlog */;

/*!50003 SET COMPLETION_TYPE=@OLD_COMPLETION_TYPE*/;

Database Object Timestamps

SQL Server

The following query can be executed to return a listing of objects including database views, procedures, functions, tables, and extended procedures within a database.

```
(select sob.name as 'object', sch.name as 'schema', type_desc,
create_date, modify_date from sys.all_objects sob,
sys.schemas sch WHERE sob.schema_id = sch.schema_id and
sob.type IN ('V','P','FN','U','S','IT','X')) UNION (select
name, '', 'Db_User', createdate, updatedate from sys.sysusers)
UNION (select name, '', 'Login', createdate, updatedate from
sys.syslogins)
```

Sample results are as follows

```
[SSFA]|pangolin_test_table|1429580131|09/12/2012
11:12:23 AM|09/12/2012 11:12:23 AM|U |USER_TABLE|1|False

[SSFA]|Vacation|2137058649|08/12/2012 1:52:37 PM
|08/12/2012 1:52:37 PM|U |USER_TABLE|5|False

[SSFA]|PastEmployee|2121058592|08/12/2012 1:52:37 PM|
08/12/2012 1:52:37 PM|U |USER_TABLE|5|False

[SSFA]|Employee|2105058535|08/12/2012 1:52:37 PM|
08/12/2012 1:52:37 PM|U |USER_TABLE|5|False

[SSFA]|sysftstops|85|09/07/2008 4:20:01 PM|09/07/2008
4:20:01 PM|S |SYSTEM_TABLE|4|True

[SSFA]|syscompfragments|82|09/07/2008 4:20:01 PM|
09/07/2008 4:20:01 PM|S |SYSTEM_TABLE|4|True
```

Oracle

The following query can be used to return a list of database objects including tables, views, and procedures ordered by modification and creation date both in descending order.

Select object_name, object_id, object_type, created, last_DDL_time from dba_objects ORDER BY LAST_DDL_time DESC, created DESC;

Sample query results can be seen in Fig. 6.7.

Administrator: Command Prompt - sqlplus.exe system/rdsora1@localhost/

OBJECT_NAME	OBJECT_ID	OBJECT_TYPE	CREATED	LAST_DDL_
RLM$SCHDNEGACTION	58851	JOB	03-NOV-11	25-JAN-12
RLM$EVTCLEANUP	58850	JOB	03-NOV-11	25-JAN-12
ORA$AUTOTASK_CLEAN	12704	JOB	03-NOV-11	25-JAN-12
PURGE_LOG	12582	JOB	03-NOV-11	25-JAN-12
SM$CLEAN_AUTO_SPLIT_MERGE	13255	JOB	03-NOV-11	25-JAN-12
RSE$CLEAN_RECOVERABLE_SCRIPT	13254	JOB	03-NOV-11	25-JAN-12
MQCP001	77255	TABLE	24-JAN-12	24-JAN-12
USR	77254	TABLE	24-JAN-12	24-JAN-12
HOST	77253	TABLE	24-JAN-12	24-JAN-12
WRH$_MVPARAMETER_PK	77251	INDEX PARTITION	23-JAN-12	23-JAN-12
WRH$_OSSTAT	77234	TABLE PARTITION	23-JAN-12	23-JAN-12
WRH$_TABLESPACE_STAT_PK	77231	INDEX PARTITION	23-JAN-12	23-JAN-12
WRH$_TABLESPACE_STAT_PK	77232	INDEX PARTITION	23-JAN-12	23-JAN-12
WRH$_TABLESPACE_STAT	77230	TABLE PARTITION	23-JAN-12	23-JAN-12
WRH$_ACTIVE_SESSION_HISTORY_PK	77227	INDEX PARTITION	23-JAN-12	23-JAN-12
WRH$_ACTIVE_SESSION_HISTORY_PK	77228	INDEX PARTITION	23-JAN-12	23-JAN-12
WRH$_ACTIVE_SESSION_HISTORY	77226	TABLE PARTITION	23-JAN-12	23-JAN-12
WRH$_SERVICE_STAT_PK	77223	INDEX PARTITION	23-JAN-12	23-JAN-12
WRH$_SERVICE_STAT_PK	77224	INDEX PARTITION	23-JAN-12	23-JAN-12
WRH$_SERVICE_STAT	77222	TABLE PARTITION	23-JAN-12	23-JAN-12
WRH$_OSSTAT_PK	77236	INDEX PARTITION	23-JAN-12	23-JAN-12
WRH$_MVPARAMETER_PK	77252	INDEX PARTITION	23-JAN-12	23-JAN-12
WRH$_MVPARAMETER	77250	TABLE PARTITION	23-JAN-12	23-JAN-12
WRH$_EVENT_HISTOGRAM_PK	77247	INDEX PARTITION	23-JAN-12	23-JAN-12
WRH$_EVENT_HISTOGRAM_PK	77248	INDEX PARTITION	23-JAN-12	23-JAN-12

FIGURE 6.7 Sample listing of Oracle database objects.

MySQL

The following query can be used to return a list of MySQL database objects.

```
Select * from ((SELECT TABLE_NAME as "OBJECT ", TABLE_SCHEMA
as "OBJECT_SCHEMA ", TABLE_TYPE as "OBJECT_TYPE ",
CREATE_TIME, UPDATE_TIME from information_schema.tables)
UNION (SELECT SPECIFIC_ NAME, ROUTINE_SCHEMA, ROUTINE_TYPE,
CREATED, LAST_ALTERED FROM information_schema.routines WHERE
ROUTINE_TYPE = 'PROCEDURE') UNION (SELECT User, '', 'DB_USER',
'', '' from mysql.user))R
```

A snippet of sample results from the preceding query can be found within Fig. 6.8.

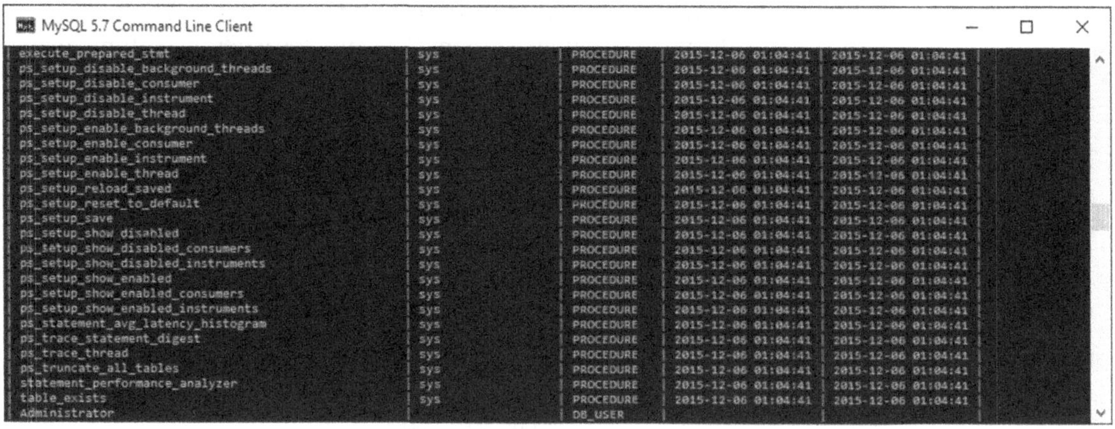

FIGURE 6.8 Sample listing of MySQL database objects.

ANALYZING DATABASE ARTIFACTS

At this point you may have tracked an intruder's access to the database or perhaps simply have a suspicion that an intruder made it to the database, this may have been through a SQL injection, or the unauthorized actions of an insider, however, the questions you likely have now is now what? Well to state the obvious, now it's time to embark on the most consuming stage of the investigation and find that needle in the haystack of collected artifacts. One or a combination of approaches can be used to perform the analysis, manually or using a tool.

Analyzing Artifacts Manually

Well whether you manually preserved artifacts or used a tool at this point you have database artifacts within text files which can be viewed using your nondatabase forensics tool of choice to analyze. SQL Server artifacts, for example, preserved by dbResponder and dbInvestigator carry a ~|~ delimiter and stored within text files with ".hal" extensions. When dealing with relational information, it is my experience that this information is best analyzed within a relational database to manage the relationships and translations from pointers and key values to human-readable values. This information can be imported into Microsoft Excel or the database platform of your choice for analysis.

Sound simple? Well analyzing some artifacts is relatively trivial, others can be far more involved. Database artifacts such as the execution cache which contains plain text information can be manually viewed and searched using any text editor and would fall into the trivial category for analysis. Other artifacts however, such as the transaction log can contain information in a mixture of plain text and hexadecimal formats and require separate metadata to interpret the log data. Further actually analyzing it requires an understanding of data types used to store the data modified as part of the transaction and on-disk data structures. This ladder example would fall into the complex category. We won't cover how to perform manual artifact analysis in this book, however, for those who would like to venture down this path please refer to the references within Table 6.5.

Table 6.5 Database Forensics Manual Artifact Analysis References

Database Platform	References
Microsoft SQL Server	■ SQL Server Forensic Analysis[a] ■ SQL Server Database Forensics[b] ■ Forensic Analysis of an SQL Server 2005 Database Server[c] ■ DoubleTrouble SQL Rootkits and Encryption Flaws[d]
Oracle	■ Oracle Forensics: Oracle Security Best Practices[e] ■ Various white papers[f]
MySQL	■ Forensic Analysis of a MySQL DB System[g] ■ Forensic Analysis of a MySQL database system[h]

[a]https://www.amazon.com/SQL-Server-Forensic-Analysis-paperback/dp/032195162X.
[b]https://www.blackhat.com/presentations/bh-usa-07/Fowler/Presentation/bh-usa-07-fowler.pdf.
[c]https://www.sans.org/reading-room/whitepapers/forensics/forensic-analysis-sql-server-2005-database-server-1906.
[d]http://www.ringzero.ca/presentations/DoubleTrouble.SecTor.Oct08.pdf.
[e]http://www.amazon.com/Oracle-Forensics-Security-Practices-In-Focus/dp/0977671526.
[f]http://www.davidlitchfield.com/security.htm.
[g]https://digital-forensics.sans.org/summit-archives/dfirprague14/Forensic_Analysis_of_MySql_DB_Systems_Marcel_Niefindt.pdf.
[h]https://uarkive.uark.edu/xmlui/handle/10826/936.

Analyzing Artifacts Using a Tool

As captured earlier in Table 6.1, there are not many database forensic tools in the market today. We will look at dbResponder and dbInspector, the only Microsoft SQL server forensics tools that acquire, preserve, and analyze database artifacts. Much of the analysis techniques we'll cover is available in dbResponder, which is a free tool. Some analysis techniques, however, will only be available in dbInvestigator, a feature-enhanced commercial version of the dbResponder tool that is planned for release later in 2016. Despite this fact, I do thinks it's important to understand how database forensic tools can be leveraged within an investigation, for fee or free.

Creating a Case File

dbResponder has integrated case management features that will allow investigators to manage multiple cases concurrently. The first thing an investigator will need to do is to create a case to hold the previously preserved artifacts.

Creating a case file can be accomplished within dbResponder by

1. Open dbResponder and select the "Analysis Workbench" link on the Analyze tab as depicted in Fig. 6.9

FIGURE 6.9 dbResponder analyze tab.

2. You will see the dbResponder Analysis Workbench as seen in Fig. 6.10

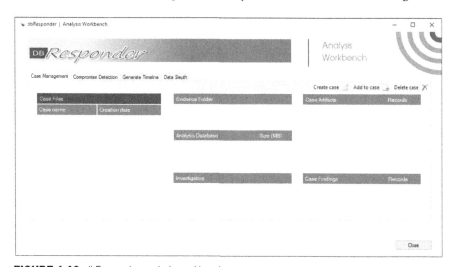

FIGURE 6.10 dbResponder analysis workbench.

3. Pressing the "create case" button within the Analysis Workbench "Case Management" form
4. Entering the name of the case and the folder containing the database artifacts to be added to the case as illustrated in Fig. 6.11

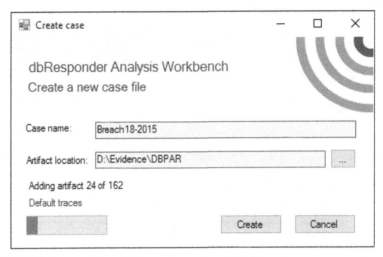

FIGURE 6.11 Screen capture of dbResponder creating a case file.

Progress on the case creation and import status is reflected by the progress bar in the bottom left of the screen. As captured in Fig. 6.12, when the case is created you will be provided a summary of the analysis database and the artifacts imported into the case. The green checkmarks within the case artifact table indicate that hash verification was completed successfully. Hashes generated at the time of artifact preservation are verified upon case creation. Artifacts with hash mismatches will be flagged with a red "x" icon.

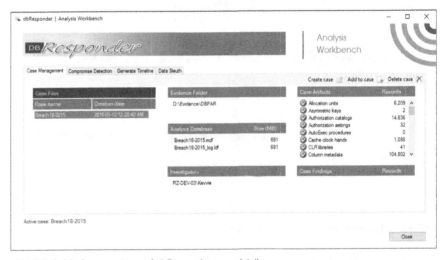

FIGURE 6.12 Screen capture of dbResponder case details.

With the case created let's look at how to analyze the artifacts added to the case.

WHAT ARE YOU TRYING TO ACCOMPLISH WITH YOUR INVESTIGATION?

It's important to ask yourself this question before you get too far through your investigation. Databases have multiple artifacts and it can be tempting to delve into the analysis. This, however, without a plan will rarely identify valuable facts with the investigation. Please refer to Chapter 4 for additional guidance on developing an investigation plan.

Two common objectives of database forensic investigations are investigating nonmalicious events or providing assurance in event of a Breach.

Investigating Nonmalicious Events

Databases are used for a seemingly unlimited number of purposes, being used by front-end applications to store data or images, storing door card access logs, to storing sensitive personal or financial data. During the normal course of business, whether due to mistakes by system users or the routine purging or overwriting of data by applications, database forensic investigations can involve determining information that was accessed, inserted, modified, or deleted from tables associated with nonmalicious activities. Nonmalicious events typically have less mystery associated with them and less demanding timelines.

Providing Assurance in Association With a Breach

Assurance is a statement or activity that improves confidence. During a Breach investigation you can investigate to improve confidence that sensitive information was not accessed as part of the Breach or that it was, however, you fully understand the scope of the unauthorized access. These for most investigations I am involved in this centers around eliminating or reducing material impact by confirming or discounting if an intruder made it to sensitive information, if so scoping it with precision to determine what records were accessed. Objectives for database investigations can range from ensuring no residents information from a selected state, province, or country was included in a Breach, a certain client's information wasn't included in the Breach or generic. One example is the EU data privacy legislation which may fine an organization up to 2% of global revenues in event of a material event, including a cyber security Breach. Proving the Breach did not include this information can save an organization millions or, in some cases, billions of dollars.

Stating what did versus what may have happened eliminates theoretical statements and reduces impact to clients. To get started, figure out the best way to use database forensics to provide assurance.

Using Database Forensics to Provide Assurance

When the panic of a Breach sets in (or subsides) and it's time, forensics Breached organizations and often their legal counsel are looking for assurance, in one form or another, to assess the scope of the Breach. Primary methods of scoping a Breach are through two types of assurance:

- Negative assurance
  A representation or opinion that facts are believed to be accurate since no contrary evidence was found during the investigation. An example of negative assurance would be an investigator who checked all database evidence and could not account for all of the attackers actions, however, could not identify specific evidence of an attacker accessing a table with sensitive data
- Positive assurance
  All statements or conclusions that the forensic investigator believes are accurate are based on specific evidence that was identified and analyzed. An example of specific positive assurance would be an investigator who reviews database evidence, can account for an attacker's actions within a database, and has evidence that shows the attacker didn't view or alter data within a table

Assurance is as good as the reputation and credentials of the individual or organization providing it. Before you go too far in the process ensure your internal or external forensic investigation team does indeed have the reputation and credentials in performing database forensics and provide you the assurance you can use to limit the impact of a Breach.

When seeking either positive or negative assurance, the common dependency for both is understanding where the sensitive information is located within the database.

Determine Where the Sensitive Information Is Located Within the Database

We covered common forms of sensitive information in Chapter 1. When criminals with no prior knowledge of a database, first gain unauthorized access, they often search the database for tables that may contain sensitive data. This approach can be time consuming and can often miss sensitive information residing within tables without descriptive table or column names. During a database investigation, you often will not know the criminal involved, whether they had insider knowledge, or not and if they were able to identify the sensitive information. Understanding where sensitive information is located is essential as you prepare or augment your investigation plan (which we discussed in Chapter 4). The unique advantage you as an investigator will have over the criminal is the ability to ask the appropriate individuals who own or maintain the database, "what sensitive information is stored within the database and where it is located?" This question will allow you to more accurately and efficiently identify the key areas of the database containing sensitive information that you'll need to analyze as you determine the Scale of Impact associated with the Breach.

Determining the Scale of Impact

Some database systems will have thousands and possibly millions of events that may need to be analyzed. Understanding where the sensitive information is within the database will allow you to determine the Scale of Impact for your organization (or client) that will allow you to understand the priority to place around your analysis. Fig. 6.13 is an illustration of a sample Scale of Impact. For example during the analysis of a transaction log you may identify thousands of transactions that could theoretically be analyzed. Identifying that sensitive information resides within a handful of tables would allow you to focus your analysis on just the transactions affecting those tables. A Scale of Impact organizes the various types of sensitive information within a database and prioritizes it by potential impact to an organization if accessed by a criminal. You can use a Scale of Impact as part of your investigation plan to help plan the activity and artifacts you wish to analyze, or you can use one to plot the type of data access associated with confirmed activity that you've analyzed to help determine the scope of access associated with a Breach.

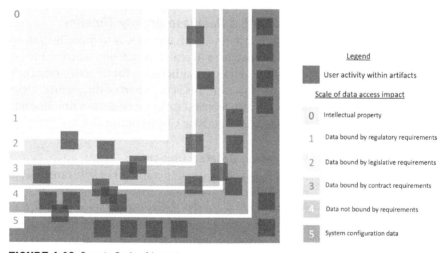

FIGURE 6.13 Sample Scale of Impact.

Each time you confirm activity within a level of your Scale of Impact it should be investigated. When you confirm an attacker did access information within a lower level (higher impact) of your scale I recommend you move to the next level, hold that line, and investigate if any activity is confirmed at a lower level of the scale. Once you have determined what level the intrusion recorded within the Scale of Impact reached you can revisit your other levels to determine the extent of the unauthorized access within each of the levels.

Once you have identified where the sensitive data is stored, I recommend you also investigate data flows for instances where the data is exported from the database via backup, replication, or other process. These data flows can also serve as a target for criminals and may be the actual source of the Breach. You can draw a proverbial box around your scope of sensitive data and hold that line, investigating all activity that enters your scope of sensitive information.

With an understanding of where the sensitive information is within the database and the Scale of Impact of the data, you can proceed leveraging your investigation to provide assurance. We will cover how the analysis of a few artifacts can be used to provide Breach-related positive and negative assurance surrounding unauthorized data access. The analysis of any artifact can be used for either positive or negative assurance depending on the type of investigation or even the analysis results. With this in mind we will cover a few examples of artifact analysis that you can apply to both positive and negative assurance scenarios as appropriate. The examples we will look at are against artifacts taken from a database server in its default configuration. No specialized logging configuration or third party tools were implemented prior to acquisition of artifacts by dbResponder and dbInspector. This underscores the importance of pragmatic science which is geared for the real world.

Developing a Database Activity Timeline

Developing a timeline is a great way to broadly look across as single or multiple database instances in search of activity, whether broad in nature or relating to a defined timeframe. Gathering a list of active objects is beneficial for an investigation, however, this is only part of the picture. Deleted database objects and logins are also relevant to an investigation timeline and can themselves serve as Indicators of Database Compromise (IoDC).

Recovering Deleted Objects

Similar to operating systems and other software that store, retrieve, modify, and delete information, when activity occurs such as deleting or modifying data, traces are left scattered across the database platform and underlying operating system. We will focus on how tools can help retrieve this previously deleted information that resides deep within the internals of a database server.

It's highly recommended that recovering deleted objects is performed prior to developing a database activity timeline as the timeline will not be complete in the absence of the deleted object data. The following is an example of how a dbInvestigator can be used to recover database objects.

1. Select the "Data Recovery" tab
2. Select the instances you would like to recover data on
3. Select the type of data you would like to recover
4. Press the "Scan" hyperlink within the "Scan files for deleted data" label

dbInvestigator will recover data from collected database artifacts, reconstructing previously deleted data objects, logins, and Common Language Runtime (CLR) libraries. Results are populated in real time as deleted items are identified and recovered. Fig. 6.14 illustrates this data recovery and that dbInvestigator has recovered two deleted logins (both named "L0pht") and several deleted tables named "pangolin_test_table" each with a different object ID. The names of these tables are consistent with those used by the Panolin SQL injection tool and the large number of tables carrying the same name but with different ID's further support that they are part of a successful SQL injection attack. SQL Injection tools often create and routinely delete tables in an effort to frustrate forensics and conceal their past actions. The identification of this activity within a database investigation would be positive assurance that an attack did happen and that the criminal was able to execute commands within the database. Transaction log analysis, which we will cover later in this chapter would be needed next to help identify what specific information was extracted from the database via the Pangolin tool.

FIGURE 6.14 Sample recovered database objects viewed within dbInvestigator.

With previously deleted data now recovered a holistic timeline can now be created to provide a broad view into past activity that occurred on the database server. Deleted objects recovered by dbInspector will be incorporated into the database activity timeline. dbResponder can also be used to create database activity timelines, however, only those created within dbInvestigator will include recovered database objects. Timelines generated by dbInspector and dbResponder are populated with all events from collected temporal artifacts providing a very granular view of activity within the database server including server logins, failures, user activity, and internal database platform activity. This level of events will include the routine activity such as the login\user who executed an INSERT, UPDATE, or DELETE operation. However, it will also often show activity associated with the execution of SELECT queries. SELECT queries are viewed by many as an action that if not explicitly logged will go unnoticed. SELECT queries, however, often will create temporary objects needed by the database server to sort interim results before presenting the results to the requesting user. Looking at a timeline you can actually observe a logged SELECT query within an execution plan, for example, and then look at the internal tables created by the database platform to temporarily manage the interim results, or the generation of internal statistics used by the database platform for performance reasons. This level of analysis even with a tool is complex and should left for experts to perform. Fig. 6.15 illustrates table statistics that were created in response to a SELECT query.

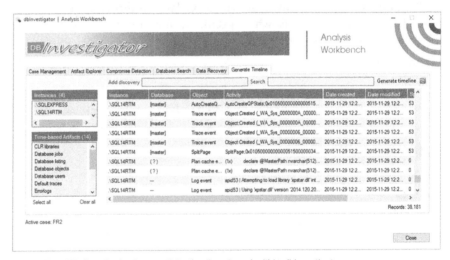

FIGURE 6.15 Sample database activity timeline viewed within dbInvestigator.

The activity within the database is often one of many sources of events for a timeline. Events from the network, operating systems, and other middleware applications should also be factored in. To facilitate this interaction the database timeline generated by dbInspector or dbResponder can be exported and added to other timeline data that you may have.

1. Right clicking on any record within the timeline will provide an export option as seen in Fig. 6.16 that when selected will output the entire timeline within a delimited text file that can be incorporated into a broader timeline you may be creating

Some events within the timeline will need further analysis to understand their full context to your investigation. For example, an entry in the timeline indicating a DELETE operation was executed signifies that a record within a table was

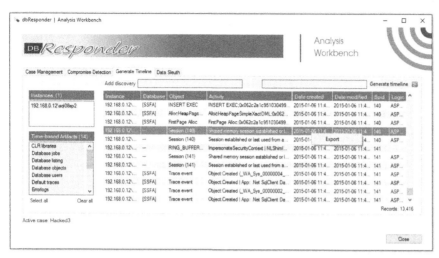

FIGURE 6.16 dbInspector export feature.

deleted; however, this can mean different things within the context of an investigation. Because database platforms manage metadata that describes the objects that database servers maintain in order to function such as user accounts, tables, configurations, and even login attempts database operations can take on different meanings from table to table. In a table storing metadata about objects the DELETE operation could signify that a database table or login was dropped from the system or if the operation was executed against a table used by a middleware application it could mean that a customer record was deleted (for example). Further, understanding that something happened is part of the context you need, but understanding what data was actually deleted would complete the picture which we'll cover a little later in this chapter. Events within your timeline should be further explored to understand context and relevance within your investigation.

Identifying Previously Executed Database Statements

Execution plans (referred to as the plan cache within SQL Server) is another great artifact that will allow you to reconstruct previously executed user queries and statements. dbInvestigator has an "Artifact Explorer" tab that provides a listing of all collected artifacts and performs a variety of pre-analysis and correlation that make database artifacts easier to analyze. We however will focus on how to manually view collected artifacts through the "Data Sleuth" tab which is included in the free dbResponder tool and will be accessible to broader range of people. The following query can be executed from within the "Data Sleuth" tab to return a listing of all execution plans collected.

SELECT * from plch_data

This query executed from within dbInvestigator and sample results returned from the query can be seen in Fig. 6.17.

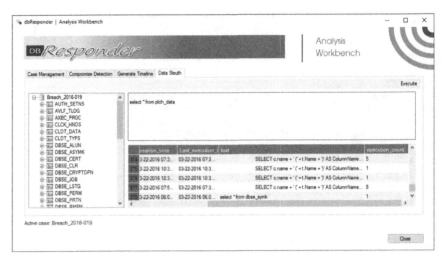

FIGURE 6.17 Sample SQL Server plan cache entries viewed within dbResponder.

It is important to note that the type of query identified within the execution plan can also indicate how the attack occurred. For example, in the scenario of an insider attack if a database administrator had access to a database server and used the Query Analyzer, within SQL Server Management Studio (default GUI database client) to query a table and export the results to a file, the syntax within the executed query will have distinct characteristics associated with that database client which would vastly differ than the same query executed via another SQL client. This finding would show that the data was viewed interactively using Query Analyzer. Cross referencing this with login activity can provide you the logged on user at the time of the interactive query and identify the login account used during the incident.

Note that all collected artifacts can be viewed directly through the "Data Sleuth" feature of dbInvestigator. Please refer to product documentation for additional details.

These have been only a few examples of how artifacts can be used to provide negative assurance regarding data confidentially, integrity, and availability in conjunction with a Breach. We'll now shift to looking at a few examples of using database forensics to achieve positive assurance.

Positive Assurance

The following examples are of how database forensics can be used to provide positive assurance, statements, or conclusions that can be proven due to the analysis of evidence.

Identifying Indicators of Database Compromise

Selecting the "Compromise Detection" tab within dbInvestigator will provide you with options on detecting IoDC's. A single case contains all database instances that have been preserved. During an investigation you may wish to analyze artifacts across all instances or a selected subset of them. The following steps can be used to detect IoDC's within a case.

1. Select the instances you would like to search for IoDC's within the "Instances" section of the form
2. Select the Indicators of Compromise that you would like to include in the search (SQL injection attacks, Brute-force attacks, and High-risk activity)
3. Press the "Identify" button to search for IoDC's across collected artifacts

Fig. 6.18 illustrates sample returned IoDC's and shows database compromise by the Pangolin SQL injection tool.

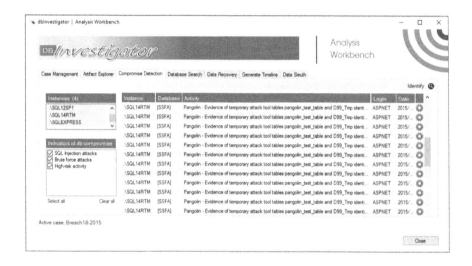

FIGURE 6.18 Sample Indicators of db compromise viewed within dbInvestigator.

IoDC's are indicators of malicious activity, however, context is needed to deem or discount the event as material to your investigation. dbInvestigator displays orange context wheels when there is information contained within other artifacts that will help the investigator add context to the specific activity under investigation. Right clicking on a record with an orange context wheel will display a menu with the additional context available as illustrated in Fig. 6.19.

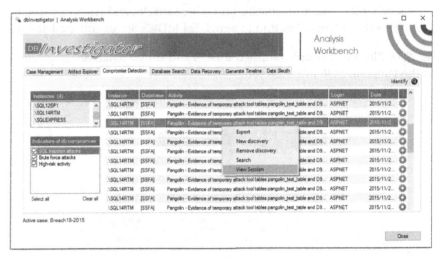

FIGURE 6.19 Sample database session recovery within dbInvestigator.

Fig. 6.20 shows the session that dbInvestigator has recreated belonging to the database login associated with the IoDC. The session shows the creation of "Pangolin_test_table" which as we covered earlier is a table associated with the Pangolin SQL Injection attack tool.

Scrolling through the session also shows that the login has loosened the database server hardening by enabling high-risk database functions "OLE Automation Procedures" and "Ad Hoc Distributed Queries" as captured in Fig. 6.21.

Following the session or separately analyzing the transaction log data can yield additional insight into what the attacker did on the system. So how can INSERT, UPDATE, and DELETE statements be helpful in an investigation? Well almost anything that happens on a database platform will have the need to write or retrieve data from disk (directly and indirectly). Take, for example, when investigating SQL injection attacks they are often executed through an SQL injection attack tool (which can be obtained publicly on the Internet). These tools identify vulnerabilities within applications, enumerate the database system to identifying user rights, database versions, and the metadata of the database in an effort to determine where sensitive information is stored. These tools then allow attackers

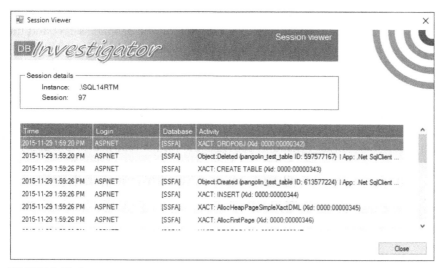

FIGURE 6.20 Reconstructed session results viewed within dbInvestigator.

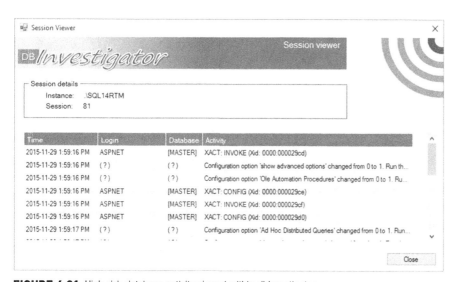

FIGURE 6.21 High-risk database activity viewed within dbInvestigator.

to easily exfiltrate data from the database or even jump out of the database server into the registry or filesystem of the database server and even connect to other networked machines. The behavior of these SQL injection tools is that a temporary table is created on the compromised database server and populated with information taken from other database tables, the registry, or the filesystem. A SELECT query is then run by the tool to return data to the attacker. Analyzing the transaction log can identify the creation of these temporary tables but more importantly the data inserted and deleted out of them which can provide an exact account of the commands the attacker executed on the database server and the specific data that was returned to the attacker during the Breach.

The below screen captures illustrate how dbInvestigator can analyze the transaction log to precisely scope a Breach resulting from a Pangolin SQL injection attack.

Fig. 6.22 shows an SQL Server transaction involving one INSERT operation. Reversing the INSERT operation provides the results returned to the attacker after issuing an arp command through the database server to the OS command prompt of the compromised database server. This activity is typically performed during reconnaissance to learn the network environment of the newly compromised database server.

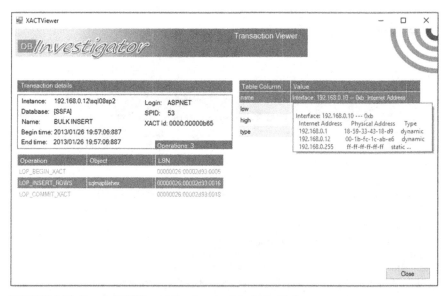

FIGURE 6.22 Sample INSERT operation viewed within dbInvestigator.

The sqlmapfilehex table referenced in the transaction highlighted in Fig. 6.22 is a table associated with the SQLmap attack tool. During the course of an investigation this fact can help fine-tune your analysis looking for artifacts typically left by the tool.

Fig. 6.23 shows another example of an attack via the Pangolin tool. Reversing the INSERT operation shows the file read by the attacker during the attack. This file is located within the filesystem of the compromised database server and was accessed through the database and returned to the attacker.

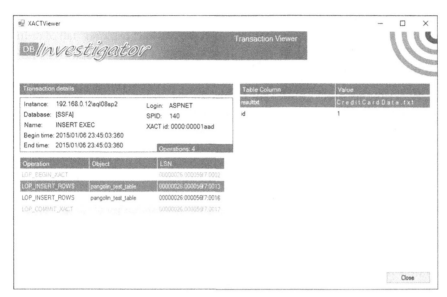

FIGURE 6.23 Directory enumeration of the Windows file system via the Pangolin SQL Injection attack tool.

The data read from within the CreditCardData.txt file captured in Fig. 6.23 can be found within Fig. 6.24.

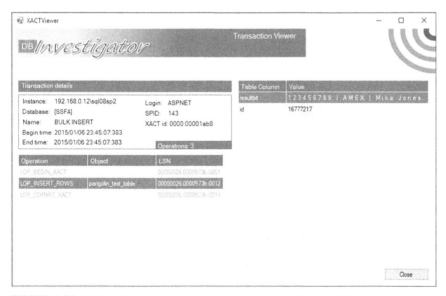

FIGURE 6.24 Windows file system data read by an attacker via the Pangolin SQL Injection attack tool.

We just explored reversing a transaction of interest. There will be several instances where you will need to look more broadly to identify the transaction activity on a system generally and associated with specific objects. This can be done easily (and with pre-analysis) through the "Artifact Explorer" tab of dbInvestigator. We, however, will look at how to create a summary of transactions within dbResponder, the free tool.

1. Select the "Data Sleuth" tab within dbResponder
2. Enter the following syntax into the query window to provide a summary of INSERT, UPDATE, and DELETE operations by table across all artifacts

   ```
   SELECT [Database], AllocUnitName as 'Object',
   Operation, COUNT(OPERATION) AS 'Count' from
   avlf_TLOG WHERE OPERATION IN ('LOP_INSERT_ROWS',
   'LOP_MODIFY_ROW', 'LOP_DELETE_ROWs') and
   AllocUnitName NOT Like 'sys.%' GROUP BY [Database],
   AllocUnitName, Operation
   ```
3. Press the "Execute" button

Sample results when the preceding query is run through the "Data Sleuth" tab of dbInspector can be seen in Fig. 6.25.

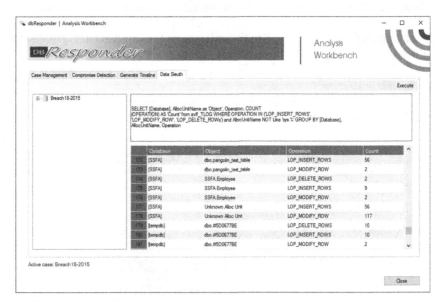

FIGURE 6.25 Sample summary of transactions viewed within dbResponder.

The last positive assurance method we'll look at is identifying a logins' past activity on a database instance.

Identifying a Database Logins Past Activity

Database timelines can provide a broad view of activity across database artifacts. However, a view of activity related to specific logins can provide a tailored view of activity of interest and allow you to better focus your analysis identifying anomalies that otherwise may have gone undiscovered. dbInvestigator will allow you, to identify activity by login, recreate past sessions and activity of the login in question and reverse related transactions to aid in your analysis.

A listing of all activity associated with a login can be gathered by:

1. Select the "Artifact Explorer" tab from within dbInspector
2. Select a login with the orange context wheel and right click within the form as seen in Fig. 6.26

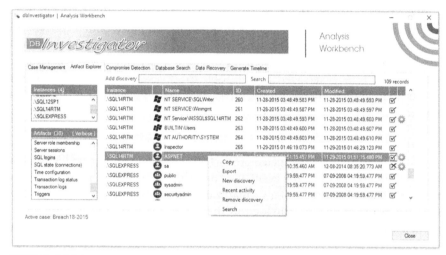

FIGURE 6.26 Generating a recent activity summary for a database users via dbInvestigator.

3. Select the "Recent activity" menu option to generate database activity by the login as illustrated in Fig. 6.27

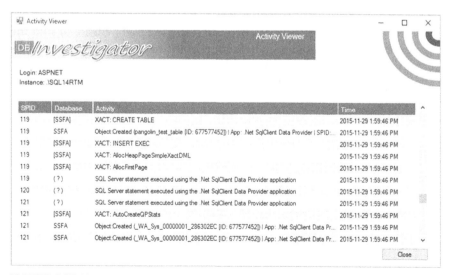

FIGURE 6.27 Viewing recent activity of a database user via dbInvestigator.

SUMMARY

In a recent investigation I found myself working with an organization who just learned that they had fallen victim to Breach. They had an on-line application with a SQL injection vulnerability that was publicly exposed. When the vulnerability was identified and patched the recommendation was made that a forensic review is performed to ensure the client was the first to identify it. The investigation was performed and coming as a surprise to the client they quickly realized they were not. 16 attackers over a 2 year timeframe found the vulnerability and exploited it. The database in question contained both sensitive and non-sensitive data. There was a tight timeline, however, database forensics was used to investigate. Database forensics was able to provide positive assurance that 5 of the 16 attackers were actually able to successfully execute commands within the database. Retracing the attackers actions throughout the database systems allowed us to provide positive assurance that no sensitive information was accessed. This allowed the organization to, classify the event as an "incident" and avoid public disclosure. Without database forensics the organization likely would have struggled precisely scoping it and therefore likely have had to publicly disclosed the event as a "Breach" which would have damage to their brand and financials. Many organizations find themselves unprepared to respond to a Breach, many can identify that an incident has occurred but struggle determining the scope and impact. The need to bring the right science to an investigation is critical in minimizing impact. Database forensic science has been practiced in limited capacities in the past and only recently has been formalized. It is a relatively unknown area of forensics and one of your most powerful allies when attempting to eliminate or reduce impact associated with a Breach. If you are part of an organization ensure your internal or external forensic response teams are knowledgeable in database forensics and applying it to reduce impact associated with a Breach. Database forensics techniques can be practiced by many, however, when the stakes are high, ensure to find the right expertise and reputation to help support the negative and positive assurance you will need in order to successfully limit impact.

CHAPTER 7

Communicating Before, During and After a Breach

Brian West

INTRODUCTION: THE CONCEPT OF CYBER RESILIENCE

No matter how strong a company's defenses are, a data Breach can still occur. Therefore a company's resilience—defined as the ability to become strong, healthy, or successful again after something bad happens—is critical and it only comes from preparation. This is the concept of cyber resilience, an immediate and appropriate response and communication after a data Breach.

Headlines trumpeting the latest victim of a cyber Breach are now almost a daily occurrence. With the integration of technology into managing the information flow for almost every aspect of a business, this no longer comes as a surprise. What is surprising though is the continued corporate misunderstanding of just who the true victim is: not the company whose defenses were circumvented, but rather the customers whose privacy—and trust in a brand—has been compromised. Every crisis needs to be viewed through the lens of those ultimately impacted, and not just that of the Boardroom or C-suite.

Yet it is these customers who are far too often considered an afterthought in both operational response and public communication. This inadequacy, amid hastily developed response strategies and tactics from affected companies suffering through intense media and public scrutiny following such Breaches, stems from their focus on managing the fallout, rather than looking to capitalize on the opportunities inherent in each and every crisis.

Make no mistake: a data Breach is a crisis in every sense of the word. It can threaten to not only damage a company's immediate financial performance but also affect long-term reputation and confidence among customers and stakeholders if not managed properly, in much the same as any other more traditional crisis scenario. Importantly, with the advent of real-time information flow, powered by social and online mediums, companies must not only react faster but also be accurate and effective from the get-go, ensuring the right audiences and messages are prioritized.

CONTENTS

Data Breach Preparation and Response. http://dx.doi.org/10.1016/B978-0-12-803451-4.00007-1

Within this context, the notion of cyber resilience, as opposed to relying on cyber security and the traditional cyber Breach response, is growing in popularity due to its broad and holistic outlook in aiding cyber prevention and post-crisis mitigation. Put simply, if we accept that a Breach is to occur, it makes for more focus on response preparation right off the bat, hence enabling a faster recovery from a crisis. While cyber Breaches might not be an inevitability for all, companies should recognize that even the strongest of cyber defenses can succumb to risk due simply to human failings—and it is in these situations that they need to have a business continuity approach, taking into account external communication, and be ready to go. It is about knowing how to effectively manage risk, rather than trying to eliminate it altogether.

Think of cyber security as the walls of a fortress; some companies might be able to raise their walls to dizzying heights and even have a moat or secondary walls around key installations in case the primary wall is Breached. However, no castle can be completely closed off from the world, and will always require people to man the defenses and keep the castle secure and operational (Fig. 7.1).

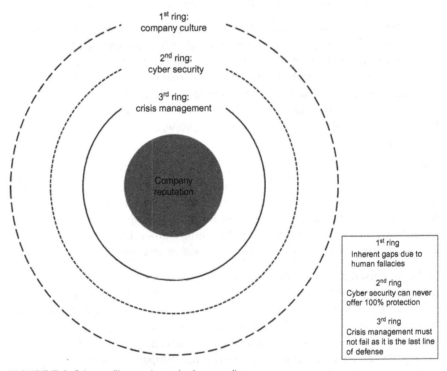

FIGURE 7.1 Cyber resilience—beyond cyber security.

With this indispensable need for human involvement comes the inevitable possibility of human failings. A guard may be lax and neglect security protocols in the interest of personal convenience, while malicious threats can piggyback or prey on unsuspecting occupants in order to gain entry to the fortress, allowing even the most robust of defenses to be Breached. Here, resilience and management of reputation becomes the key, rather than giving up and pointing at the failed first line of defense.

Even a smaller scale cyber Breach will either be trumpeted by the persons involved, or seized and sensationalized by the media when the word does get out—and yes, it will get out. While scale and severity is still the fuel for how long a crisis remains in the media and public spotlight, the initial reports can either make or break your company's reputation if communications are not managed promptly and effectively. Effectively, your company's resilience is undermined by a less than speedy response.

Additionally, the stronger your company's reputation, the higher the expectations of governments, customers, the public, and the media for you to show corporate leadership when a crisis actually occurs, leaving you with little margin in terms of time or error.

While you can't buy time in a crisis, you may be able to draw the benefit of the doubt and receive patience and understanding from your stakeholders.

Clearly, then, there is a paradigm shift towards the concept of cyber resilience, which includes a robust cyber security regime rather than relying on a solution in isolation. When your fortress is Breached, cyber resilience can be thought of as the reserve force ready to mitigate any fallout from the Breach, from pushing malicious elements back to rallying occupants (all stakeholders, and in particular, your staff—the often forgotten force) and demonstrating to outsiders that, through effective and authentic leadership, you are still the resilient and successful company you have always been.

Communication is a key element of effective cyber resilience, and effectively communicating throughout the Breach lifecycle can reduce impact and can actually stand to increase your brand equity and reputation. Let's explore some techniques that can be used to effectively communicate pre, during, and after a Breach.

BEFORE A CRISIS

Planning Ahead

When a cyber Breach occurs, your company will be scrambling to piece together what happened, assessing what was lost, and evaluating the options to take, moving forward. Against the backdrop of this confusion and panic, and with your audience and the media already hounding your company for answers, having a prepackaged and ready to go crisis communications plan significantly frees you up to manage the pressing crisis, rather than simply reacting to it.

A Crisis Playbook helps a company's management effectively navigate communications during a negative event that has or threatens to attract intense media, government, community, industrial, or non-governmental organizations' attention to its brands or products. The Playbook includes step-by-step instructions and tailorable message templates for responding to all stakeholders during an incident or a crisis. It also offers best practices, corporate policies, and other resources to help management create communications that preserves brand equity and protects reputation.

More often than not, crisis communications plans start with logistics-focused processes that outline who does what in a crisis, or who needs to be contacted. Crisis Manuals are full of "to do" lists. Many executives take this information, ask for it to be implemented, and ultimately regard the crisis management requirement as fulfilled.

While this form of preparation is a practical and essential part of addressing a problem, the focus remains passive and drives the management of operational factors only. At a time of a significant reputational challenge, the enlightened quickly realize this is not enough. In a crisis, when a company's senior executives show leadership by taking control of their destiny, they are seen to be fulfilling their responsibility and not leaving it to others to define and protect the company's reputation.

Advanced identification of crisis scenarios and strategizing how the organization would respond in these situations, along with preapproved responses, moves an organization to the next level—a Playbook. While a Playbook cannot predict all pressures from different stakeholders in a crisis, in combination with a long-term strategy or objective, it can ensure a company's crisis decision makers do not fall for the temptation of making expedient or ad-hoc decisions to accommodate pressure from specific interest groups. Attempting to put out spot fires in this way often comes back to haunt companies in their new, post-crisis reputational context.

So, if a company has made the right preparatory moves, and has understood and accepted the need to have a crisis communications plan, what exactly should it include in the context of today's crisis playing field? Modern-day playbooks, in the cyber-influenced world in which we live today, need to recognize and consider following:

- The role of social media
- The speed imperative
- How to and when to line up additional resources
- The benefits of a shortened chain of command
- Management training
- The importance of crisis simulations to stress-test plans and skills
- Understanding your organization's Guiding Light Strategy

This is the only way to achieve a holistic and comprehensive response framework and approach—widening your scope, your perspective in viewing, managing, and responding to a data Breach.

Widening Your Cyber Scope

Companies today rarely operate in isolated silos, with most having links and connections to various companies as part of their regular business undertakings. Multinational companies are particularly reliant on a vast network of suppliers, contractors, subsidiaries, and even governments.

While your company might have the most robust of cyber defenses, it is important to keep a perspective and know that not every company in your network will have the same level of cyber security that you might have. If external companies have access to your network as part of your working relationship, it is especially important to consider the possibility that cyber criminals might bypass attempts at breaking through your defenses in favor of hitting the weaker systems of partner companies.

You may also be impacted by cyber Breaches at companies that are part of your supply chain, even if they have no access to your actual network. In these cases, the media is always quick to emphasize the involvement of the most well-known entity to attract reader attention, even if that company's connection to the affected company is tenuous at best. This is especially true of social media platforms that don't have the strict journalistic integrity and fact-checking processes of traditional news publications.

Ultimately, whose crisis is it? Yours or your supply chain partner's? If you are the final contact point with the public, the customer, then you have carriage of the duty of care, and it is your crisis.

Given this context, a crisis communications plan today should actively consider how to mitigate and respond to public scrutiny regarding not only direct cyber attacks but also those of suppliers, contractors, subsidiaries, and business partners: your supply chain as indicated in Fig. 7.2.

The Role of Social Media

Audiences today have moved beyond the traditional forms of mass communication to the near-instantaneous milieu of social media. But, despite this, many crisis communications plans are stymied by a lack of consideration for and attention to these game-changing platforms.

This has drastically changed the communications landscape, and further compounds the proliferation of cyber Breaches and the devastation they create. Why? Because a crisis no longer breaks, it tweets. And in an era where crises

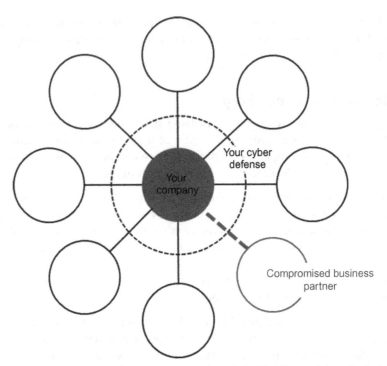

FIGURE 7.2 Widening your cyber scope—a Breached supply chain is still your crisis, as the final public touch point.

are measured by the number of tweets per second, its imperative is to be able to communicate at the same speed as your audience.

Considering that companies often discover that they have been Breached either after cyber criminals broadcast their latest conquest online or when the cache of customer information surfaces in black markets around the internet, the power of the social media can never be ignored.

However, the real-time speed at which information is distributed via social media is not just a threat. It also presents an opportunity for your company to disseminate accurate information to counter rumors and hearsay that may be floating online, while also allowing for direct and unfiltered engagement. The opportunity social media delivers for direct, unfiltered, real-time responses and proactive engagement with key stakeholders cannot be understated.

Companies, therefore have to become their own media outlet, to produce and amplify your facts and your viewpoints directly to all stakeholders via all available media platforms and using a mixture of media. Not just the written word but also utilizing the power of video and then using all paid, earned, shared, and owned media to drive traffic to your website where your story is told in an authentic way by your spokesperson.

Furthermore, journalists and reporters from reputable, traditional media publications are increasingly turning to the faster access and information flow enabled by social media to stay ahead of their competition, often adding their organization's legitimacy to what might be inaccurate or misleading information online. Executives should not be intimidated by the unfamiliarity they have with social media but, instead, should take steps to embrace the potential that it holds.

Consideration also should be given to the type of content that has the greatest impact. Anything visual—particularly video—is fast becoming the preferred medium for the growing population of digital natives, and social media outlets are prime channels for the distribution of such videos. In a crisis, this kind of content can be used against your company but, by the same token, it is one that can be used strategically to help humanize your brand's crisis communication, demonstrating your empathy, compassion, and understanding. Corporate words in the form of a written statement simply cannot achieve this as effectively—though that is not to diminish the impact the right words can have.

The Speed Imperative

Again, in an era where your audiences expect your response to be immediate and effective—and even more so in a cyber Breach where their privacy has been compromised—you cannot afford to delay. When a crisis hits, the market decides quickly whether a company is a winner or loser.

Reputational damage in a crisis is now often directly proportional to the management's response, or lack thereof, making a company's reaction in the first minutes, hours, and 24 hours absolutely critical. Yet, in a cyber attack, the first mistake managers make is thinking of the at-risk or stolen data as belonging to the company rather than to the customers actually affected, thereby approaching the crisis primarily from their own perspective.

As a result, companies delay announcing that they have been Breached until they know everything about the Breach: when it occurred, over what time frame, how much data has been stolen, is the data now secure, and so on. If they delay until they know everything though, they will never say anything. Retailers, government departments, anyone who holds data and approaches Breaches in this manner, delaying disclosure of the truth, in the process destroys their trust with key stakeholders. Those whose data has been stolen have a right to know, and to know immediately.

Compare this approach to one of transparency and speed. Instead of withholding information, a company can ensure there is no communication void being filled by speculation and unreliable sources by responding promptly, as soon as a Breach is discovered. In this way, a company can control the narrative from spiraling out of control by constantly talking about what they are doing to support their customers, mitigating the risk of the media playing on the ire of disgruntled customers who have had personal information compromised.

A successful crisis communication plan today, therefore, hinges on speed, from the initial response after the Breach is discovered to regular updates, catered to specific stakeholders. With the speed at which information—and misinformation—moves today, crisis communications must move in tandem or your audiences will simply move on to alternative information sources. Whether those alternative sources know the full picture may not be known or understood but, without question, they will not have your best interests at heart.

Lining up Resources

A key part of an effective crisis communications plan is the identification and preparation of key resources and experts that can be leveraged when a crisis strikes. Building on the speed imperative, your initial phases of crisis communications can be shortened even further with this arrangement in mind.

One of the primary resources to have at hand is a dark site, not to be confused with the dark web which we covered in Chapter 1 of this book. This dark site is a purpose built website, specifically designed to be activated in the event of a crisis and which is regularly updated so that it is ready to go live immediately when needed. Most companies with high operational risks already have dark sites in place, but the vagaries of cyber Breaches—from their targets to their methods—should prompt more companies to consider this strategy.

The reasoning is clear. Bearing in mind that your corporate website is designed to cater for different purposes and audiences, it is unlikely to be appropriate or sufficiently flexible when a crisis hits. Your stakeholders, the public, and the media will turn to your website for more information or updates, and if none is forthcoming, or the relevant information is not readily available, you will have already lost control of the narrative to other sources that may be easily accessible, but also less accurate.

Having a dark website, ready to go live at short notice, with detailed information already prepared, tells visitors to the site that you are serious about being transparent and accountable in a crisis, and have the foresight to have specific channels in place. This speaks volumes about your company, and your leadership.

As well as having a dark site ready, there are other resources that you should have lined up, including external agencies or individuals that have capabilities and resources that can be useful in a crisis. You must have external information technology and data experts on speed dial in the event of a cyber Breach, to support your internal team, and have contact details ready for an experienced public relations firm or crisis consultants, reputation management and recovery experts, and digital gurus who can lead your crisis communications initiatives in the online sphere.

It will be even more advantageous if you have taken the time to build relationships with the various industry authorities and experts, key opinion leaders, and influencers, in advance, forming a steady and reliable pool of allies to call upon immediately if you are suffering a cyber Breach. This will enable you to call on them to give voice to the integrity of the organization and its leadership, and this incident is not indicative of a systemic failing by the company.

Once again, this is all about the speed imperative. Having your tools ready or within arm's reach will help you address the issue at hand much faster than if you have to rummage for the relevant and appropriate tools when a crisis strikes.

Shortening the Chain of Command

Tied in closely with the speed imperative, companies also need to recognize that the structure and chain of command of traditional business units are one of the main hurdles that can slow down effective crisis communications. While there are countless real-world examples of contrasting approaches at work, business units that operate as silos act as a poison pill in a crisis, even if they may be successful from a purely operational standpoint.

The traditional, centralized, command-and-control structure of multinationals cannot be applied to crisis communications, and it is even more dangerous when it ignores or is ignorant of the local sociopolitical, economic, and media landscapes. Instead, executives have to empower the local first responders on their staff to action directives in the crisis communication plan in consideration of local sensitivities and heuristics, instead of forcing them to consult with central headquarters that may be many time zones away, before acting.

Companies also have to recognize that, especially in relation to cyber Breaches, there is no such thing as a local crisis. Databases are often congregated in a few sites rather than being housed at a centralized location, while the interconnectivity that is integral to information technology renders physical distance a moot point. Cyber criminals simply have to gain access at a single point of entry anywhere in the world, and they will have free rein over the entire information technology infrastructure.

Similarly, crisis communications can no longer merely focus on the physical location of the Breach, but have to be able to address stakeholders in every country in which the company has interests. Again, locally based staff, empowered to launch crisis communication plans immediately—and with the authority to localize all messages and disseminate and if needed—can help minimize long-term damage through slow responses from head office or responses that are insensitive to local mores.

Training Management

While cyber Breaches might be confined to the virtual world, your audiences are human and effective crisis communications after Breaches rely on human displays of compassion, empathy, and understanding. Executives have to be adequately trained to project these emotions, and generate *authentic leadership* that helps to cultivate the benefit of the doubt, patience, and understanding when a crisis strikes.

What exactly do we mean by "authentic leadership?" The term "leadership" implies that someone is taking charge of the situation. However, presence alone (or the display of it) of a CEO or other business leader is not sufficient. For example, a CEO who is visible but dodges questions from the media and sticks to a script derived from the corporate statements of their company does not improve your chances of reputational recovery.

Cyber Breaches can result in the loss of sensitive information of customers, creating undue stress and inconvenience on their part (whether their information is ever used or not). Too often, companies fail to display the empathy and compassion needed in these circumstances. Conversely, a CEO who is quick to take and display leadership of an unfolding crisis, and even takes personal ownership in managing the incident when necessary, resonates well with the public and the media. Apart from taking ownership, a leader who displays genuine care and compassion for compromised customers can go a long way to ensuring the damage is limited to the crisis itself.

Authentic leaders in a crisis step away from traditional styles of leadership. Top-down, one-way public communication models are abandoned in favor of two-way symmetrical models. And the measure of their success is how personal, highly involved, compassionate, transparent, and empathetic is their communication.

Running Simulations

It is also important to run regular simulations of your crisis communications plan. In the same way that your cyber security systems need to be regularly checked and evaluated, testing and trial runs of your crisis communications have to be conducted to test for flaws and weaknesses—especially when there are new cyber security updates. In much the same way, crisis communications plans also have to be regularly updated and it is prudent to run simulations based on the latest iteration.

Companies have to start moving beyond the mindset that having a crisis communications plan, even if it is updated regularly, is more than sufficient when a crisis hits. If the plan itself has not been stress-tested, the chances are that your company will be mired in disarray and confusion (especially with the limited time factor in play). Confidence in working with a crisis plan can only be gained if your crisis communications team is comfortable and familiar with its content and approach.

The concept of cyber resilience is dependent on how fast you can react when a crisis strikes, and your reactive force should be drilled, prepared for and confident in repelling threats, restoring faith, and reinforcing relationships right from the get-go.

Guiding Light Strategy

The last, and arguably the most important point, is to have a "guiding light" strategy when formulating your crisis communications plan. A cyber Breach, much like any other crisis, will see its share of vociferous stakeholders, and each group will be clamoring for attention from the crisis management team and the company's leadership (Fig. 7.3).

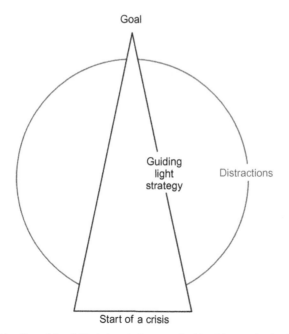

FIGURE 7.3 Using the guiding light strategy to focus on the big picture and cut out the noise.

A guiding light strategy forces you to take a long-term view while fighting the various fires you may want to put out immediately. It pushes you to ask yourself how you want your company to be viewed 2, 5, or even 10 years after the crisis, helping to guide your actions rather than giving in to ad-hoc, expedient demands just to get a particular group off your back.

A guiding light strategy also presents an opportunity for you to fulfill your corporate vision, motto, values, and principles. While every company has some form of corporate speak ostensibly guiding their company, a crisis invites scrutiny if your company is actually failing to fulfill what it purportedly stands for.

Your corporate ethos should be a point of consideration in deciding how far you should go to cover the costs incurred by customers or staff in the event of a cyber Breach and loss of their personal information, from identity recovery services to credit cover. Rather than hastily trying to find solutions to placate affected stakeholders, a guiding light strategy helps to ensure all the actions are strategic and helping fulfill an overriding objective.

Doing so not only engenders perceptions that you are serious in making amends for the Breach, but that your company's published principles are more than simply corporate speak.

DURING A CRISIS

Embracing the concept of cyber resilience also involves understanding the communication trajectory of a crisis. Every crisis situation has a specific arc, as do the resulting news coverage and social media conversations (Fig. 7.4).

Bearing in mind that crisis communications can no longer be guided by a one-size-fits-all approach, nor be characterized by a list of tasks simply to be checked off and completed, there are still three general stages of managing a crisis effectively:

- Assess
- Resolve
- Control

Assess

Before jumping into crisis mitigation immediately, it is essential to draw some time, no matter how limited, to assess the situation. Firstly, there is a need to classify the problem, in terms of the severity, the people involved, and whether

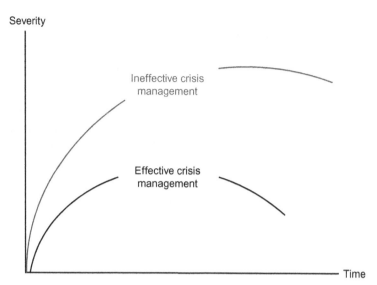

FIGURE 7.4 Every crisis has an arc; management's response can either compound fallout or demonstrate resilience.

the Breach itself has been resolved or is still ongoing. Some crises will require aggressive measures to stall hostile reporting and negative sentiments before they spiral out of control, while others might require a gentler approach to connect better with stakeholders and customers, especially when consumer data is Breached.

Every company might have communications staff designated as go-to crisis responders, but whoever is immediately available may not be the best fit for the specific crisis. By gaining an understanding of the problem at hand, the right team to manage the crisis and help guide the response might require a more diverse group of people (such as your risk, IT and HR departments), and companies have to be flexible enough to recognize and draw upon the right skill sets with the appropriate expertise and on-ground knowledge.

Additionally, the team should be identifying potential risk scenarios, including evaluating the likelihood of these scenarios occurring, and creating appropriate measures to address them.

Each crisis will see a range of stakeholders with competing interests and conflicting demands, seeking to influence a company's crisis response. In addressing these competing demands, a company must identify which of the many communication mediums available to them are best for getting their message across to the various stakeholders.

Again, they must recognize that simply pouring messages into traditional media channels is sufficient of itself. Yes, they are perceived as more legitimate and can reach mass audiences, but the latent power of social media to spread not only accurate information but also misinformation should not be downplayed.

Given that you often know you have been Breached when someone alerts you online, or from the buzz generated by cyber criminals and their bounty, there must be social media monitoring in place as well as tracking of traditional platforms. Media monitoring should also not be restricted to English language mediums or the local top tier media outlets.

Therefore, a robust crisis mitigation plan should not be a rote set of tasks, but a tailored, measured, and comprehensive approach covering as many avenues and possibilities as possible.

Resolve

Once the foundation has been built and the team knows what it is dealing with, it can move on to tackling the crisis itself. In a badly managed crisis, proceedings can quickly degenerate into a blame game, with parties involved pointing fingers while ignoring the growing damage to the reputations of all involved.

To effectively resolve the confusion generated from the myriad conflicting viewpoints or information, the affected company must quickly seize the authority to get accurate information out to the appropriate audiences, using the most appropriate channels.

Authority can be established by crafting and sharing regular public communication to keep stakeholders informed, rather than withholding information from them—which can give inaccurate gossip and slander undue airspace. Key messages should also be crafted as part of short- and long-term strategies while managing the different challenges emerging from a crisis, challenges that ideally should have been identified during the Assess phase.

Information that is disseminated by your company should be consistent and accurate. Instead of reactively waiting for questions to come, a proactive approach is advantageous in ensuring that your stakeholders, the public, and the media are getting accurate facts and figures straight from you, rather than from other, unreliable sources.

Trained spokespeople are crucial in maintaining influence and sway over the dissemination of information, and a spokesperson who displays calm authority makes all the difference in convincing the media, stakeholders, and the public that their faith and trust in the company are well placed.

It is also important to frame the challenge in terms of how your audiences are viewing the crisis. Cyber Breaches are the result of any number of reasons, from poor cyber security systems to insider threats or large-scale state-sponsored attacks. It is important to take a step back and view the way in which the manner of the cyber Breach is perceived by the different audiences and then tailor the messages for each of them rather than relying on a broad-brush approach that might not resonate or gain acceptance with all or any. The message is the company's view or statement as tailored for each audience which is then delivered via all media platforms—traditional media, online via media releases, tweets, blogs, and videos (Fig. 7.5).

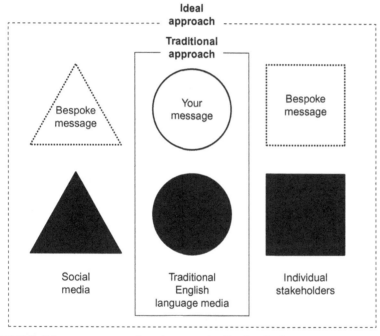

FIGURE 7.5 Tailor your messages; there is no one-size-fits-all method.

For example, if a cyber security vulnerability is found, a company's initial responses should not be overly technical in explaining the reasons for the security compromise if they are communicating with nontechnical audiences. Customers will be focused on the implications for them and what follow-up actions the company intends to take.

Maintaining trust is also key when engaging in communications outreach during a crisis. If you are unable to maintain the trust that has been afforded to you, or even destroy goodwill, this will take your company from the victim box to the culprit box. You will not be read the Miranda rights by your audience but the onus will be on you to convince the jury of public opinion that you are a victim as well, and you must take the initiative to act and speak quickly.

Control

Effective crisis communications cannot be a rote set of tasks that can be checked off and considered complete. Even with public statements and tailored key messages, authority can still be drained away and eventually lost by hostile actions from industry rivals or players hoping to capitalize on the affected company's misfortune.

When a major automaker was struggling with the fallout from its recall because of the sudden acceleration of its vehicles, competitors and even lawyers paid for advertisements on Google Search, playing on the reliability and liability perception gaps that were forming. It took some time for the automaker to regain the initiative by bidding aggressively for advertising space on Google Search via a search engine marketing campaign, and enacting effective search engine optimization to ensure that consumers and interested parties were directed to the website created to help manage the recall, rather than being diverted to other, hostile websites.

In a crisis, all your paid, earned, shared, and owned (PESO) platforms should be utilized and be similar in tone, creating a consistent and authoritative presence in the minds of your stakeholders, the public, and the media, showing that you are firmly in control. They should be used to amplify your message and also drive traffic to the website where you host the full array of facts and tactics, including video, in addressing the crisis.

Control can also be maintained with the formation of "truth squads." These groups of roving information seekers roam the traditional and social media landscapes, trawling comments and sentiments shared by the public and the media at large. In this social media era, where everyone is a publisher—or even propagandist and marketer—your truth squads need to be on hand to correct inaccurate information immediately and to mitigate misinformation, spread deliberately or otherwise, so that you remain in control of the crisis communication narrative.

Maintaining control is also reliant on successful integration through all four PESO channels. There should not be four separate thrusts along each channel, but a unified message that affirms the authority behind effective crisis communications. Again, simply putting messages out there is not enough; there has to be constant evaluation and monitoring of responses to the messages, and the flexibility to modify or even test a new angle if the results do not pan out as expected.

AFTER A CRISIS

While the immediate crisis may fade over time, you should not make the mistake of assuming that the worst has blown over and crisis communications can cease. With the frequency at which cyber Breaches occur, the media is likely to continue quoting your action or inaction when your company was Breached, especially if you are a reputable or well-known entity.

There are potential crises in the making as well, with various experts and subject authorities picking through your management of the crisis, your security measures, and whether you should even have been holding the data that was Breached. Appropriate communication is needed to justify your actions, so it is prudent to retain a small team dedicated to managing crisis communications, even after the main phase has concluded, to ensure that aftershocks do not develop into earthquakes in the future.

Discovery-to-Notification Time Gap

One of the first things the media may seize upon, even while the crisis is unfolding, is the discovery-to-notification time gap in the wake of a cyber Breach. Some companies might be fortunate enough to discover the Breaches while they are operational and online, but oftentimes it is only when the harvested information surfaces on the internet that companies realize that they have even been Breached at all.

Again, the speed imperative comes into play. It is vital that you prove to your stakeholders that you are serious about cyber Breaches by communicating to them in the very first instance, followed by regular updates. Remember that if you wait until you know everything, in the end you will not say anything. Your silence not only forces the media to turn to other, less reliable sources, but makes you appear culpable for the Breach instead.

In crises, the natural human instinct is—and often reinforced by legal counsel—to know more about what has happened before saying anything. This is an unsustainable position: those that trust you and your brand need to hear from you, to know that you are in control and will resolve the crisis. Silence is not golden, it can be damning, leaving the field open to others to define your reputation.

While your initial response and notifications to stakeholders may be swift, every second of the Breach that goes unnoticed can be a point of condemnation, calling into question your cyber security safeguards and processes that should have picked up on the Breach, even if they were unable to prevent it.

Adequacy of Safeguards in Place

As your company picks up the pieces after a cyber Breach, there will no doubt be internal assessments on how your cyber defenses were Breached in the first place. Similarly, the way in which you go about showing how you reacted and, if the Breach was not the result of lax security, proving your innocence, may very well affect the decision of your stakeholders to continue putting faith and trust in your company.

Security experts and the media may not have the full picture about your cyber security system and it might be unwise to overshare the specifics. There is a very fine line to tread in showing the elements of your system that support your stand that your cyber security safeguards were adequate at the time of the Breach, while not revealing so much that you might be further compromised in the future.

While high walls do not guarantee invulnerability, you must point to them as manifestations of your due diligence in trying to prevent cyber Breaches. Although you are still ultimately responsible for the Breach, your stakeholders must be persuaded that your systems and safeguards were effective in mitigating the threat, and that a similar Breach will not occur again in the future.

Appropriateness of Data Held

The Big Data trend is proving to be a double-edged sword for companies; while the information collated is immensely useful for your company operations, a cyber Breach will result in hard questions on whether you should even be holding so much information in the first place.

Given that there is no 100% guarantee that your databases will not be Breached, it is prudent to curate the information that you decide to store very carefully and be able to justify its continued retention. You must also understand that even if you are not holding particularly sensitive information on your customers, such as medical records, the information siphoned can still be used for other purposes, especially when we use similar or identical login details for different websites.

Expert Analysis of Your Preparation and Response

Finally, keep in mind that while the trauma of the crisis you have undergone may fade, scars will be left behind in the form of industry experts using their analysis and commentary on your management of the crisis to burnish their own credentials and thought leadership. That is to say, you become a case study for others.

What this means is that your handling of the crisis will continually be held up as either a lightning rod for criticism and a prime negative example, or as a paragon of what effective and appropriate crisis management should be like. In either case, the repercussions will continue impacting your reputation long after the crisis itself has concluded.

Summary

If a crisis came calling today, are you comfortable that your company has the right plan and the right people in place, fully prepared to respond swiftly to communicate clearly and consistently and therefore effectively in the event of a data Breach – all in order to show authentic leadership? Or are you simply in a position to check boxes off a list in managing your crisis, rather than taking leadership of your company's reputation? These are questions—and realities—that need to be confronted before it's too late.

Your management's response and its messaging and positioning during a data Breach either compounds or mitigates the reputational impact. Preparing before a Breach actually occurs, allows for rapid and authentic communication when mitigating crises. A company which is able to do this reinforces their cyber resilience: the ability to become strong, healthy, or successful again after something bad happens.

CHAPTER 8

Restoring Trust and Business Services After a Breach

Kevvie Fowler, Chris Pogue, Paul Hanley

INTRODUCTION

When news of a data Breach spreads across an organization, the immediate focus is on containment which is effectively stopping the bleeding. Shortly after the incident is contained, focus shifts to restoring business operations which may have been taken offline during the containment of a Breach or in an effort to protect the organization from (at the time) any unknown threat that may have been spreading within the environment.

Each minute that key systems are down is revenue that is not being generated, employees that are being less productive and are clients who aren't being serviced. Recovery is of paramount importance to an organization suffering a Breach; however, providing some degree of assurance as to the scope and severity of the Breach or when business services can be expected to resume is equally important to internal stakeholders, clients, and third parties such as partners and vendors.

When thinking about compromised hosts, finding the impacted systems, remediating the vulnerabilities associated with the Breach, and recovering from the attack may seem like a pretty straight-forward activity in theory, until you find yourself actually face to face with this daunting task; that's when uncertainty sets in. How do you identify the compromised hosts? How do you ensure you got the scope of the Breach correct? What standard should you use to rebuild the systems? How do you know if you have effectively recovered from the Breach? This chapter will provide you with answers to these questions, as well as additional guidance that will assist you in detecting compromised hosts, isolating and recovering them to a trusted state, and restoring business services.

THE DIFFERENCE BETWEEN CONTAINMENT AND RECOVERY

The words containment and recovery are often used interchangeably; when discussed however, they are truly different activities driven by different

CONTENTS

187

Data Breach Preparation and Response. http://dx.doi.org/10.1016/B978-0-12-803451-4.00008-3

objectives. Within the scope of this book, containment and recovery are defined as follows:

> *Containment*—Removing or isolating compromised hosts and severing unauthorized access within an environment.
> *Recovery*—Removing, rebuilding, or restoring systems and networks to a trusted state.

To draw an analogy, if a team of horses got out of their barn and were running loose within a farmer's lot, closing the main gate to the road would contain the incident by preventing the horses from spilling out onto the main road or adjacent yards. Recovery on the other hand would involve returning each horse to their individual stall within the stable in the barn and securing them properly so they don't escape again. Stopping the bleeding (containment) and restoring order (recovery) are both essential steps in restoring trust within an environment and resuming business operations.

RECOVERING YOUR ENVIRONMENT

During a Breach getting the victim organization back to normal business operations is a core priority for responders. At this stage you will likely have your suspicions about what may be compromised and whether there is unauthorized access actively occurring within your environment. It's fine to have a hunch of what you "think" is going on but when stabilizing your environment, a good rule of thumb is to trust nothing and take nothing for granted. In the words of the late great American President, Ronald Reagan, "Trust but verify."

Getting back to business will be a journey requiring focus, patience, and experience. This journey will begin with regaining control over what is likely to be a very dynamic environment with several people or teams actively involved to try and ascertain what happened.

Regaining Control Over the Environment

Often when news of a Breach hits, several people who aren't part of the CSIR Plan will try to insert themselves into the response, whether communicating with senior executives about the Breach, response teams on priorities or even leading independent aspects of the investigation themselves. During a crisis, it's basic human nature to want to help, however, this sort of "help" can be counterproductive if shared CSIR Team resources are focused investigating the wrong things or if the inaccurate information is being circulated about the Breach internally or externally to the organization. To this end, two disciplines must be exercised early in the Breach life cycle. The first is that your organization must establish a communication path to ensure updates regarding the

Breach are managed by one individual who will coordinate with the appropriate internal stakeholder(s). This is normally the public relations director or general counsel. The second is to control access to the environment where the Breach has taken place (or is believed to be). Both of these should be outlined within your CSIR Plan; however, in my experience these are two areas that most often become strained. With these foundational elements under control the following additional measures can be executed to further regain control over the environment.

Halting All Changes Within the Environment

The last thing you need when trying to restore trust are other IT employees or contractors installing software on hosts of interest, logging in and applying patches to systems, or restarting machines as part of their scheduled changes. All of these activities can contaminate the "crime scene" by introducing additional evidence, while diluting or destroying existing evidence such as volatile information, file system activity, and Registry last write times. Without question, this will increase the complexity of your investigation. Halting changes also allows you to ensure evidence is preserved on in scope hosts, perform assessment activities such as scanning hosts for vulnerabilities or evidence of unauthorized access (which we'll discuss later in this chapter) and determining anomalous changes which can serve as activity relevant to the investigation.

Isolating Systems

Whether identifying a system believed to be compromised or a system you would like to isolate in an effort to prevent it from being compromised, *don't power them off!* They can contain valuable volatile data such as active processes, port mappings, logged in users, and active network communications—all of which are lost once the system is shut down. This is an active crime scene and may contain evidence that helps prove a system you are disconnecting to prevent compromise—either wasn't compromised or that a system you believed was compromised wasn't actually compromised at all.

Logically, segmenting systems can support containment and at the same time in most cases will not jeopardize evidence relevant to the Breach. We'll cover some methods that can be used to determine which ones to collect evidence from later in this chapter.

Changing System and Application User Credentials as Needed

Credentials allow both interactive and remote access to systems and applications and are often used by attackers that use them as a form of back door to maintain a foothold within an environment, even after the initial point of entry has been remediated. Your investigation earlier in the Breach response life cycle should have identified accounts that were disclosed or identified to have been used as part of the Breach. The passwords, and if possible the usernames, should be changed to severe the exposure or unauthorized access within the environment; this is true of user accounts as well as service accounts. It should be noted that changing user or service accounts linked to application can have an adverse affect on application stability. Testing should be performed after account changes to reduce the livelihood of impact. Changes made to accounts as part of containment or recovery should be reflected in your investigation notes and discounted from your analysis.

Controlling Access to Backups as Needed

The need to secure and preserve backups is critical in event of an investigation as well as restoring trust to an environment. Backups can be used to restore files in event of an incident, however they can also serve as a material source of risk in hindering the restoration of trust within an environment or even undoing trust that has been restored to an environment. The following are just a few examples of why it is critical to secure and preserve backups during an incident:

- Online backup can be at risk of network threats such as ransomware that can infect a machine and also online network backup files that may be present
- Allowing backups to continue on compromised systems can overwrite last known good data with those of compromised systems. Ensure to understand the backup retention period and use the known timeline of the attack to identify if data from compromised systems is included in backups you may be hoping to use to restore systems or business services
- Backups can be requested by multiple business units for a variety of purposes. In event of an incident ensuring that backups containing compromised systems are identified and removed from the backup retention/rotation will help prevent the reinfection of a threat within an environment
- Backups can contain system and application logs as well as temporary files and swap memory that can contain evidence of lateral movement within an environment by an intruder
- During a Breach it's easy for someone to request data or information they normally would not be allowed access to

Deploying Monitoring Equipment

Network monitoring is an invaluable step in identifying malicious or suspicious activity for further investigation. Existing equipment within your environment may or may not have capabilities needed for the network monitoring. Alternatively, you may have spare monitoring devices that have yet to be connected to the environment in question which you may choose to leverage for the network monitoring. Even if you do have the requisite equipment, and it does have the necessary capabilities, you will likely be dealing with an environment where you don't yet know the scope of the Breach and therefore may not be able to trust the devices within your environment, or you would be gathering network packet captures in such volume that storage and analysis could become unwieldy. Another alternative is to leverage trusted equipment on a temporary basis from a vendor or your forensic services provider. Regardless of the source, ensure to use trusted equipment as part of network monitoring or you run the risk that evidence obtained from it may not be accurate and can't be relied up on within your investigation or for future legal proceedings.

Secondary Communication Channels

Until the integrity of your email and VOIP systems can be confirmed, you should find alternative methods to communicate about the incident. This includes the technical response teams as well as executives, legal counsel, and even members of the Board. Criminals have been known to compromise communication systems in past high-profile attacks.[1] There are vendors such as Crisis Response Pro,[2] AtHoc,[3] or iPR Software[4] that provide software solutions specifically designed to provide secure communications in a crisis situation.

You should set guidelines for the type of information that should be documented and emailed regarding the Breach, especially if the secondary communication channel is a cloud email provider; which can introduce additional risks to manage. As part of preBreach planning, identifying this secondary Breach communication channel will hopefully have occurred and the risks associated with assessing the security and risk with using the third party has been assessed.

With control over you environment regained, you can proceed with identifying the compromised hosts and expelling the known evil presently within your environment.

Identifying Compromised Hosts

Identifying compromised hosts is not a trivial task. Attacks today are often stealthy and advanced, making them extremely hard to detect. To draw an analogy, if you look at allergic reactions, in some cases the first time a person suffers a reaction they definitely know from the physical symptoms they are having a reaction, however it can sometimes be very difficult to immediately identify the specific product they consumed, touched, or smelled that triggered the reaction. Coming back to the cyber realm, you will know a Breach has been experienced; however, finding the source and the systems and data involved can be a challenge. Further complicating things, missing just one compromised host can

[1] http://www.theguardian.com/technology/2012/feb/03/anonymous-hacks-call-fbi-scotland-yard.

[2] http://crisisresponsepro.com/.

[3] http://www.athoc.com/.

[4] http://iprsoftware.com/solutions/crisiscomm.

leave a backdoor to the environment that will allow the criminals to retain their foothold within the organization which can lead to a subsequent Breach. You need to find out the infected hosts, and do so in an efficient manner. A great approach at accomplishing this feat is using Indicators of Compromise and Indicators of Attack.

Using Indicators of Compromise and Indicators of Attack

The term Indicator of Compromise was coined by the government and defense contractors back in 2007 when hunting advanced persistent threats (APTs). An IoC is simply an artifact that is left on a system or network that signifies a known threat or attack has occurred. The evolution of IoCs are Indicators of Attack (IoA), which focus on the activity a criminal would use after they've penetrated a system or device. Simply put, IoCs look for traces of payloads or signs of an exploit that was used in an attack and IoAs look for traces of activity that are typically seen after a system is exploited. There is debate within the industry which is the better solution to detect traces of the complex attacks of today. It's my opinion that it's an "and" solution not an "or" solution. Both IoCs and IoAs have benefit in a Breach investigation and I think to choose one over another during an investigation will result in missing relevant indicators that can better determine scope of the Breach. Fig. 8.1 shows an abbreviated attack life cycle with examples of the phases that IoCs and IoAs could help detect activity within.

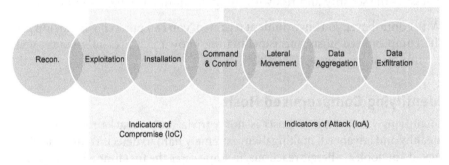

FIGURE 8.1 IoC and IoA scope of coverage during an example investigation.

Depending on the nature of a Breach, IoCs and IoAs can apply to more or less stages of the attack life cycle; however, Fig. 8.1 provides an example to help illustrate the differences between the two.

We won't be able to do a deep dive on IoCs or IoAs within this chapter. In order to provide the most meaningful content for you, we will focus on IoCs which are more mature in the industry and are associated with a wider range of tools and frameworks.

Developing an IoC can be as simple as writing a Windows batch script to execute at logon and identify specific registry entries on a Windows server. On the opposite end of the spectrum, IoCs can also involve identifying anomalous egress network activity, account activity, registry and file changes, login activity, and file access. IoCs should be specific and generate minimum false positives in order to provide value during an investigation.

There are a few industry frameworks that standardize the format of IoCs and ensure tools and products can interpret, execute, and analyze the data returned from an IoC search (which we'll cover later in this chapter). The following are some of the popular frameworks at the time of this writing.

OpenIOC. Developed by Mandiant, OpenIOC definitions are XML and provide over 500 terms that can be used to identify a threat. There are limited commercial products that leverage this standard.

Mitre standards (CyBOX, STIX, TAXII). Cyber Observable eXpression (CybOX), Structure Threat Information Expression (STIX), and Trusted Automated eXchange of Indicator Information (TAXII) are three XML-based IoC standards that were developed by Mitre and are being accepted by a wide range of industry's leading providers with STIX and TAXII seeing the widest adoption.

For the examples in this chapter we will use the OpenIOC framework[5] which comes with over 500 IoCs prebuilt and there are other several sites that publish and share IoCs developed through the community such as IOCBucket[6] which publishes hundreds or additional IoCs. The threat at the source of your Breach may not be known, so you may be patient zero, and need to develop your own IoCs to search for across your environment to identify compromised hosts. The easiest way to do this is through tools.

Tools

As we covered earlier, there are multiple ways to create an IoC; you could write a custom IPS signature, a regex-based script to search a filesystem for keywords within a file or leveraging a framework. Looking squarely at The OpenIOC framework, there are tools that have been developed and released to assist in the development and execution of the IoCs as well as interpret and analyze the results. Two free tools for doing this are IOC Editor,[7] a tool developed to allow the creation and viewing of IoCs and Redline,[8] a tool for collecting host information and searching it for the IoCs.

---

[5]http://www.openioc.org/.

[6]https://www.iocbucket.com/search.

[7]https://www.fireeye.com/services/freeware/ioc-editor.html.

[8]https://www.fireeye.com/services/freeware/redline.html.

Regardless of the tool used, the IoC is only as good as your understanding of the threat and the indicators to include within the IoC that will return relevant information with minimal false positives.

Determining What to Search for

I find when looking for the source of the Breach you start broad and work your way back to a precise number of hosts of interest. Starting broad includes looking for anomalies across both the network and the hosts within the compromised environment.

On the Network

Review broader network logs looking at traffic patterns to get a sense of what normal looks like so that it will be easier for you to identify when something is abnormal. You hopefully will have Netflow or other traffic that can be analyzed against a known good baseline. In addition, it's a good idea to look for connections to geographies that you do not do business with or remote systems that normally wouldn't be interacting with systems in your network. It's important to set the scope at both ingress connections (those originating from abnormal places) as well as egress connections (connections originating from your network to remote abnormal locations). In addition to firewall logs, Security Information Event Management (SIEM) systems and security controls such as Network Antivirus and Network IPS systems can be helpful as well in identifying a Host of Interest (HoI) on the network.

On Hosts

Your organization should have master images of servers/devices, per type, frequently referred to as "Gold Standard Images." For example, a webserver image, a corporate desktop image, etc. These images should be trusted and have the hardening of software and files for each type of system within the untrusted environment. Using this gold standard and hashing each file with SHA-2 or another secure hashing algorithm will allow you to generate a standard for what "known-good" looks like. You can use this standard and compare all other devices of that class, against, to identify anomalies.

Checking Identity and Access Management systems or equivalent (Windows Active Directory, etc.) for large volumes or patterns of failed login attempts followed abruptly by a successful login and newly created user accounts or existing accounts that have had privileges augmented can also identify HoI's and activity that can be incorporated into your timeline which will likely be dynamically updating with events and activity as you go through recovery.

When a HoI is found, it should be imaged and analyzed to discount or confirm if it indeed has been compromised. When you identify suspicious activity that appears to be associated with the incident, look at that activity in relation to a timeline of events to determine what other activity occurred on the system or network on or around the same time. This should include host activity, network activity, email, or social media communication and the access of registry and database object timestamps. At this point you should have an indicator of systems, common files, registry entries, or communication patterns that have been deemed as malicious. These can serve as the details needed to develop an IoC or IoA that can be helpful in identifying other HoIs compromised using the same methods.

Developing Indicators of Compromise

With an understanding of the IoC XML schema to use (we're using OpenIOC in this chapter) you can create an IoC using any text editor such as Notepad. IoCs however are typically developed using tools which provide a GUI-based interface to the wide range of available indicator terms and simplify the development of the XML files. A few principles that can be applied to develop a good IoC are as follows:

- *Focus on the elements of an attack that are difficult to change.* Attack tools are hard-coded to use specific files and registry entries in addition to allowing an attacker to specify the name of output files, etc. Developing an IoC looking for the default name of an output file that the attack tool would use that is easily changed by an attacker would be an example of a poorly developed IoC. It may have a low degree of false positives; however, it could be easily circumvented. In contrast, developing an IoC to look for hardcoded elements an attack tool is designed to use would not so easily be circumvented, requiring an attacker to alter the attack tool binary
- *Known registry entries and files that are directly linked to malicious threats.* Also consider opportunities to whitelist as well opposed to blacklist. Instead of looking for a known bad file, look for the existence of a file in a directory where it shouldn't be
- *Have a low number of false positives.* IoCs should be developed and tested to ensure they operate as expected and don't generate a large number of false positives

With the above in mind, let's look at how IOC Editor[9] can be used to develop an IOC.

1. Install and launch IOC Editor
2. Select **File | New** from the menu
3. Add search terms based on the behaviors you have seen on your HoI. Please refer to the guidance covered earlier in this chapter on developing good IoCs. Fig. 8.2 contains a sample IoC that searches for files containing the strings "Mikaela Fowler" or "Isaiah Fowler" or having an MD5 hash of 016da6ee744b16656a2ba3107c7a4a29

---

[9]https://www.fireeye.com/services/freeware/ioc-editor.html.

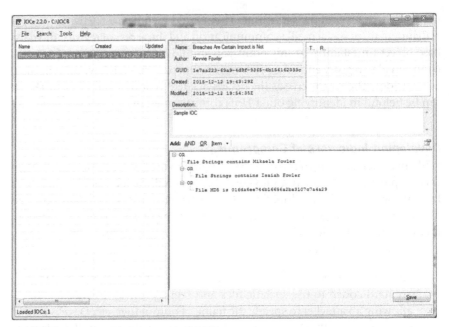

FIGURE 8.2 Sample IOC viewed within IOC Editor.

4. Pressing the **File** | **Save** option from the menu allows you to save the IoC into an.ioc file. The contents of the IoC file created in the previous step can be seen in Fig. 8.3

```
<?xml version="1.0" encoding="us-ascii"?>
<ioc xmlns:xsi="http://www.w3.org/2001/XMLSchema-instance"
xmlns:xsd="http://www.w3.org/2001/XMLSchema" id="1e7aa223-69a9-4d9f-9365-4b156162333c"
last-modified="2015-12-12T19:54:35" xmlns="http://schemas.mandiant.com/2010/ioc">
  <short_description>Breaches Are Certain Impact is Not</short_description>
  <description>Sample IOC</description>
  <authored_by>Kevvie Fowler</authored_by>
  <authored_date>2015-12-12T19:43:29</authored_date>
  <links />
  <definition>
    <Indicator operator="OR" id="bd313e98-ec3d-4198-852a-58bacb43b1ec">
      <IndicatorItem id="dd40e33e-834c-4ec8-9327-8f9ae0cc4885" condition="contains">
        <Context document="FileItem" search="FileItem/StringList/string" type="mir" />
        <Content type="string">Mikaela Fowler</Content>
      </IndicatorItem>
      <Indicator operator="OR" id="e97f9dfb-52c7-4f31-829f-8258b056f04c">
        <IndicatorItem id="73427bfc-fcba-4e99-94bf-fef8dffb625f" condition="contains">
          <Context document="FileItem" search="FileItem/StringList/string" type="mir" />
          <Content type="string">Isaiah Fowler</Content>
        </IndicatorItem>
      </Indicator>
      <Indicator operator="AND" id="bfd0a808-29f5-43c2-bcaa-3e7591a82078">
        <IndicatorItem id="d2ddd40b-2eae-46cb-a7fa-d0fdd252b52e" condition="is">
          <Context document="FileItem" search="FileItem/Md5sum" type="mir" />
          <Content type="md5">016da6ee744b16656a2ba3107c7a4a29</Content>
        </IndicatorItem>
      </Indicator>
    </Indicator>
  </definition>
</ioc>
```

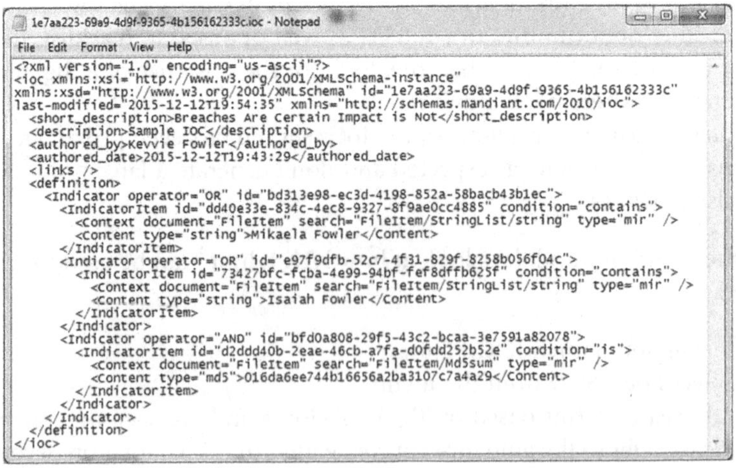

FIGURE 8.3 Sample OpenIOC-based IoC.

At this stage you will have your IoC(s) developed and we'll look at using the Redline tool to gather data and search for the IoC(s).

Searching for Indicators of Compromise

As we covered earlier in this chapter, Redline[10] is a freeware tool that can be used to gather data from hosts and scan for developed IoCs.

1. Install and Launch Redline
2. From the main you will be able to create a collector which will gather information from HoIs that you have identified. In our example, we'll select **"Create an IOC Search Collector"** from the main screen. Entering the location of the created IoCs will load them into RedLine as captured in Fig. 8.4

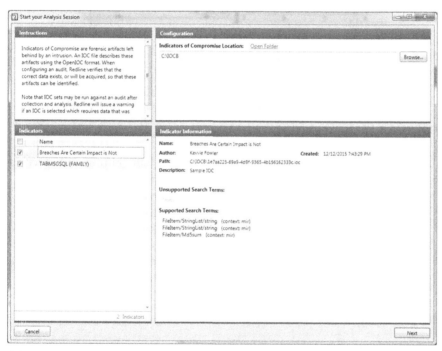

FIGURE 8.4 Sample redline collector viewed within Redline.

3. Selecting the **Next** link and then the "**Edit your script**" link will present you with a number of options of artifacts that can be selected for collection on targeted hosts. Fig. 8.5 shows the displayed options

---

[10]https://www.fireeye.com/services/freeware/redline.html.

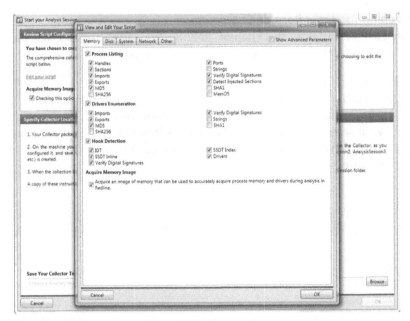

FIGURE 8.5 IoC collector script options within Redline.

4. Once options have been selected, press the "**OK**" button and specify a location to store the created collector followed by "**OK**." When complete close the displayed Collector Instructions dialog box
5. The "**RunRedlineAudit.bat**" file and supporting files will be stored within the specified output directory. Copying these files to removable media such as a USB key is recommended
6. Attaching the USB key (or other removable media) to the HoI, execute the "**RunRedlineAudit.bat**" file which will initiate the collection of artifacts on the HoI as seen in Fig. 8.6

FIGURE 8.6 IOC Collector execution on a Windows computer.

7. Once complete, move the result files to your forensic workstation and launch Redline
8. Selecting "**Analyze Collected Data**" from the Redline logo at the top left of the window supports the import and analysis of the data retrieved from the HoI. You can also enter the directory of the IOC(s) and press the **Next** and **OK** buttons as seen within Fig. 8.7

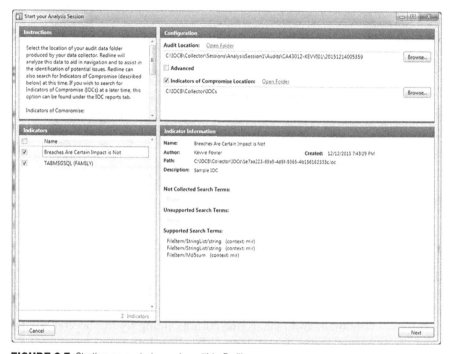

FIGURE 8.7 Starting an analysis session within Redline.

9. Data collected from the HoI is now imported into Redline for analysis as seen in Fig. 8.8
10. Once imported, you will have several analysis options including selecting an "**IOC Reports**" which will determine if the IOC was found on the HOI. Please refer to tool documentation for full features and options

We took a very high level view at using IOC Editor and Redline to build an IoC, gather data from a host of interest, and scanning it for the developed IoC. In addition to using purpose-built IoC tools, you can use security infrastructure tools to also search for IoCs.

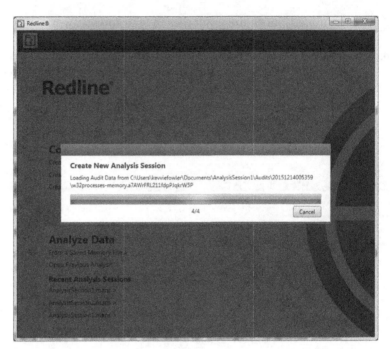

FIGURE 8.8 Importing collected data into Redline.

Using Existing Security Infrastructure

Tools like Redline are great to assess single systems. In an enterprise environment, you will want to leverage other tools better geared for execution of IoCs across an environment and manage the corresponding results. Several SIEMs, Firewalls, Intrusion Prevention Systems (IPS), Host Intrusion Prevention Systems (HIPS), and other security tools allow for either the support of IoC frameworks or the conversion of the IoC into a vendor-specific framework. Please consult the vendor of your security tools for guidance on the support of IoC frameworks within your security tools. Once you identify HoIs or confirmed compromised instances, it is important to quickly isolate and investigate them.

Isolating and Recovering Compromised Systems

When you identify a HoI or confirmed compromised system, do not power it off until volatile information can be preserved. The following steps can be followed to minimize disruption and extract artifacts relevant to better understanding the threats used in the Breach as well as the proper scope of it.

1. *Remove network connectivity.* It's better to remove the network cable or disable the wireless card if it is wireless-enabled as this prevents the further spread or compromise of the device. Powering the device off will destroy volatile information that need to be collected during the next step
2. *Capture system information* that you can use to help build new or refine IoCs. It's a good practice to also capture volatile data, forensic images, and memory to support future forensic analysis if needed. Scopes change, the listing of systems storing sensitive data also often changes. Capturing data will allow you to go back and investigate in response to changes in the scope or direction of an investigation
3. *Take one or more long-term recovery measures.* Some recovery measures are provided below in the order of recommended priority in permanently recovering compromised systems or accounts
   - Rebuild the system or device from a known good image
   - Patch or Reconfigure the system to close the exploited exposure
   - Permanently remove the system, device, or account if it is no longer needed
   - Reset user account passwords that have been confirmed to have been misused or disclosed

Unfortunately an option not on the preceding list, but an approach I've seen taken more times than I would have liked, is the "Do nothing" option. One example is an organization that had their webserver defaced and pages of content rebranded by a cyber terrorist group to promote their cause. The organization skipped steps one and two above and jumped to step three where they simply restored correct web page versions to the server and closed the incident ticket. This effectively was taking the "do nothing" approach by not identifying or addressing the root issue.

You may not decide to take an all or nothing approach; you may rebuild some systems, remove others such as systems that were scheduled to be decommissioned anyway, and patch or reconfigure others. The reasons will vary but ensuring business and system owners are involved in making the final decision and understanding the risk associated with patching or reconfiguring versus rebuilding is known. When decisions are made, options taken for each compromised host (for example all servers within a given subnet were patched instead of being rebuilt for a specific reason) and justification for doing so should be captured. Subsequent incidents or Breaches may arise and understanding how previous systems were recovered will come in helpful in investigating or in future litigation. We cover some additional guidance on how to rebuild, reconfigure, or patch servers in Chapter 5 which you can refer to for additional guidance.

CERTIFYING YOUR ENVIRONMENT

The better you prepare for a Breach the greater the likelihood you can deter, detect, and respond to it. Many organizations experience more than one public data Breach, in some cases in close proximity to each other. In these cases, I often think, who put their hand up to attest:

- The Breach was correctly scoped, managed and recovered from
- There are no other indicators of additional Breaches that have yet to be detected
- You will be able to better prevent, detect, and respond to Breaches in the future based on learning and additional measures put in place after the Breach

The above are very powerful statements, especially in a cyber landscape with threats that experts have long acknowledged can't be detected and will result in Breaches that have and will continue to go undetected. The only hope we have is better responding to them. This can be a difficult statement for anyone to make especially under the pressure to restore business operations efficiently. Some C-Suite executives and Board members have turned to third party service providers to help them ensure they have scoped, responded to, and recovered from the Breach successfully, as well as provide some level of assurance in making the preceding statements that we just reviewed.

Certifying your environment is not going through a formal certification process, rather certifying your environment after a Breach is having an independent individual or team:

1. Review the background of the Breach and how it was scoped
2. How compromised hosts were identified, contained and recovered
3. How gaps in Breach response and management were identified and overcome allowing improvement in event of a repeat Breach

Completion of this review should be done by someone independent from the CSIR Team who managed the Breach, but by a group or individual competent to review, identify gaps or incorrect remediation activity, and provide recommendations on how to correct it. Many organizations bring in an independent third party Breach response team to do this review. Some organizations that have in-house response personnel have their internal cyber response teams complete this step. Regardless of who performs this step, it's important to ensure they are independent. This activity also helps protect the individuals in the trenches who managed, scoped, and recovered the impacted systems. In the heat of a Breach, responders often, despite working in shifts, are running on little sleep with elevated levels of stress, may get too close to the incident in order to maintain independence about what and why certain actions were taken and how required recovery objectives were achieved.

Confirmation from both the Breach response team and the certifying team can be presented to senior management to provide confidence that recovery has been achieved and you're ready to restore business services.

RESTORING BUSINESS SERVICES

With the known evil expelled from your environment you can focus on restoring business services. During the management of the incident logging levels likely have been altered to be more verbose. Devices that were removed from the network may now be introduced with nonstandard settings to support additional verbose logging. This additional logging creates a heightened demand on your network, logging server or SIEM solution and health monitoring should be implemented to ensure this additional load and the normal load of business can run concurrently without impact. A phased approach is recommended turning on the most critical business systems first, monitoring for health, and introducing more systems in order of priority based on business criticality.

When all systems have been restored, heightened monitoring should continue for a period of time to ensure the health of the environment so that there is no malicious activity. A separate response process should be implemented to ensure clarity when suspicious or anomalous network or host activity is identified during this period. When verbose logging is disabled, a new baseline of network and system activity can be generated to use future compromise detection and troubleshooting.

When services have been restored and things begin to return to a state of normalness, it's important to conduct what is known as a postmortem review.

CONDUCTING A BREACH POSTMORTEM REVIEW

A positive outcome associated with each Breach is the opportunity to learn and improve your ability to prevent, detect, and respond to future incidents. This learning however will be embedded within the minds of each member of the CSIR Team, who each filled different roles and encountered issues and success throughout the management of the Breach. Conducting a postmortem review (also referred to as an After Action Review or AAR) allows you to extract the key takeaways from all involved stakeholders and share it with other members of the team for reinforcement of what worked well and improvement in areas requiring focus in the management of Breaches.

The Breach postmortem review should happen as soon as possible after the recovery of an incident to ensure thoughts, challenges, and successes are still fresh in the minds of those involved. The following guidance is also recommended for consideration:

- Attendees should be aware of the purpose of the meeting in advance and instructed to bring any Breach-related notes or documentation that they may have
- Avoid the blame game. Reflect and improve, don't deflect and blame others or yourself for the Breach
- Ask open-ended questions. The goal is to share, not dictate

A sample that can be used for the Breach postmortem meeting is:

1. *Introductions* (you may have run multiple response teams or shifts resulting in members of the CSIR Team not officially meeting)
2. *Clarify the objective of the meeting* is not to lay blame but to reflect and improve in future response
3. *Review Breach events*
4. *Discuss opportunities for improvement and action items*

When reviewing the Breach response, it's important to replay the events from the point you first learned about the Breach through Breach containment and finally to recovery and business resumption. This should be done while stepping through each phase of the Breach life cycle (up until the present which will likely be the Postmortem phase) based on the Breach life cycle we discussed in Chapter 1. Table 8.1 contains sample questions that can be asked to the postmortem attendees to help identify Breach management success and areas for improvement.

Table 8.1 Sample Postmortem Questions

Phase of Breach Response	Postmortem Questions
Preparedness	- Did you self-detect the incident? - Did you have a SOP to manage the incident?
Detection	- When was the indicator of Breach reported? - When was the Breach qualified?
Invoking the CSIR Team	- When was the CSIR Team engaged - How long did it take them to assemble? - Was the incident prequalified by the CSIR Team?
Qualification	- When was the incident classified as a security incident? - When was the security incident classified as a data Breach?

Table 8.1 Sample Postmortem Questions—cont'd

Phase of Breach Response	Postmortem Questions
Engaging third parties	■ How long did it take to gain voice contact with the required third party? ■ Did the third party experience any challenges in fulfilling their documented role? (procurement, approvals, R&R confusion)? ■ Were applicable investigation updates delivered to and from the third party as expected?
Breach investigation	■ When did the investigation begin? ■ How long did it take? ■ Did the Breach scope change, if so why? ■ Were you able to precisely scope the Breach? ■ Did you have the right skills and equipment to perform the investigation? ■ Did you identify root cause of the Breach?
Containment	■ How long did it take to contain the incident? ■ Did you meet defined Breach containment timeframes (Priority/Severity 1 – 4)?
Notification and inquiry management	■ Did notification and escalation happen as documented in the CSIR Plan?
Postmortem	■ How long after the incident did the postmortem meeting occur?
Recovery	■ Were required system build books, gold images and software available to rebuild systems? ■ Was data needed for recovery available and successfully restored?
Environment validation and business resumption	■ During environment validation, was an issue identified that was missed by the initial incident response effort?
General	■ Was the CSIR Plan followed effectively? ■ Was the CSIR Plan effective in managing the incident?

Ensure to document the meeting minutes including action items so stakeholders have a record and can report back to the group with progress and updates. Some organizations use internal audit teams to track and ensure remediation of assigned action items.

One of the objectives for the meeting is to identify areas for improvement. As we discussed earlier in this book, organizations are sometimes sued not for negligence in protecting information but rather for managing the detection, management, and notification associated with the Breach. Some of these details may come out in your postmortem review, so it's important to ensure that this information and the meeting minutes are protected appropriately in order to limit their potential inclusion within future litigation.

■ Refer to the guidance in Chapter 9 and more importantly, speak to your legal counsel about how best to protect the communication under privilege

- Control distribution—limit the number of people who will receive or come in contact with the meeting minutes
- If third parties are engaged in the postmortem review, ensure that contracts are in place and they are retained through a lawyer to shield Breach-related findings and communication

The postmortem review is the last step in the short-term recovery of the environment. Following this moves into the long-term objective of improving cyber security.

IMPROVING CYBER SECURITY AFTER A BREACH

The silver lining associated with a Breach is the ability for an organization to improve their overall cyber security posture. In the wake of a Breach, the visibility and renewed focus on the importance of cyber security couldn't be more evident, however, in the immortal words of Stan Lee, "with great power comes great responsibility." Investments should be made wisely and will often be accompanied by expectations from management that the investment will improve the organization's cyber security posture or reactive capabilities. Avoiding the following pitfalls can help ensure you are picking the correct initiatives to improve organizational cyber security posture and meet management's expectations:

1. *Deploying unnecessary security tools.* There are a lot of security tools in the industry. These tools are developed for different organizations at different levels of cyber security maturity. Ensure to first develop a strategy of what you want to achieve, then look for specific solutions that will provide those tactical capabilities. Your organization may not be at the right state of maturity to deploy some of the new cutting-edge technology products in the market today without first implementing a litany of dependencies that will prepare them for these more advanced solutions. One example is deploying Data Loss Prevention (DLP) without first identifying and classifying your data. To improve security you will need a strategy (which we discuss later in this chapter) and some technology may be the right solution; however, it's more than simply throwing money at the problem, despite what you may hear from security vendors. To truly improve upon your organization's post Breach security posture, you need a combination of strategy and the right solutions at the right time
2. *Focusing solely on the root cause of the recent Breach.* Focusing on the one exposure at the source of your recent Breach will only help your organization if you can go back in time, and will only protect you against that specific attack. Looking forward, there is no guarantee that the next attack will target the same exposure as your recent Breach (in fact, if

that happens, your post-Breach remediation efforts have failed miserably). Your organization likely has a number of exposures and vulnerabilities that may have a higher likelihood of exploitation. When looking to improve your cyber security posture, it's important not only to address the vulnerabilities that permitted the recent Breach but also assess, identify, and remediate any other threat vectors within your organization that could potentially be exploited in the future

In the wake of a Breach, it's important to go back to basics of IT Hygiene. I'm not saying you need to disregard your entire security program but you do have to start at the beginning and look at the information you are trying to protect, the best way to protect this information and how you can demonstrate you were doing the right things (should the need arise—and it likely will). This is referred to as establishing a Cyber Defensible Position.

CREATING A CYBER DEFENSIBLE POSITION

It is difficult to identify how much time, resources, and money an organization should dedicate to tackling cyber security issues. There is no "one size fits all" solution and as such each organization needs to decide on the right balance for themselves. However, there are some best practice approaches that can help to provide an organization with the right balance to assist in proactively preventing a Breach from occurring, or to adopt following a Breach. The approach is called identifying and achieving your Cyber Defensible Position.

Why would you need a Cyber Defensible Position? A Cyber Defensible Position can be defined as a posture that your organization has implemented, given your organization's assets and specific Cyber security risks and threats, to significantly reduce the impact should a Cyber security Breach occur. In the event of a Breach, a good Cyber Defensible Position can provide:

- A reduction in the likelihood of fines and lawsuits from clients, regulators, and Government bodies
- A strong foundation upon which to defend your actions should the case move to litigation
- A reduction in the backlash from customers who may otherwise take their business elsewhere
- A reduction in the impact to share price and the reaction to this from shareholders
- Less attention paid to your Breach by the media
- Overall protection of your brand

In addition, the exercise of obtaining your Cyber Defensible Position will by its very nature reduce the likelihood of a successful Breach occurring in the first place.

Cyber Defensible Position Benefits

The exercise to establish your Cyber Defensible Position is a structured approach to reduce the overall cyber security risk posture within your organization.

In addition, identifying and creating a good Cyber Defensible Position will provide a clear advantage to the organization should it experience a cyber security Breach in the future. Doing so will help the organization to articulate the following:

- We kept the Board and senior executives apprised on cyber risks internally and relevant emerging industry threats
- We followed good cyber security governance practices, using an internationally recognized standard
- We used external experts to help review and improve our security
- We regularly reviewed our risks, keeping up-to-date with the latest threats and vulnerabilities
- We had strong technical controls
- We used good patch management of all software and firmware within the infrastructure
- We had good cyber security awareness training program across staff, clients, and partners
- We conducted cyber Breach simulation exercises utilizing the expertise of an external service provider
- We conducted realistic, human-driven security technical testing of our systems and infrastructure
- We detected, managed, and recovered from other incidents in a timely and forensically sound manner
- We mapped our security controls to the prevention, detection, and reaction to security incidents

By adopting this approach, it means that staff, partners, regulators, and the public can clearly see that your organization took security seriously and attempted to implement the correct level of due diligence and attention to prevent, detect, and recovery from Breaches.

Achieving Your Cyber Defensible Position

To obtain an effective Cyber Defensible Position, an organization must be able to demonstrate that it takes security seriously. Part of this is demonstrating that it performed more than simply a cursory glance and doesn't treat it like a "tick box" exercise.

As a minimum prerequisite to achieve your Cyber Defensible Position, an organization must:

- Identify critical data assets (we reviewed how to do this in Chapter 2)
- Identify the specific risks, threats posed to this data
- Assess how current practices compare to established industry standards and best practices
- Put a plan in place to mitigate or accept the risks

There are a number of steps to take for achieving a good Cyber Defensible Position, summarized in Table 8.2.

Table 8.2 Obtaining Your Cyber Defensible Position

Step	Activity	Approach
Step 1	Plan	■ Planning activities to ensure the assessment is completed in an efficient and effective manner ■ Identify the scope of activities, including the controls in scope, the geographies and locations to be assessed, the key stakeholders, and key success criteria
Step 2	Identify your present state of Cyber Security	■ Understanding and evaluating your organization's current cyber security status (example, how comprehensive your cyber security program is when compared to the industry standards and best practices of other organizations of similar size and industry) ■ Use recognized security frameworks to complete an assessment ■ Perform realistic, human-driven security technical testing
Step 3	Identify your target state of Cyber Security	■ Determining your preferred future maturity rating, together with observations and recommendations (example, what is your organization's target level of security practice (the desired Defensible Position of Reasonableness)) ■ Define a target state of security ■ Accept or mitigate risks
Step 4	Develop a plan to achieve your target state of Cyber Security	■ Helping formulate a high-level action plan to address recommendations (example, what needs to be done to address any gaps to include the work needed to achieve these targets). Ensure a program is put in place to implement the mitigating controls. Key Performance indicators (KPIs), post implementation testing, and other security metrics should be identified to ensure the controls are functioning as expected

The following sections discuss the steps outlined in Table 8.2 in more detail.

Phase 1: Plan

The formation of an appropriately scoped and agreed upon plan is critical to the success of the engagement. Some of the most critical activities during this phase include:

- Agreeing on the timeline
- Identifying the systems, networks, controls, and activities in scope
- Agreeing on the detailed approach that will be followed (will you be looking at design of controls, effectiveness of controls, or both?)
- Agreeing on the geographic regions in scope (organizations operating in multiple countries will have some unique local challenges that should be understood)
- Understanding other key activities that should be taken into account during the review (such as system upgrades and maintenance freeze periods)
- Identifying key personnel who will be involved in the engagement
- Defining key milestones

An output from this step is typically a detailed work plan of required tasks, timeline, and an initial list of documentation that will assist with the review.

Phase 2: Identify Your Present State of Cyber Security

During this step, a number of inputs are typically analyzed prior to the detailed analysis. These inputs include, but are certainly not limited to:

- Identification of the most sensitive type of data in your organization (often referred to as Crown Jewels information)
- Identification of business-specific cyber risks and threats
- Identification of specific security regulatory, legislative, and contract compliance requirements

With this background information, the Cyber Maturity Assessment and Red Team activities can begin.

Perform a Cyber Maturity Assessment

The baseline to use when performing the Cyber Maturity Assessment needs to be agreed upon prior to actually beginning the assessment. There are many internationally recognized best practice security standards and methodologies that can be used for this purpose including ISO 27001,[11] NIST Cyber Security Framework,[12] SANS Critical Security Controls,[13] Payment Card Industry Data Security Standards,[14] HITRUST,[15] and the OSFI Cyber Security Self-Assessment Guidance.[16]

---

[11]https://en.wikipedia.org/wiki/ISO/IEC_27002.

[12]http://www.nist.gov/cyberframework/upload/cybersecurity-framework-021214.pdf.

[13]https://www.sans.org/critical-security-controls.

[14]https://www.pcisecuritystandards.org/document_library?category=pcidss&document=pci_dss.

[15]https://hitrustalliance.net/hitrust-csf/.

[16]http://www.osfi-bsif.gc.ca/eng/fi-if/in-ai/pages/cbrsk.aspx.

For some organizations, it may make sense to combine multiple parts of these standards to create a consolidated list of requirements to measure against. This will help prevent against "cyber assessment fatigue," where many organizations feel like they are being perpetually measured against multiple different standards. It is also important to identify whether the framework will be used to assess the effectiveness of the design of security, the effectiveness of security, or both. The level of detail should also be identified, and the level and type of evidence may be collected as a result.

Once the framework to measure against has been agreed upon, a current state assessment should be performed, which involves devising the best way to gauge your organization's security capability within each area of the framework. As part of the review, you will ask stakeholders across the organization a series of questions, review provided documentation, and ask to see evidence of any such processes to ensure that they are in place, being followed, and having the desired impact. The insight gained during this review will allow the assignment of a maturity score across each area of the framework, and gaps and weaknesses to be documented and used as part of Phase 3.

Conduct a Red Team Assessment

The second part of identifying your present state of cyber security is to complete a realistic, human-driven, hands-on technical testing (Red Team Exercise). This should not be confused with penetration testing as this activity goes beyond the value of a penetration test, using multiple methods to gain access to systems or data (such as social engineering, client-side attacks, spear phishing campaigns, or physical access), and operates in a manner more closely associated with how a large scale, coordinated criminal syndicate may operate.

It is recommended that the technical testing be tailor-made for your environment. It should be intelligence led, and should be adapted during the exercise based on findings and customer needs. If the approach is too "prescriptive," then it will lack the fluidity and realism of a real world threat simulation and the value will be eroded. Using this "all-sources," realistic method of attack allows the approach to be as close to an actual incident as possible, and allows for areas of weakness to be identified as well as areas of good practice.

Red Team testing includes the following elements.

Intelligence Collection. Use multiple sources to identify information related to the cyber security controls, systems, environments, and employees who may serve as good targets for social engineering. Open Source Intelligence (OSINT) can be used to gather publically available information that could aid or accelerate an attack.

Processing and Analysis. The intelligence collected in the previous step can be analyzed to identify points of vulnerability and exploitation and utilized in the creation of an attack plan.

Attack Planning. Planning is critical for an effective attack to be executed. The team performing the test often uses attack trees to document the environment, exposures, and the attack path with the highest likelihood of success. These should include multiple attack methods with multiple approaches in the event that one avenue leads to a dead end. Typical attacks include USB sticks with malware preloaded on them and left around the car park or other strategic location, social engineering (via phone and email) and application, and network penetration tests. Focused testing can also include 0-day vulnerabilities and custom exploits that are developed for the purposes of the test (the inclusion of this level of service is not typical and will only be offered by teams with advanced technical capabilities).

Execution. The activities from the previous phases will then be used during the execution phase. The attack path and plan is executed by the testing team, commonly in a manner to avoid detection.

Typically there are multiple methods of attack during the execution phase (technological, physical, social), agreed at the onset of the engagement. The team should be clear on the activities they are performing and ensure that any activities that are not covered in the statement of work are discussed with the client prior to inclusion in the testing. Should any such activities not be covered by the indemnification letter, they can be seen as a violation of the contracted agreement, or worse, illegal. Know your boundaries and do not cross them. When performing physical site testing, it is important for testers to carry a letter of authorization with them explaining their role and containing contact details (email address, office phone number, and mobile phone number) of senior individuals that can attest to their permission to conduct the activities. I have witnessed first-hand these letters requested by company security as well as local law enforcement and can say without hesitation that having that letter on my person most certainly kept me out of jail.

Evaluation. This involves an analysis of the results of each attack and determining the level of success of each scenario. Analysis will include an evaluation of the quality of the results, assessing the underlying circumstances of the attack, and identifying any outlying test conditions. The success or failure of each attack devised by the Red Team will be evaluated in detail.

The cycle begins again when the evaluation process results in a key finding that can be exploited and tested further. The process is repeated and the next steps are identified and laid out, until either the objective has been achieved or a defined milestone date has been reached.

Geographic challenges With Red Team activities. It should be noted that certain geographic regions impose legal restrictions on the type and nature of the Red Team testing performed. For example, if a team member is tailgating an employee to try to gain physical access to the site, laws in certain countries mean that they are not permitted to lie if they are challenged. As a consequence, it is critical to ensure that all aspects of the Red Team engagement are considered in advance. As part of this due diligence, it is important to review the terms and conditions of the engagement with legal counsel, and when applicable, local law enforcement. It's far better to have these conversations and so as to understand the nuances of local legislation rather than to be surprised during testing and end up in handcuffs.

Phase 3: Identify Your Target State of Cyber Security

At this stage, the organization should use the combined information from the Cyber Maturity Assessment and the hands-on Red Team assessment to determine the maturity rating of each area in scope.

To identify "how much" security is enough, the organization should identify where it wants to be as a firm, for example, middle of the pack compared to similar organizations, slightly ahead, slightly behind? While there is no formal definition of "how much" is enough, there are indicators and benchmark reports[17] that can be used. In addition, independent security consulting firms can also give their opinion as to how performance is compared to peer organizations based on their knowledge and experience, together with costs and approaches to enhance security maturity. Caution should be used at this point: just because you appear to have the best security among your peers does not mean that it is the right level for you to address the true risk. Global knowledge and experience, together with analysis of trends and predictions for the future, can help guide your organization as it progresses in the security maturation process.

A workshop with the firms' senior management (which could include Board members) should be held to help outline their roadmap to achieve their Defensible Position of Reasonableness. This should include a discussion on the maturity ratings, as well as observations and recommendations which will help management in determining where they expect the organization should be in terms of their Cyber maturity. This also allows the right people to make the right risk-based decisions on Cyber security: either accepting a risk or mitigating it.

---

[17]https://www.bitsighttech.com/hubfs/Insights/Q315_BitSight_Insights_Energy_Utilities.pdf?t=1442931636227&utm_campaign=resource+center&utm_source=hs_automation&utm_medium=email&utm_content=22205572&_hsenc=p2ANqtz-83uH0gdym1fXT2Z6ioyv1QeKOatlAJqHyyiWQ7ANVC2mbi.

Phase 4: Develop a Plan to Achieve Your Target Cyber Security State

Following the agreement of cyber risk appetite (within Phase 3), pragmatic, risk-based observations and recommendations can then be identified and designed to achieve strong cyber security practices.

These activities should form the basis of a project plan, with defined activities, responsibilities and accountabilities, budgets, milestones, and success criteria.

Remediation activities should be regularly tracked, and progress updates provided to senior management. In addition, effective internal security teams should keep up-to-date with the latest cyber threats and vulnerabilities, and should be feeding this information back into the plan on a continuous loop. While adjustments to the plan may need to be made based on this information, the reasons for doing so should be clearly identified.

Following the successful execution of the plan (including the implementation of all mitigating controls), the output will then be a defined Cyber Defensible Position. Defined KPIs and metrics must also be defined and measured even after the implementation of all controls to demonstrate that they are still functioning as required and to make any future enhancements as necessary.

Identifying and obtaining your Cyber Defensible Position is one of the best and pragmatic approaches for an organization to adopt to help reduce the risk of post Breach litigation, as well as government-driven inquiry. It has proven valuable to organizations across all sectors and industries that have adopted it, and for those that believe they have a mature security practice as well as those that are still in their infancy.

SUMMARY

Recovery is not a trivial task. During recovery, systems may look the same by their IP addresses/ranges and builds; however, in reality some are compromised while others may not be. Figuring out which is which can be challenging and at times you can (and will) find yourself not trusting your own judgment. This reminds me of a story from my earlier days in my career. While responding to a rapidly spreading Code Red[18] worm I observed large enterprise switches physically melt after a fan failure and the increased burden of managing worm-related traffic. I've seen a system administrator see the devastation first-hand of the worm and unplugged the network cable from his corporate computer before getting ready to go on vacation. About half way to the door, I then observed him turn around and walk back to his desk and actually unplug the power cable of the computer from the wall while stating "you can never be

---

[18]https://en.wikipedia.org/wiki/Code_Red_(computer_worm).

too safe, huh?". He was trained, knowledgeable but based on what he had recently witnessed no longer trusted his own judgment and his understanding of the threat at hand.

After a Breach, systems and infrastructure are relatively easy to rebuild. You can reinstall software, reimage systems, and redeploy them across the enterprise with relative ease. Trust however is something much more difficult to rebuild and extends far beyond just technology. Yes, data Breaches do involve technology however the loss of trust in technology has a cascading impact to a much broader spectrum. Services that are unavailable when needed or sensitive data intended to be private and secure that is exposed can have a devastating impact on trust with internal employees, business partners, investors, and the general public. When a Breach happens, you can't roll back the hands of time. There are no do-overs. You can however effectively and efficiently respond to minimize the impact to your organization as well as the individuals impacted. The information in this chapter has provided you the guidance needed to contain a Breach, recover from it, and hopefully restore trust within an environment and in turn limit the impact to your organizational brand.

CHAPTER 9

Preparing for Breach Litigation

George S. Takach

INTRODUCTION

Thus far in this book, we have looked at how to prepare for a Breach by developing tailored Breach response processes and selecting and equipping CSIR Teams with the right skills, resources, and training to efficiently and effectively manage a Breach. Part of this Breach management is using advanced database forensic practices to precisely scope a Breach. All of these disciplines share a common objective, to limit the impact of a Breach. One of the most damaging forms of impact associated with a Breach is litigation.

I have two objectives for this chapter. First, to raise your awareness level to the types and extent of Breach litigation. And second, to provide practical recommendations for action to help you avoid Breach litigation (or at least to manage it more effectively if you couldn't avoid it). These two objectives will allow you to go from Breach litigation awareness to action.

Due to the nature of the content in this chapter, I am going to try something new. I will talk about some of the key take away points and then jump into the background behind them.

In terms of awareness, the take away points are:

- We are seeing a rise in the amount of Breach litigation that corresponds with the increase in the number of Breaches
- The kinds of legal liability that support a Breach case are varied, and growing
- Most of the material litigation is framed as a Breach class action case, which can raise the stakes considerably

With the takeaways behind us let's jump head first into Breach litigation, the topic everyone likes to talk about but no one wants to experience firsthand.

217

BREACH LITIGATION

Not every Breach will result in litigation against the organization or company who experienced it, but many do, and therefore it is entirely appropriate for you to prepare as if your Breach, when it occurs (note, not "if" it occurs—but "when") will indeed be accompanied by legal action. In this regard, Fig. 9.1 illustrates the steady growth in the number of privacy Breach incidents in the United States over the past 10 years.

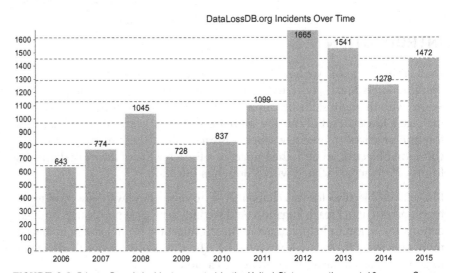

FIGURE 9.1 Privacy Breach incidents reported in the United States over the past 10 years. *Source: http://www.datalossdb.org/statistics.*

The legal claims that flow from these incidents reflect multiple "theories of liability." Many include various types of negligence—essentially, that the organization failed to take adequate measures to secure its computing facilities, whether through state-of-the-art Internet firewalls or other measures. In other cases, contract claims can figure prominently, as when a collection of clients or customers are given contractual confirmation that their personal information will be safeguarded.

There are many other heads of alleged liability that are asserted in these cases. The lawyers acting for plaintiffs in these cases are nothing if not imaginative. In some ground-breaking research, recently, several US law professors studied 230 federal court litigation cases that were brought in the United States between 2005 and 2010 ("Empirical Analysis of Data Breach Litigation," *Journal of Empirical Legal Studies*, Vol. 11, Issue 1, 74–104, March 2014, Sasha

Romanosky, David Hoffman, and Alessandro Acquisti ("Empirical Analysis")), and they found they contained 86 distinct causes of action. They slotted them into the categories illustrated in Fig. 9.2.

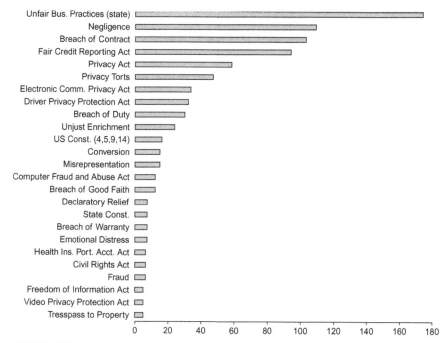

FIGURE 9.2 Causes of Breach-related litigation cases within the United States. *Source: Empirical Analysis, p. 101.*

Canadian Breach litigation cases are also exhibiting creativity by plaintiffs' counsel. In a recent Canadian Statement of Claim arising out of a Breach matter, the document contained the following bases for alleged liability: negligence, Breach of confidence, Breach of privacy, Breach of fiduciary duty, Breach of contract, unjust enrichment, negligent misrepresentation, Breach of the *Sale of Goods Act*, Breach of the *Consumer Protection Act*, and Breach of the *Competition Act*.

In one fairly recent case, where one bank employee accessed the personal financial records of another bank employee, the court in Ontario created a new theory of liability called "a right against intrusion." The court awarded the individual plaintiff damages of $10,000, which might not seem that significant—but one always has to be mindful of the potential multiplication of this sort of an amount when the case is brought as a class action (see the section Class Action Cases).

In another recent case, a bank in British Columbia mistakenly changed a customer's address, with the result that two letters from the bank were sent to an incorrect address, and the incorrect address also went to a couple of credit agencies. Given that no actual financial harm was incurred, the court only awarded $2000 in damages—but again, the risk profile would increase dramatically to the organization if the erroneous address mix up were replicated among a large group of customers, again given the dynamics of class action cases discussed below.

Another trend that is fairly recent, particularly in the United States, is for plaintiffs' counsel to bring shareholder derivative suits that include claims against directors and officers of the company personally. While in a recent high-profile case, this particular claim was dismissed, it is likely that this trend will continue. Therefore, it is not enough that a public company's senior management take various proactive steps to deal with the risk of Breaches, but that Boards of directors do likewise.

In light of this shareholder derivative claim litigation involving Board members personally, here's a short list of steps that your organization's Board could consider:

- The Board should retain, from time to time, experts in cyber/IT security to review the company's state of IT security, and to recommend improvements
- Review carefully the recommendations in these reports, and the remediation suggestions that are made
- Make cyber and IT security a regular topic at Board meetings, or at least at a subcommittee of the Board, until the material deficiencies surfaced in these reports are remediated
- In addition to reviewing these external reports, the cyber/IT security discussion topic can include presentations by the company's CIO, General Counsel, chief security officer, chief risk officer, and others as appropriate, on the state of readiness of the organization in these areas from a Breach perspective. For example, this would include a periodic update on the organization's CSIR Plan, and recent experience with the testing or operational use of such plan
- Ensure that all incidents involving Breach, and even merely allegations of Breach are reported to the Board, and that the company's response to each (including any eventual remediation measures) is well documented
- Decide whether lead responsibility for the Board's oversight of cyber/IT security should rest with a subcommittee of the Board (like the audit committee), or whether a specific, cross disciplinary subcommittee should be established to deal with the matter, at least until the maturity of

the organization in the cyber/IT security space increases to a sufficiently reasonable level

- consider what D&O insurance the company carries relative to cyber/IT security and Breach risk (note: many such insurance policies contain an express exclusion for Breaches, so this review must be carried out carefully)

Class Action Cases

Full disclosure: the author, George S. Takach, is a partner with McCarthy Tétrault, and this law firm, institutionally speaking, defends organizations against these claims, and does not bring them. Rather, the plaintiffs (as the persons are called who are bringing these claims) are represented by "plaintiff law firms." Moreover, the plaintiff law firms invariably bring these claims as "class action lawsuits," which is an important aspect of privacy Breach litigation.

In a typical non class action lawsuit, one person or entity is bringing a claim against one other. Given the cost and hassle of modern litigation, however, it's not worth it for a single plaintiff to bring a claim if his or her recovery will be limited to a few dollars. What class action litigation allows for, however, is many little claims arising from the same problem or event, to be aggregated together. That changes everything.

An example I like to use to make this clear is the class action lawsuit, a number of years ago against the makers of computer monitors. The marketing material said they were 14″ wide, which in the computer hardware world is measured diagonally, from one corner to the opposite corner. When an engineer one day by chance measured his monitor, it was just a tad short of 14″; he calculated his "damages" to be $6.00 (six dollars).

This paltry amount is simply not worth going to a lawyer about—but how many computer monitors do you think have been sold in the United States? You guessed it! Quite a large number. And so plaintiffs' legal counsel brought the litigation and settled for about $67 million. Of which, about 1/3 (or over $20 million) went to the plaintiffs' lawyers. And the rest, if it's too small to deal with on a per claimant basis, simply gets donated to a charity.

This non Breach litigation example makes it clear why most Breach cases are brought as class actions. And, as noted above, there have been many of these cases launched over the last number of years.

What's very interesting, however, is that most of these cases settle once the class action is certified—that is, once a judge decides the case is indeed appropriate to proceed as a class action matter. What is fascinating is how few of these cases then go to trial in order to be decided on its merits.

In the *Empirical Analysis* study noted above, the researchers asked the fundamental question: what factors result in Breach litigation? and what elements tend to drive settlement in these cases? Their findings are very interesting and have implications for you as you approach the planning and management of Breaches and resultant prospective litigation.

Different Types of Data Make a Difference

The *Empirical Analysis* research concluded there was a heightened correlation between the type of data that is compromised, and the likelihood of an ensuing Breach litigation. For example, Breaches involving financial data, and especially credit card numbers, generated the highest likelihood of subsequent litigation. One driver for this result is that in the United States, the Gramm-Leach-Bliley and Fair Credit Reporting statutes mandate fairly strict security controls, while the collection and sharing of credit card data is strictly governed by contracts administered under the Payment Card Industry Data Security Standard.

Again, therefore, the lesson from this finding is the requirement for situational awareness and action—namely, if you are dealing with financial information, and especially credit card data, you have to be thinking in terms of an extremely robust level of security for that data. The same also goes for medically oriented data, given that the US Health Insurance Portability and Accounting Act also prescribes a fairly stringent set of requirements, including patient consent, before health information can be shared across healthcare facilities.

FROM CLAIM TO SETTLEMENT

Relatively few litigation cases actually proceed to trial, and in this respect Breach litigation is not much different than other types of lawsuits. However, the Empirical Analysis research also considered what factors particularly drive settlement in the Breach space.

The researchers found that 76% of the Breach litigation cases in their 2005–10 study period were class actions. Moreover, successful certification as a class results in a 30% greater likelihood of settlement. Again, this is perhaps not surprising. More interesting, though, is the finding that plaintiffs are also 30% more likely to settle when they experience financial loss.

It is important to note that the lack of a finding of identity theft is one reason often given by judges in dismissing a Breach lawsuit. That is, the court is not convinced that a sufficient "actual" harm has occurred to warrant the litigation. At the same time, however, particularly if the class is able to get certified, often the defendant settles simply to avoid the additional costs of litigation, or to attempt to stop the negative publicity, or merely because the litigation has taken a significant amount of senior management's attention that could be put to better, more productive use.

It is also worth noting that the likelihood of settlement increases 10 times in the case of hack attack caused Breaches when contrasted with hardware items that are stolen or lost. And in terms of the sensitivity of data, when the litigation relates to medical data, there is an increase of 31% probability that the case settles.

As with most class action litigation, one cannot underestimate the importance of class action litigation lawyers, who tend to propel these cases forward. The *Empirical Analysis* research was able to ascertain that the mean payment to plaintiffs' legal counsel for a settled class action Breach case was $1.2 million, with the maximum being $6.5 million. At the same time, the mean award to members of the class was $2500, with most settlements providing roughly $500 per plaintiff. In many cases, the total amount of financial redress per claimant is so small that the bulk of the award (after satisfying plaintiff counsel fees) was paid to charities.

THE VOLUME OF BREACH LAWSUITS

Overall, the *Empirical Analysis* research noted earlier in this chapter found that in the 2005–10 period, in the United States only about 4% of Breaches resulted in litigation claims. This is fairly consistent with the findings for litigation rates in other types of American personal injury litigation.

It is interesting to speculate, however, whether this percentage, in Canada, will rise with the relatively new mandatory Breach notification requirement that was added to Canada's federal privacy law in mid-2015. Also, from a potential litigation perspective, the recent amendments to the Personal Information Protection and Electronic Documents Act (PIPEDA) now require companies to keep track of the precise records implicated in a Breach. Again, presumably this will assist plaintiff's legal counsel in the mounting of Breach litigation claims.

The More Records, the More Lawsuits

The *Empirical Analysis* research data uncovers a number of conclusions about when it is more likely that a Breach ends up in litigation. One of the most prevalent factors is the number of records implicated. In short, the greater the number of records that were disclosed in an unauthorized fashion, the greater the likelihood of the Breach resulting in litigation. Bottom line, the research found that a 10 times increase in the number of disclosed records increases the probability of a lawsuit by 8%. For example, the research found that the mean number of records in nonlitigated Breaches is 98,000; but for those that are litigated, the mean number of records is 5.3 million.

This finding has important implications for your organization. It means you have to analyze your databases, and understand which ones are most vulnerable, and the relative size of each. Obviously, your "hardening" measures should be implemented for all of them, but if you have some very large ones, you should expend extra effort on protecting them. Incidentally, many investigations of Breaches lead to the database, and due to the investigation team's inability to properly scope what information was involved, are forced to assume all database data may have been compromised. This sometimes unwarranted assumption increases the impact of the Breach. Please refer to Chapter 6 of this book for advanced database forensic practices that can be used to more precisely the specific records involved in a database Breach which can then reduce the scope and impact of a Breach.

PREPARING FOR BREACH LITIGATION

When dealing with a Breach what you do, say, and uncover can be used against you in a court of law. The first critical step when responding to a Breach is protecting Breach-related communication.

Operationalize Attorney-Client Privilege

The principle—and the importance—of attorney-client privilege has already been discussed in Chapter 4 of this book. In a nutshell, certain communications that flow between you and your lawyer (including emails) are "privileged," which means they do not have to be disclosed to plaintiffs' legal counsel, or to regulators. They remain, in effect, private communications between you and your lawyer.

Accordingly, once a Breach comes to light, while you have the obligation to preserve all relevant evidence (as discussed above), at the same time you do not have to turn over any privileged material to regulators or plaintiffs' counsel. Thus, one subexercise you will work through with your legal counsel soon after the Breach is detected is determining which evidence is protected by attorney-client privilege.

It is worth noting that if the legal retainer includes an analysis of the Breach itself, then it is likely that any materials prepared by technical experts for the lawyers (which technical expertise is used as an input to the legal assessment of liability, etc.) would also likely be subject to legal privilege. Accordingly, at the commencement of the response to the Breach, when legal counsel first appears in the picture, the assessment of privilege requires a quick but thorough consideration so that the organization's options are not foreclosed.

Determine What Caused the Breach

When managing a Breach, proper containment requires identifying what caused the Breach and eliminating the vulnerability or exposure. We covered steps on how to do this in Chapters 4, 5, and 8 of this book. Keeping this in mind, let's look at some factors that highlight the importance of determining what caused the Breach and the implications this has on Breach litigation.

The *Empirical Analysis* research noted earlier shows that it matters to prospective plaintiffs (and their legal counsel) what the actual cause of the Breach was. In the survey period (2005–10), lawsuits were more likely to follow when there was a highly negligent act, such as mistakenly throwing tax records into a dumpster, than when there was an attack on the organization's computer network by a hacker. Presumably, the former was considered more a "fault" of the organization than the latter, with the startling result that the improper disposal of data is three times as likely to lead to litigation, relative to when the data is stolen.

I wonder, however, whether this distinction is as clear cut in the 2010–15 period. Over the last 5 years, the mechanisms for managing external threats over the Internet have improved, such that a series of best practices for this have developed—witness the cyber security policy issued in the United States by the National Institute of Standards and Technology, or in Canada by the federal Office of the Superintendent of Financial Institutions in Ottawa. On the other hand, the number of hackers has increased as well, and their expertise is improving, with the result that the number of Breach incidents has increased markedly over these past 5 years relative to the previous half decade; for example, have a look again at the datalossorg chart presented earlier in this chapter: in the United States, during 2006–10, there was an average of 805 Breaches a year, while in the 2011–15 period, the number increased to 1411 a year.

Identify the Type of Harm

The *Empirical Analysis* research also shows that it matters what type of harm actually befell the plaintiffs. Most critically, if actual financial harm was experienced, particularly through identify theft, then that led to a much more likely litigation result. Interestingly, the research uncovered that 22% of the federally-litigated Breach cases in their 2005–10 sample period involved financial loss (while 78% did not). Considered from another perspective, the results of this research indicate that the likelihood of a company being sued increases by a factor of 3.5 when its customers experience actual financial harm.

By the same token, the likelihood of litigation drops by a factor of six if the organization provides free credit monitoring promptly after the Breach. This is why, for example, one often sees the express remedy of the provision of free credit monitoring hard wired into an outsourcing agreement between a financial institution customer and its IT services provider, with the remedy to kick in immediately upon the service provider experiencing a Breach that impacts the customer's client data. Indeed, for some time now, it has been considered a standard, best practice to have credit monitoring commence immediately following a Breach (eg, this is recommended by the US Federal General Accountability Office). As for how long you should continue the monitoring, that depends on a range of factors.

Preserve the Evidence

From the moment your organization first detects that it may have been the victim of a Breach—you must preserve all evidence surrounding the Breach. This point cannot be emphasized enough. You must, to use the official terminology, institute a "litigation hold" on all your evidence the nano second you find your systems or data have been compromised.

The reason for the litigation hold is quite simple. Without the appropriate evidence, you will be unable to prove in court, or to a regulator, what actually went on surrounding the Breach. And in that case, it will be open for the judge, or jury, or the regulator, to draw the inference that you destroyed evidence in order to cover up some incriminating deeds or misdeeds on your part.

Therefore, as you work with your IT department, and the incident response and computer forensic experts, and others, getting to the bottom of what went on, you must very consciously keep track of and preserve every item of evidence. For example forensic experts should collect evidence and then create a duplicate copy of the evidence for analysis.

Showing Empathy, But Within Limits

One of the toughest judgment calls you will have to make in the course of dealing with the legal fallout from the Breach is how to respond to your customers (or employees) if any of their personal information was compromised during the Breach. On one hand, you will likely want to communicate early with them, and, if appropriate, you may well want to take an approach of empathy—even regret—at the events that have unfolded and caused them anxiety and perhaps worse.

On the other hand, however, your legal counsel will likely caution against too much empathy, especially if it begins to border on an apology, because that may well open you up to a claim for legal liability. In effect, you don't want your statements to be making the case for the plaintiffs' lawyer in the class action suit.

The resolution to this conundrum is usually somewhere in between. Your public relations expert will typically prevail in getting you to "show a human side" in response to what is a difficult situation, but this should only be done, and the actual message should be carefully vetted, with the assistance of experienced litigation counsel.

Whatever the content of your message in the hours, days, and weeks following a Breach, you have to try to make sure that you and the CSIR Team manage the communication around the Breach as closely as you can. As a first step, it is often prudent to notify the senior management, and (among other things) to remind them not to speak to the media, or participate in social media, about the Breach and the fallout (if any) radiating from it. You will want to tightly control the messaging.

Once news of the Breach gets out, particularly if it is a high profile one (and is gaining some play in the mainstream media), one option is to communicate to a broader circle of managers, reminding them not to talk to the media about the matter, and not to participate in social media on it either. Reassure them that the management team handling the Breach has the situation in hand, including any required communications involving customers or the general public. More guidance on communicating pre, during, and after a Breach can be found in Chapter 7 of this book.

Determine Whether to Notify Data Subjects?

Breach-related notification is highly driven by regulatory and contract requirements that may be in place with partners, cyber insurers, and other organizations. These requirements often specify who should be notified and within what timeframe. Despite these requirements, one of the judgment calls you'll be confronted with during a Breach is whether to notify the data subjects whose personal information may have been compromised. In Chapter 2 of this book, we discussed the importance of developing a compliance inventory of sensitive data and requirements to protect and notify associated with it. If for some reason this has not been complete or has become outdated, you should ensure you compile a list of all those jurisdictions where you have personal information originating from, and determining whether or not your organization has Breach notification obligations in those jurisdictions. That is, the majority of US states have such a requirement, as does the newly amended federal privacy law in Canada (that was updated in July, 2015 largely to update the statute for this specific purpose). There have been several recent cases where organizations who suffered a Breach were sued, not due to their inability to adequately protect sensitive information, but the manner and timeframe in which they chose to notify the victims of the Breach. Notifying victims of a Breach is not a task to be taken lightly, it will involve multiple CSIR Team members such as external legal counsel, government relations (GR) and public relations (PR) experts as well as stakeholders from across your organization to determine who should be notified, within what timeframe, and the best way to notify the individuals, whether via a banner on a website, social media, mail, newspaper ad, or a number of other methods. Notifying people within required timeframes and in a manner that proves effective against the demographic you are trying to reach (we discuss this further in Chapter 7 of this book) are all factors to consider while notifying data subjects.

BREACHES AND THE BOARD

An organization's Board of directors has transitioned from a group that was simply advised on serious Breaches to one that wants to know about pre-Breach protection measures. They are also becoming actively involved in Breach preparedness. In June 2014, SEC Commissioner Luis Aguilar spoke to the New York Stock Exchange about cyber security risks in the Boardroom, noting that cyber security incidents have become more frequent and sophisticated, and also more costly to companies.[1] He emphasized the role of Boards of directors, noting that "ensuring the adequacy of a company's cyber security measures needs to be a critical part of a Board of director's risk oversight responsibilities."

Courts have also begun to consider the role of directors in managing cyber security risk. On October 20, 2014, a New Jersey Court dismissed a shareholder derivative suit that sought damages notably from the directors and officers of Wyndham Worldwide Corp. (WWC) for several Breaches. This decision is the first decision issued in the United States in a shareholder derivative claim arising out of a Breach. The decision provides examples of approaches to Breach risk oversight that directors and officers may implement to help shield them from liability in the context of a Breach (Table 9.1).

---

[1]See "Boards of Directors, Corporate Governance and Cyber-Risks: Sharpening the Focus", available at <http://www.sec.gov/News/Speech/Detail/Speech/1370542057946>.

Table 9.1 Sets Out Examples of Steps That Could Be Taken By a Company's Management and Board of Directors to Identify and Assess an Organization's Cyber security Risks	
Actions of Directors and Officers[a]	
Policies	**Endorse cyber security policies**, procedures, and internal controls, including when and how to disclose
	Oversee governance frameworks to protect against and to detect the occurrence of a cyber security event
Appointments	Management and Board members could discuss the appointment of a **chief information security officer** with the expertise to meet regularly with and advise the Board on cyber risk
	Consideration could be given to appointing a **Board member with cyber security expertise** and experience (or the Board should seek out an expert who can provide presentation(s) to the Board in this regard), and to appointing an enterprise risk committee
Reviews and reports	The Board should review annual **budgets for privacy** and **IT security programs**
	The Board should receive regular **reports on** Breaches and cyber risks
	The Board should have a clear understanding of **who in management has primary responsibility** for cyber security risk oversight and for ensuring the adequacy of the company's cyber-risk management practices
Direction	Consideration should be given to which risks are to be addressed and mitigated directly and which may be transferred through **insurance**

[a]Drawn from the WWC case, presentation by SEC commissioner Luis A. Aguilar's, dated June 10, 2014 and by the National Institute of standards and technology's "Framework for Improving Critical Infrastructure Cybersecurity." Available at <http://www.nist.gov/cyberframework/upload/cybersecurity-framework-021214-final.pdf>

As part of the Board's risk management mandate for Breach preparedness, consideration should also be given to ensuring compliance by the organization with any applicable regulatory guidance, such as that from bank regulators, if your organization is a financial institution. If you are in the United States, you may have to deal with the Federal Trade Commission from a general privacy regulatory perspective; in Canada the equivalent would be the Privacy Commissioners in Ottawa (for the Canadian federal privacy law) and in BC, Alberta, Manitoba, and Quebec for provincial counterparts. And if your organization uses payment cards, then you need to be current on the guidance in this area from the Payment Card Industry Security Standards Council, and particularly their PCI-DSS requirements. The key point of all of the foregoing is that an important element of any subsequent litigation is demonstrating that you discharged the all important requisite "standard of care." You must be able to prove your actions were consistent with industry best practices, as found in regulatory pronouncements. Doing so can limit direct, indirect, and system costs for specific organizations as well as the industry as a whole.

SUMMARY

Some things in life are certain, such as paying taxes and according to many, suffering a Breach. For most organizations, the exposure associated with the

Breach has long been resolved, the organization has restored business operations and improved their level of cyber security to try and prevent a repeat occurrence. Despite all of this, Breach litigation often looms on the horizon and will, sooner than later, need to be endured. This chapter has provided you a glimpse into the world of Breach litigation and how to prepare for and manage it effectively. Please keep in mind that this chapter was merely a glimpse into what can be a lengthy process involving many experts, some lawyers, and a material demand of resources within the Breached organization. Engaging experts experienced with Breach litigation and involving them early in the process can help minimize impact. This being said, the number one thing you can do to limit the impact associated with a Breach is to be prepared for it. Don't wait for notification from opposing counsel. The guidance in this book will help ensure preparedness which will limit financial, operational, and brand impact associated with the Breach, including the following:

- While you need to harden all your IT environments, particular emphasis should be put on your largest databases holding sensitive personal information
- Be extremely careful with the disposal of IT equipment, and the practices you employ to wipe them clean of personal information
- Pay particular attention to potential Breaches that might cause financial harm to your customers, and where there is such a Breach, be quick to offer credit monitoring
- From the moment you suspect a Breach, you must preserve all evidence relating to it, but also very early on you should organize your process for preserving attorney-client privilege
- Once you understand the parameters of the Breach, you need to consider what message you send to affected customers, including whether to notify them formally of the Breach

Appendix

Digital Evidence Chain of Custody Tracking Form
Data Breach Preparation and Response
www.BreachesAreCertain.com

Case Number: _____   Type of Case: _____

Submitting Investigator: (Name)
_____

Client:
_____

Date/Time of Seizure: _____   Location of Seizure:
_____

Description of Evidence		
Item #	Quantity	Description of Item (Model, Serial #, Condition, Marks, Scratches)

Chain of Custody				
Item #	Date/Time	Released by (Printed name, title, signature)	Received by (Printed name, title, signature)	Comments/Location

Evidence Chain of Custody Tracking Form
(Continued)

Chain of Custody				
Item #	Date/Time	Released by (Printed name, title, signature)	Received by (Printed name, title, signature)	Comments/Location

Final Disposition/Disposal Authority

Authorization for Disposal

Item(s) #: _____ on this document pertaining to (client): _____

is(are) no longer needed as evidence and is/are authorized for disposal by (check appropriate disposal method)

☐ Return to Owner   ☐ Auction/Destroy/Divert

Name & ID# of Document Authorizing Disposal Attached: _____

Signature: _____   Date: _____

Witness to Destruction of Evidence

Item(s) #: _____ on this document were destroyed by Evidence Custodian _____ ID#:_____

in my presence on (date) _____.

Name & ID# of Witness to Certificate of Destruction Attached : _____

Signature: _____   Date: _____

Release to Lawful Owner / Law Firm / Business / Entity Name

Item(s) #: _____ on this document was/were released by Evidence Custodian _____ ID#:_____

to:

Name _____

Address: _____ City: _____ State: _____ Zip Code: _____

Telephone Number: (_____) _____

Under penalty of law, I certify that I am the lawful owner of the above item(s).

Signature: _____   Date: _____

Copy of Government-issued photo identification is attached. ☐ Yes ☐ No

This Evidence Chain-of-Custody form is to be retained for one (1) year by [Company]

Evidence Collection and Processing Worksheet

Data Breach Preparation and Response
www.BreachesAreCertain.com

Evidence Collection

Investigator: (Name)

_____

Case number: _____   Date/Time of Collection:

_____

Item number: _____

Evidence Information	
Evidence Name	
Make	
Model	
Serial Number	
Expected evidence contained within	

Evidence Processing

Processing Information	
Name of investigator conducting analysis	
Date of analysis	
Material analysis findings	
Relevance of analysis findings within the investigation	

Incident Triage Checklist
Data Breach Preparation and Response
www.BreachesAreCertain.com

Document Initial Facts of the Case (Who, What, When ,Where, Why & How)		
Completed (date/time/ initials)	**Task**	**Notes**
☐	What is the nature of the Incident?	
☐	Who detected the incident? • Name: • Number: • Title: • Details Reported: (obtain copy)	
☐	How was the incident discovered?	
☐	When was the incident discovered?	
☐	When was it reported? How and to whom?	
☐	Who knows about the incident? Who needs to know about it?	
☐	Is there any information protected by regulatory or legislative requirements believed to be involved in the incident? (Credit card data, etc.)?	
☐	What is the present scope of the incident? • Number of systems or accounts presumed to be compromised? • Type of data?	
☐	What actions have been taking in response to the incident?	
☐	Are there any 3rd parties involved? (Lawyers, hosting providers, law enforcement, insurance companies, IR/Forensic providers)?	
☐	What data is available • Network logs • Host logs • Application log • Database logs	
☐	What are the objectives of the investigation (identify the scope, responsible parties, etc.)	
☐	Are there recent vulnerability assessment results available?	
☐	What logs and other artifacts are available • Network firewall logs • Database • VPN logs	

Incident Triage Checklist
Data Breach Preparation and Response
www.BreachesAreCertain.com

Completed	Task	Notes
	• Netflow • Security device/Appliance • SIEM • DNS • LDAP/Active Directory • Host • Application • Cloud • Host-based security software (HIPS, AV, FIM, etc.) • Physical evidence (CCTV, facilities, etc.)	
☐	What is the retention of log data? (On-line and off-line storage)	

Critical Infrastructure		
Completed	**Task**	**Notes**
☐	Is the organization aware of any intelligence they received that may be relevant to the investigation?	

Logistics to Establish		
Completed	**Task**	**Notes**
☐	Determine reporting distribution list, frequency, etc.	
☐	Reporting distribution list, frequency of updates and level of detail within	
☐	How information security should be managed during the engagement (secure email transfer, etc.)	
☐	Obtaining a "war room" in which to lead the Breach response and investigation	

Incident Triage Checklist
Data Breach Preparation and Response
www.BreachesAreCertain.com

General Checklist Guidance

1) Set expectations regarding follow-up.

   a. When will you speak to them again?
   b. How will you contact them?
   c. Who will be contacting them?

2) Inform your leadership to get resources allocated, unless you have this responsibility, do not attempt to own this or assign resources.

3) Remove all data from the above sheet that you do not need. These questions may provide sample responses or ask questions that are not relevant to your specific case.

4) Be as clear as you can. The responder who needs to act on this information may be different than the person who fills out the form. The information needs to be clear enough to be understood by everyone who reads the form.

Index

Note: Page numbers followed by *f* indicate figures, and *t* indicate tables.

Printed in the United States
By Bookmasters